The
Elements
of Banking

The
Elements
of Banking

F. E. Perry

Methuen *&* Co Ltd
in association with
The Institute of Bankers
LONDON

First published *1975* by Methuen & Co Ltd
11 New Fetter Lane, London EC4P 4EE
Reprinted with revisions and supplementary notes *1976*
Second edition *1977*
Reprinted with revisions and supplementary notes *1978* and *1979*
© *1975*, *1977*, *1978* and *1979* The Institute of Bankers &
F. E. Perry
Printed in Great Britain by
Richard Clay (The Chaucer Press) Ltd, Bungay Suffolk

ISBN 0 416 85880 5

The author is anxious to stay in touch with teachers
of this subject and expressly requests that any
teacher with criticisms or suggestions should write
to him care of the publishers, Methuen & Co Ltd.

Contents

iv Contents

Part Two The business of banking

Note to the Second Impression

In this reprint of the second edition of *Elements of Banking* the text has been brought up to date. Additional new information is given in the Supplementary Notes (pp. 396–401). Readers are referred to these notes by asterisks and footnotes in the text.

Acknowledgements

The author acknowledges the helpful information derived from the following books and periodicals:

Central Office of Information: *British Banking and other Financial Institutions* (HMSO, 1974)
Confederation of British Industry: *Sources of Finance for Industry and Commerce* (CBI, 1974)
ANDREW D. CROCKETT: *Money – theory, policies and institutions* (Nelson, 1973)
NICHOLAS FAITH: *Money Matters* (Hamish Hamilton, 1973)
J. L. HANSON: *Money* (English Universities Press, 1953)
International Banking Summer School 1964: *Banking Trends in Europe Today* (Institute of Bankers, 1964)
F. E. PERRY: *Law and Practice Relating to Banking* (Benn, 1977)
ROBIN PRINGLE: *Banking in Britain* (Charles Knight, 1973)
JACK R. S. REVELL: *The British Financial System* (Macmillan, 1973)
LAWRENCE S. RITTER and WILLIAM L. SILBER: *Money* (Basic Books, 1973)
H. P. SHELDON: *Practice and Law of Banking* (Macdonald and Evans, 1972)
W. THOMSON: *Dictionary of Banking* (Pitman, 1974)
D. P. WHITING: *Finance of Foreign Trade and Foreign Exchange* (Macdonald and Evans, 1973)
GEORGE WINDER: *A Short History of Money* (Newman Neame, 1959)
Journal of the Institute of Bankers
The Bankers' Magazine

Preface

I am very conscious of the fact that responsibility for good communication rests with the teacher or author, and in writing this introduction to banking, which is intended for young people starting a commercial career, I hope that I have been able to arrange the subject matter for them in a way which they will readily understand, and that it will serve as a kind of induction course for them. The fascinating business of banking has now become so very diverse, and the pace of change is so rapid, that an up-to-date review should be helpful. I hope indeed it may be so.

Each chapter except the two last has a series of multi-choice questions for self-testing and a number of subjects for discussion. The latter are not necessarily based on the chapter which they follow, but are based on all the chapters up to that point. It is hoped that these will be used as material for study groups.

This second edition has been slightly enlarged and updated. In a new section in Chapter 2 the consequences and aftermath of the Competition and Credit Control measures, introduced in 1971, are described and discussed in some detail, together with the new thinking on the supervision of banks and deposit-taking institutions. More emphasis is also placed on the role of the banks in the community and on the banker's duty of secrecy. Several more banking services have been added to the list in Chapter 10; and changes in the opportunities offered by the various savings media have been noted. A number of amendments have also been made as the result of helpful suggestions by teachers and students.

Explanation has, I hope, proceeded step by step with discussion, so that the book remains comprehensible to the younger and less experienced readers for whom it is primarily intended and will give them a good grounding for their further studies, their branch or departmental work, and their future careers.

I am glad to acknowledge the continuing assistance given to me by Mr Eric Glover, Director of Studies, and Mr Peter Spiro, Assistant Secretary, of The Institute of Bankers, particularly in connection with the appendix on the Institute; and also the help that I was given by the library of The Institute of Bankers. Apart from the many friends and organizations whose valuable assistance was acknowledged in my preface to the first edition, I should now also like to thank Mr M. A. Maberley, Managing Director of Credit Factoring Ltd, for his advice and help with the section on factoring, which has been largely rewritten as a result; and Mr P. H. Spencer, Head of Corporate Planning, National Westminster Bank, who supplied most of the information on which the section on the aftermath of Competition and Credit Control is based.

I am obliged to the National Westminster Bank for permission to reproduce the bank's balance sheet and the diagram on p. 68; to Barclays Bank for the diagram of the organization of the bank's United Kingdom Management Company; to the Phoebus Publishing Company for the diagram on p. 99, which originally appeared in *Knowledge Encyclopaedia*; and to the *Daily Telegraph* for permission to reproduce its articles on a career in banking, published in April 1975 and May 1976. The first of these was written by Mr K. Hirst, Personnel Development Manager, Lloyds Bank International Ltd, who has also kindly signified his willingness that this article should be reproduced in this book.

Any names used in the examples in this book are fictitious, and are not intended to refer to any existing person or company.

London, 1977   F. E. Perry

Part One

The
Background

What is money?

Many parents have children at school who do not seem very bright at their schoolwork. Annual reports contain phrases such as 'tries hard, but finds it difficult to take in' and 'finds this subject hard to understand'.

Yet the parents observe that, however dull their offspring may appear to their school teacher, there is one subject over which they have complete mastery, that is, money. They have had no difficulty in learning the sub-divisions of the pound, they recognize the coins instantly, they can check their pocket money in the twinkling of an eye, and they know exactly how much their money will buy. Moreover, they learnt all this at a very early age.

Why is this? Surely it is because the subject of money is one which concerns us all very closely. We have a personal stake in the subject, so we are interested. Because we are interested, we learn.

But what exactly is money? To answer that question, we have to go back in time.

Barter

Today we buy, say bread, or clothes with money in the appropriate shop. These are goods; we exchange our money for goods which others sell to us. Today we travel on a train or bus, or maintain a banking account, or consult our solicitor about some legal matter, and we pay the charge or fee demanded. These are services; we exchange our money for the services which others provide for us.

But in a primitive community where there was no money, goods and services were obtained by barter – we called it 'swapping' at school. In very early times the Phoenician traders of the Mediterranean reached Cornwall and the Scilly Isles to barter their spices and dyes for the tin mined in the West.

But as primitive communities develop into more advanced societies people specialize in what they can best do, and barter becomes a clumsy method of exchange. The cobbler who wanted to advertise his shoes had to find not only a printer to print the handbills, but also a printer who happened to want a pair of new shoes. This was called the 'double coincidence of wants'. Even then, what is to be the 'rate of exchange'? How many handbills should be printed for a pair of shoes?

There had to be some commodity which could be used as a medium of exchange. Anything would do as long as everyone accepted it in payment. This acceptance was crucial. The 'money' did not have to be attractive for its own sake, although it often was. In this connection everyone instantly thinks of cowrie shells, which were rather handsome rose-tinted shells found in the Indian and Pacific oceans. But other parts of the world found other things to use as a medium of exchange. In early Rome men used sheep, and in Greece cattle. In ancient Egypt if a man was well disposed towards another, or wished to impress him, he would make him a present of one or more slaves, for there a man's status was measured by the number of slaves he had.

These were rather large units, difficult to match up with some small article the herdsman or farmer might want. Neither were they very convenient for carrying about. Also of course, there were healthy, fat cows; and poor, thin cows.

There might be trouble from a seller expecting to be paid ten fat cows when he was offered ten thin ones.

Nowadays we know that the units of money must be homogeneous – that is, they must all be of the same kind, look the same, weigh the same, all be of the same type, shape, size and quality. They must also be durable. Cows die sooner or later.

Many things have been used as the medium of exchange – corn, furs, rice, tobacco, salt, tea, rum – there is no end to them. Man is an animal with a gift for trading, and when conditions are primitive – i.e. when there is no money – barter will reappear. Thus cigarettes were used in prisoner-of-war camps and in the black markets in post-war Germany. They are still used by convicts in HM prisons.

In time it was generally realized that metals were superior to the commodities previously mentioned, because coins made from metal are homogeneous, portable, and easily divisible by weight. However, coins did not come immediately, and sellers had to be in a position to check the weight of a bar of the metal offered in payment. So every market place sported its weights and scales, and we can find many instances of their use in the Bible and in other records of early times. Metals also had the advantage that if they were not required as money they could be melted down and used to make something else, such as spear blades or ploughshares or goblets.

Among the Ancient Britons, and in Greece, iron was used, and copper in Rome, but gradually silver and gold emerged as better than the other metals because they keep indefinitely – iron rusts – and they provided a greater value in a smaller bulk. That meant that merchants had to carry less weight about with them. Another advantage was, and is, that all gold and silver of a certain weight and fineness is the same.

Coinage

The advent of coinage marked another step forward in the increasing efficiency of the medium of exchange. It became possible to list the things which money should be. We have seen that as a medium of exchange it overcame the problems of barter – the double coincidence of wants.

Most commodities depreciate as time passes: gold and silver do not. Therefore, money made from them can be used as a 'store' of wealth. Instead of spending money as fast as we get it, we can save some of it in the expectation of using it at a future time.

Possession of a store of money gives power – the ability to get things as and when you want them. Of course, money may depreciate in the sense that inflation may progressively reduce its value. In this way a store of money may buy less and less as time goes on, and if this tendency gets really bad another store of wealth may have to be considered such as investing in land or buying equity shares (a 'hedge' against inflation). Money serves as a common unit in terms of which all other commodities may be valued.

We can summarize all this quite easily. Money is a necessary part of any civilized society. It serves as:

(1) a medium of exchange
(2) a store of wealth
(3) a measure of value

Let us also repeat another basic principle:

Money must be generally acceptable in exchange for goods and services. The form which money takes (shells, cigarettes, banknotes) is unimportant as long as it commands confidence. The use of metal which had to be checked for weight and fineness progressed to the use of metal which had been cut into pieces of a fixed weight, and then into coins. The first coins are credited to China round about 1000 BC. They were not round, but fashioned in the shape of knives, having holes in the handle, which presumably made it easier to string a number together. These were of bronze and gold. Later other coins of irregular shapes were manufactured one at a time from dies, struck out with a hammer. Eventually, of course, the most convenient shape was found to be a circle. It was realized that the State must accept responsibility for both the manufacture and the quality of coinage, and first the Greeks, and then the Romans, issued gold coins which carried an impression guaranteeing the weight and the purity of the metal in the coin.

In this country in the early middle ages, the local barons carried out most of the functions of government in their own areas. They had their own mints and struck their own coins, which were accepted locally. Other important people did the same.

At that time there must have been a great variety of coins from different sources circulating in Europe. Some of them were of such undoubted purity that they gained universal acceptance, while others no doubt were not so readily taken. Among them were coins called librae, solidus and denarii, names which had come down from the Romans. The denarius was a penny, and twelve of them were equal to a solidus. Twenty solidus made a libra. These coins gave us our £ s d, and the subdivisions of a pound lasted until decimal coinage was adopted in 1971.

The early British coinage was based on silver, probably because gold was scarce and expensive. There were, however, gold coins from time to time, particularly one struck by the extrovert Henry VIII which bore his figure. This was called a sovereign, and the name persisted, to describe our chief gold coin in later years.

Towards the end of the seventeenth century gold became more plentiful and golden guineas and florins were struck. The guinea was first coined from gold brought back from the coast of Guinea, whence its name. The florin (now 10p) is named from the city of Florence, where florins were first coined. These proved very useful in a period of expanding trade, and over the next hundred years or so they became more important than the silver coinage. The golden guinea has had its value fixed at twenty-one shillings (now 105 pence) and it commanded great respect. In 1816 a Coinage Act was passed establishing a gold standard. In future there would be a sovereign worth twenty silver shillings. The exact weight and fineness of the gold were specified. The sovereign became available five years later, some time after the end of the war with France, and served as the sole measure of value right up until the outbreak of the Great War in 1914.

Copper and bronze coins, the farthings, halfpennies and pennies, originated because of a shortage of coins of small values. Tradesmen got in the habit of issuing copper tokens for small transactions, much as drapers' shops used to give out a packet of pins as change in place of a farthing. Of course people could not be allowed to issue their own coinage and the tradesmens' tokens were stopped. But the need had been recognized, and in 1672 the mint began to issue copper coins. In 1860 bronze coins were substituted, containing ninety-five parts copper, four parts of tin, and one part of zinc. These bronze coins were very much better, and were in use up to the changeover to decimal coinage, except the farthing which was discontinued in 1961. The passing of the old penny was greatly regretted. Three of them weighed exactly an ounce, and this was a very useful thing to know when one was wondering what the weight of a letter might be.

The decimal coinage was called 'new pence', to distinguish the new coins from the old ones. The use of the word 'new' has now disappeared, and the new halfpenny will probably be discontinued as prices continue to rise, so that we shall once again be left with only 'pence'.

During the nineteenth century most nations adopted the gold standard, and virtually the whole of the trading world had the advantage of a common basis to their monetary systems. The gold coinage in almost universal use had the advantage that its supply could not be quickly increased, and this made for stability of prices. In the Victorian era there was no serious change for a considerable period of time in the quantity of goods which a gold sovereign would buy, and so people in those days never spoke of changes in the value of money. It is only since the gold standard has been abandoned that the forces of inflation have been set loose. This is shown by constantly rising prices. The value of commodities can be measured in money – this is one of the functions of money – but the value of money itself cannot be measured in monetary terms, but only in terms of the prices of goods.

Debasement of the coinage

Coins are free from most of the disadvantages of earlier forms of money, but if the coinage is to retain its value and the confidence of those who use it certain dangers must be guarded against. But before we see what these are we must be clear what sort of coins we are talking about. The original or early coinage was more or less worth its stated face value in its content of metal. Thus if you melted down a number of silver coins, you could sell the silver for about what the total value of the coins had been. While this was so the merchants who used them no longer had to check their weight on scales, but could rely on the guarantee of the government implicit in the imprint, and check them only by the (much quicker) process of counting them.

The later coinage tended to be token coinage, that is to say, it might be made from cupro-nickel instead of silver. The value of the metal in the coin would be nowhere near the face value of the coin. Nevertheless the governmental imprint still appeared on it, certifying that it was a true coin of the realm, issued under governmental authority. In this case the value of the coin depended upon the confidence of the public in the government and its conduct of the monetary system. Token coinage is used in mature and developed communities. Let us call these the earlier coins, and the later coins.

The earlier coins had intrinsic – genuine – value, and if they could be copied cheaply, and the cheap copies substituted for the genuine article, there would be a profit in it for those who made the substitution. So forgeries appeared. Bad forgeries gave themselves away, good forgeries could be detected only by weighing or bending them.

Because of the dangers which always follow any tampering

with the monetary system of the country, the dangers that
the public will lose confidence in the coins, and trade will be
thereby hampered, the State has invariably imposed relatively
severe penalties for the crime of forgery, and the search for
the culprits has always been undertaken with the utmost
vigour.

Another profitable operation used to consist of clipping or
shaving a little metal from the edge of the coin, and then
passing it on to the next person a little smaller than it was
before. To defeat this the device of the milled edge was
introduced and from the second half of the seventeenth century all coins coming from the London Mint were so protected.

Then there is, of course, normal wear and tear. Coins get
steadily thinner and lighter as they continually get handled.
When the wearing away had got to a point where the coin
was no longer acceptable, the government had to recall it and
replace it with a new coin. This maintenance of the coinage
is an expensive business which no government wishes to
carry out more often than is absolutely necessary, and the
practice grew up of minting coins with an alloy of a harder-
wearing metal to give longer life without, however, signifi-
cantly reducing the amount of valuable metal in the coin.

Finally, there was the risk that the government itself would
deliberately mint the coins with a value less than their face
value. In a way, it is a disadvantage that the government of
a country is responsible both for issuing the coinage and for
maintaining its value. A phrase comes down from the
Romans—many of whose emperors debased their coinage –
'quis custodiet ipsos custodes?' – who will supervise the
supervisors?

Kings, emperors and governments in need of money have
never been reluctant to debase the coinage. That is, they have
withdrawn good coins containing the proper amount of
metal they were supposed to have, and have replaced them
with lighter coins containing less metal, pocketing the difference. Any such manœuvre has always resulted in a depreciation in the value of the coins, forcing merchants to resort

again to the practice of weighing the metal. The depreciation in the value of the coinage is shown by a general rise in prices. It was not really that prices were going up so much as the fact that the value of the coinage was going down.

While this process of debasing the currency is under way, coins of the proper weight and value will circulate side by side with the 'light' coins. ('Good' money and 'bad' money.) When this happens people will tend to hoard the good coins and pass on the bad ones. This tendency for debased coins to drive good coins out of circulation is called Gresham's Law, after Sir Thomas Gresham, Queen Elizabeth I's financial adviser, who seems to have been the first official to note the working of this tendency.

It is not necessary, however, for all coins to be worth their full face value of metal. This would be possible only if the metals used maintained their prices unchanged, i.e. if the country were on a gold or silver standard. So we come to the later or token coinage.

These coins are free from the risk of forgery, for that is not worth anyone's while. Nor is anyone going to bother to clip the edges. In spite of this the token coinage may well still incorporate the milled edge, partly through convention and habit, and partly to make the coins look as much as possible like the old ones which had intrinsic value. Nor is the government likely to embark on the sterile project of trying to debase them. Wear and tear will still continue, but this cannot be avoided.

These are all advantages. The disadvantage is that there is no automatic check on the value of the coinage, which is therefore free to depreciate according to the inflationary conditions which now appear to have become normal throughout the world.

An example to illustrate these principles comes from the silver coinage of this country.

Originally this consisted of thirty-seven parts of silver to three of alloy. At the outbreak of war in 1914 the market value of the silver in a shilling (now 5p) was fivepence. This low figure was the result of a world-wide fall in the value of silver.

After the war the price of silver rose considerably and because of this it became too expensive to maintain the ratios quoted above. At the new price of silver the cost of the silver in a shilling piece was in excess of one shilling. The silver content of the coins was therefore reduced to one half, or twenty parts of silver to twenty parts of alloy.

After the second World War there was a world-wide shortage of silver and the price of silver rose again. During the war the government had borrowed from the USA 88 million ounces of silver on lease-lend, and this now had to be repaid. It seemed a good plan, therefore, to withdraw the silver coinage, melt it down, extract the silver, and so discharge the debt. This was accordingly done, and cupro-nickel coins were substituted. These looked much the same, still had milled edges, but had a negligible metallic value, consisting of three-quarters copper and one-quarter nickel. The cupro-nickel coins maintained their value, not because of their intrinsic worth, but because of the national confidence in the monetary system.

The present 5p and 10p decimal coins are of a similar composition.

Development of paper money

After coins came notes. These were developed almost by accident. Accustomed as we are in these days to the security of our banking system, we may find it hard to imagine a time before there were any banks, and to understand that the hardest problem for anyone with money then was to find somewhere safe to keep it.

In the seventeenth century many people in this country held their wealth in gold, for a great deal of that metal had been brought back from America during the Elizabethan Age. During the Civil War people were very frightened of being robbed. If they lived in or near a large town it therefore seemed sensible to look around for someone who had to have vaults and safes for their own business, and then to ask them to look after the money. Gold and silversmiths had such safes, for their trade was traffic in coin and bullion, and they needed somewhere secure to keep their stocks. (Bullion is uncoined, refined gold or silver, generally in bars called ingots; or gold or silver, including coined metal, when exported or imported.)

So it came about in the seventeenth century that goldsmiths took these deposits for safe keeping, issuing a receipt which acknowledged the deposit of the money and incorporated a promise to return it on demand. More and more people came to hold these receipts and they began to circulate for value among merchants. Originally the merchant A, wishing to buy something from B, would take his receipt back to the goldsmith, surrender it, and get his money back. Then he would buy the article from B. As like as not, B would then take his money and deposit it with a goldsmith, either the same one, or another.

It was quicker and more convenient for A to pass the goldsmith's receipt on to B, who could either keep it or 'cash' it at the goldsmiths. Where the goldsmith's name was well-known and his reputation good, such circulation became commonplace. To pass the right to the ownership, or title, on to B, and to guarantee that the transaction was bona fide and in order, the merchant 'endorsed' the receipt before passing it on to B, that is, he signed his name on the back of it.

In time B found it more convenient to pass the receipt on to C rather than to cash it. The receipts came to be issued in convenient amounts – £5, £10, £100, etc. to facilitate this passing of the paper from hand to hand, and the goldsmith began to write on the note his personal promise to pay any bearer of the note the stated sum when he was asked to do so 'on demand'. As the receipts were now expressed to be payable to bearer, that is the person in possession of the receipt, the need for endorsement disappeared.

Thus the original function of the receipt became obscured

as its function as a promissory note – a note which promised to pay – became all important. People stopped calling them receipts, and began to describe them as goldsmith's notes. So the goldsmiths began to exercise some of the functions of a banker. They kept money and valuables on safe deposit, and they issued notes. It was not long before they developed another important banking function, that of lending.

In the beginning the merchant who deposited his money with the goldsmith expected to pay a fee, or commission, for having his money kept safe. In time the goldsmith learned that he need not keep the whole of the money left with him, in case it was demanded back, because as long as his name and reputation remained good, demands for repayment were always less than the total deposited. In other words, some of his receipts were always out, circulating in the hands of the merchants. So the goldsmith always had some cash in hand, and he started to lend this out, charging interest.

This turned out to be a profitable business, and the gold-smith, far from making a charge for keeping money safe, began to offer interest, so as to get more money deposited, which he could then profitably re-lend.

This is exactly what the banks are doing today. 'Deposit rate' is an inducement to customers to leave their money with the banks. Then the banks will re-lend it, profitably, to other people. They can do this safely because they know, just as the goldsmiths used to know, that it will never happen, while the banks' names and reputations remain good, that all their depositors will come in at the same time and want all their money back.

This is a description of what happened in the towns, where goldsmiths could be found. In country places the banking functions developed a little differently, but the same principles held good. The main occupation was, and of course still is, agriculture. The farmer's life revolved around an annual cycle of sowing, growing, reaping and harvesting. When the produce was sold, but not before, he had money. For the purchase of seeds and manures, and to provide the wages of his labourers who did the harvesting, he needed to borrow, repaying out of the sale price of the crop.

As there were no banks to go to, it was usual for the farmer to approach the most prosperous and best established trader in the country town, and ask him if he would lend the money, which he usually did, of course charging interest. At first perhaps a mere side-line to the normal business of the trader, this lending grew year by year and became more and more profitable. Soon the trader, like the goldsmith, was encouraging people to deposit money with him, so that he would have plenty to lend, and issuing his notes for such sums deposited. This was the beginning of the country banks.

The place of banks in the community

We have seen how banking started in this country. In the United States the origins of some banking services were quite different, being romantically associated with the Gold Rush. The first and greatest gold strike occurred in California in 1848, and prospectors and mining camps proliferated. In the wake of them came the problems of carrying mail and gold dust over hundreds of miles of wild trails beset with marauders of all kinds.

An advertisement in a San Francisco newspaper late in 1849 announced that a concern called Adams and Company had opened an office in that city, and was preparing to provide an express mail and stage-coach service to the mines. At that time the Californian constitution provided that no corporation could be set up for the purpose of banking, so therefore the duties of a banker devolved upon the express companies, not only in Sacramento and San Francisco, but in every mining camp also. The express company received the miner's gold for the purpose of shipment, and then had to assay it, weigh it, give a receipt for it, and assume responsibility for its safety. Thus the express company's iron safe became the local bank.

We read also that in Sacramento about this time a group so

far ignored the Californian laws as to open a bank in a stone house abutting on the river. The new bank took in up to one hundred and fifty pounds of gold dust in a day. There were three clerks, all armed with Colt revolvers and knives, and the banking hours were from six in the morning until ten at night.

It was in 1852 that Wells Fargo and Company was born. In the July of that year two of its senior men had arrived in California, one to be responsible for the express services, the other for the banking. The company advertised that it would 'forward packages, parcels and freights of all descriptions' between New York and San Francisco, and would also 'purchase and sell Gold Dust, Bullion and Bills of Exchange, and attend to the payment and collection of notes, bills and accounts'. Iron chests were provided for 'the security of treasure and valuable packages'.

Nothing could superficially have been more different from the goldsmiths and their notes. And yet the basic functions of providing security, accepting deposits, paying and collecting bills, were exactly the same.

All that has happened since has been merely a development of these basic functions. A community cannot exist without banking services unless it is to remain in a primitive state. It needs the secure place in which to store money and things of value, an efficient method of payment of debts, an ability to borrow in cases of need, and a collection service. In modern times we have to add to this a facility for paying or receiving in overseas currencies (to pay for our imports and our foreign holidays), insurance and investment services, and many others. The banks must serve to channel the savings of the people and they must develop lending services. They must serve all sections of the community, the local agricultural community as well as the businesses and financial institutions of the cities. They must be reliable, punctilious, and utterly honest. When the people see the name 'Bank' they must know beyond doubt that they can never lose their money.

The Bank of England

Now we turn from goldsmiths' notes to banknotes. The Bank of England was founded as a private joint stock company in 1694, in the reign of William III. It was not the first bank in the world, but it was the first joint stock bank in this country. The principal purpose of the Bank at that time was to lend money to the government for the prosecution of the current war against France. The suggested scheme for the formation of the Bank was the work of a Scotsman, William Paterson, who submitted his ideas to the Treasury, which accepted them. Parliamentary sanction was obtained for the issue of a charter creating a corporation styled 'The Governor and Company of the Bank of England', with a capital of £1,200,000. It was to lend this money to the government at an annual interest of £100,000. To secure payment of this interest a duty upon ships, according to their tonnage, and upon certain liquors, including ales and beers, was levied. The Bank was modelled on the pattern of existing continental banks and was to have power to issue its own notes.

The Bank was a success from the word go. There was no difficulty at all about finding the necessary capital, and amongst the money paid in exchange for the shares in the Bank that were issued, there were many goldsmiths' notes which the Bank immediately presented for repayment. From the start, therefore, the Bank was in competition with the goldsmiths' banking business, and when it started lending its own notes against all the types of security which were normally accepted by goldsmiths this competition became still more marked.

These early banknotes were convertible on demand, that is, they could be exchanged at the Bank for gold coins. Because everyone knew that this could be done, they did not very often bother to do it. Instead, they used the notes in their trading, confident that a £5 note was indeed worth £5 in gold. Such 'convertible paper' is not strictly money, only a claim to money.

In 1708 the Bank was given a near-monopoly of the issue

of notes in England. No other corporate body, or banking partnership of more than six persons, could issue notes payable on demand, or payable at any time less than six months ahead. Thus parliament protected the Bank from possible competition from other joint stock banking companies, by forbidding their formation. Banking partnerships of less than six people were permitted, because it was thought that no such partnership, however rich the partners might be, could possibly amass sufficient funds in total to be a serious competitive threat to the Bank. The Bank doubtless reckoned – correctly, as it turned out – that such small concerns would in time disappear.

In Scotland, where the monopoly granted to the Bank did not apply, joint stock banks were formed and made rapid progress, issuing their own notes. These, however, were not legal tender in England. Legal tender is any means of payment that a creditor is obliged by law to accept in settlement of a debt. Thus while a debt may be settled by cheque, or by postal order, this is at the option of the creditor. He cannot be compelled to accept a cheque, or a postal order, for neither are legal tender. He can be compelled to accept Bank of England notes, for they are legal tender to any amount. As to coins, commonsense dictates that limits must be placed on their use in the payment of debts. No one would want to be paid £100 in 5p pieces. So 50p pieces are legal tender up to £10, other cupro-nickel coins up to £5, and bronze coins up to 20p.

After the Act of 1709 the goldsmiths and the private bankers in or near London deposited their cash with the Bank and used its notes instead of their own. In the country areas banking had been slower to develop, and the banking partnerships there were on a smaller scale. Limited to partnerships of not more than six persons, hundreds of small banking businesses had come into existence, all issuing their own notes, many of them with quite inadequate financial resources and doomed to fail at the first economic or monetary crisis.

The Gold Standard

At this period there were the banknotes of the Bank of England, the banknotes of the country bankers, and gold coins, all circulating together. The coins were gold florins and guineas until 1816, when the gold sovereign was substituted for them as the legal standard unit. All the notes were convertible into gold. They all incorporated a promise to pay bearer. Those of the Bank of England were signed by the Chief Cashier, as they still are today.

This system of notes backed by gold was called the Gold Standard. The system was in use in most developed countries abroad and this facilitated the settlement of international trading debts because all the countries concerned had confidence in gold as a unit of value and were willing to accept payment for their exported goods in gold or claims to gold.

The three essential conditions for a gold standard to work properly are:

(1) that there must be free mintage of gold into the standard legal coins (i.e. any person may take a bar of gold to the mint and require it to turn the bar into the legal gold coins of the realm, without charge, and to hand the coins back to him);

(2) that gold must be allowed to come into the country, or to go out of it, without restriction;

(3) that the legal paper money of the country must be convertible into gold by the central bank on request.

Apart from the period between 1797–1821, when the Bank was forced to suspend payments of gold because of the Napoleonic wars, this system lasted until the outbreak of the Great War, when gold payments were again suspended. A modified form of the Gold Standard, called the Gold Bullion Standard, was reintroduced in 1925. Single notes could no longer be exchanged at the Bank, for there was by now no gold coinage, but a gold bar of 400 oz. could be obtained in exchange for notes to the value of the gold, about £1,555.

In this way important economies were made in the use of gold, while at the same time the currency was still kept convertible. The value of gold was fixed at £3.17.10½d per standard ounce, eleven-twelfths fine.

The Gold Bullion Standard was an excellent scheme but it had a short life, for in 1931, in the worst economic crisis the world has ever known, the Bank was again forced to suspend gold payments. The reason for this was the same as on the previous occasions – the gold reserves of the country were not sufficient to meet the demands from foreign financial centres.

Since 1931 the banknotes of this country have been inconvertible. In themselves they have no value, they are just bits of paper. The promise to pay still appears on the front, but since 1931 the only way in which the Bank of England could pay for a £5 note would be by another £5 note, or five £1 notes, or £5 worth of coins. As with the milled edges of our cupro-nickel coinage, the promise to pay is a relic of former days.

People still accept the paper notes as good. Banknotes are now money in their own right, no longer merely claims to money. The nation which uses them daily has a massive belief that they may be accepted in payment for goods supplied, or services rendered, in the full assurance that they may in turn be passed on to others in exchange for their goods or services. Although the link with gold of a specified weight and fineness has been broken, and although the number of notes in circulation is no longer limited by the amount of gold which the central bank formerly had to keep by way of cover for the note issue, the public confidence in the banknote issue shows that it does not matter whether the medium of exchange is gold, paper, rice, tea, or cigarettes, as long as it is generally acceptable in exchange for goods and services.

The form which money takes is irrelevant, so long only as it commands the confidence of those who use it.

If people lose confidence in banknotes, it is either because they have lost faith in the bank which issued them, or because they have lost faith in the currency of a country as a whole.

In the great expansion of banking in the eighteenth and nineteenth centuries many of the smaller private banks, particularly in the provinces, got into difficulties through lending so much out, usually in the form of their own notes, that they left themselves insufficient reserves to meet the demands for repayment of their notes or deposits, or to pay bills falling due. On these occasions word quickly got around and the unthinkable happened – all their depositors demanded the repayment of their balances at the same time. There was a run on the bank, and confidence in the bank's note issue rapidly diminished. Eventually the bank was forced to close its doors and announce that payment was suspended. This was a local loss of confidence, often unhappily only too well founded.

On a national scale the result is infinitely worse. What happens then was demonstrated in Germany after the first world war, when prices rose with such speed that the tickets in shop windows had to be altered several times daily, and stamp collectors saw with amazement that over a period of weeks, and then days, the cost of posting a parcel in Germany escalated from 50 marks to a fantastic fifty thousand million marks. At that point the currency collapsed completely. Nobody would accept the notes any longer for anything at all. They had become completely worthless.

This has never happened in this country. The notes issued by the Bank of England have sometimes lost part of their value through devaluation as against gold or foreign currencies, or because of inflation, but the public have never lost confidence in them to the point of refusing to accept notes in payment of debts.

Bank deposits

So far we have identified as money banknotes and coins. (This is also what we mean when we talk about 'cash'.)

The balances held by banks in their customers' names are also money, and these balances are much, much greater in total than all the banknotes and coin put together.

The argument that bank deposits are money is quite a simple one. Suppose that A has £100 in £1 notes. With these he opens a banking account. When A has paid his money in to the cashier and all the formalities are complete, A has no money in his pocket, but he has, or can have on request, a bank statement to the effect that he has £100 deposited with the bank. He will also have a cheque book. He can get all or any of his money out when he wants to, by drawing a cheque for some or all of the balance.

The bank which now has his money has nowhere put into writing its promise to repay (as did the Chief Cashier of the Bank of England on A's hundred £1 notes) but this promise is nevertheless a well understood term of the banking contract between A and his bank.

So is A's money any less money because it is now in a banking account? Let's try again.

A and B both have banking accounts in credit. A owes B £100. Some of the ways in which A can pay B are as follows:

(1) A can draw £100 out of his account in cash and take it to B at B's office. B can then take the £100 to his bank, and pay it in to his account.

(2) A can send B a cheque for £100. When B gets this he will pay it in to his banking account and his bank will collect the proceeds of the cheque on his behalf from A's bank. When this has been done, A's account will be less by £100, and B's account more by the same amount, just as in (1) above.

(3) A can write a letter to his bank asking it to transfer £100 from his account to the credit of B's account at B's bank, and A's bank will comply. Again the end result is exactly the same – money has been deducted from A's account, and added to B's. In the first case actual notes were used, in the other two cases the matter was settled by book transfer between the two banks.

Some earlier writers used to compare the promise to repay on the face of the banknote with the bank's promise to repay, which was recorded only by an entry in the bank's ledger. I think the comparison was a false one, for the bank's promise to repay is not recorded anywhere – it is an unwritten term in the banking contract. The ledger record was simply evidence that there was something to repay. In these days, when bank ledgers have all but disappeared, it would be hard to imagine promises to repay somewhere inside various computers up and down the country!

Fortunately this is not necessary. We can conclude from the examples given above that bank deposits serve the same ends as banknotes, or can be made to, when it comes to transactions between parties where one pays another. The bank deposit has acted as a medium of exchange, and, as the saying is, 'money is as money does'. It is money if it does the work of money.

We can learn one or two more lessons from these examples. First, the cheque itself in example (2) is not money. It is a claim to money. In this it resembles the early convertible banknotes. Like them it is only a piece of paper. So was the letter from A to his bank in example (3). Perhaps we can identify one common factor which is responsible for the remarkable effects these pieces of paper have.

The bank note is worth its face value because the public rely on the government to maintain the value of the note issue – more or less – in terms of other commodities. In other words, the government's credit is good in the eyes of the public.

The cheque is taken by B because he has confidence that when it is presented on his behalf to A's bank, it will be duly paid. If he did not think this, he would not accept payment by cheque. He does not have to, for cheques are not legal tender. But with him, A's credit is good.

The letter would not be acted upon by the bank unless it had confidence in its customer A. This does not necessarily mean that A has to have at least £100 on his account with the bank. He might have less than that, but the bank knows that A is both willing and able to see that the bank does not lose over the transaction. A's credit is good at the bank.

The common factor, then, is credit. We will come back to this in a minute.

Not only are bank deposits money, created when bank customers pay sums into the bank, but banks themselves can be said to create money when they agree to lend.

Suppose A negotiates an overdraft of £500 from his bank. What happens? The bank marks A's account to the effect that his cheques may be honoured up to a total of £500 more than he has actually got. A goes away from his bank knowing that he can now draw cheques, up to £500, which will be honoured by the bank although they would not have been so honoured before the agreement on the overdraft facility.

No new money has been created yet, but as soon as A draws his first big cheque – say it is for £200, payable to B – the process begins. B gets the cheque and pays it in to his bank. A's account now shows figures in red, but B has £200 worth of disposable money which was not there before, and would not be there now had it not been for the decision by A's bank, to lend money to A. Where did this money come from? Not from A, for he did not have any. It has come from the bank, who marked A's account. By this marking the bank has created money. So far it has created the equivalent of £200 which is now to be found in B's bank.

But the story does not end there. We know that bankers rely on the fact that not all of their depositors will come in at the same time to demand the return of their money, but only a proportion of them. Therefore the bankers do not have to keep all the deposits ready to repay, but only a proportion of them. The rest they can lend out profitably, just like the goldsmiths did. By long experience the bankers discovered that only 8 per cent of their deposits need be actually in their tills in cash, ready to honour their depositors' cheques over the counter as and when they are presented.

So coming back now to B's bank, which has just received

£200 from B, we know that B's bank must keep £16 in cash in its till in case B wants to draw some of his money out across the counter, but can then, if it wishes, lend the other £184 to someone else. This deposit would in its turn create a further lending ability of £170 and so on.

Those of a mathematical turn of mind may care to work out what is the maximum amount of new money which can be created from A's bank's decision to lend A £500. As it is quite a considerable sum, it is clear that this decision by the bank cannot have been lightly taken and on reflection we can come to the conclusion that the factor of overwhelming importance for the bank was that A's credit was good. Without that belief in A's credit no money would have been created. In one way, then, A and his bank acted together to create the new money, and both credit and willingness to lend were factors.

An even simpler way of summarizing it would be to say that credit was turned into money, or to say that spending power surrendered by one person is passed on to another person who wants to use it immediately. In this way banks, by lending money to credit-worthy customers, create money, or spending power.

However, a bank cannot create spending power indiscriminately. As we shall see later on there are many checks and controls. One of the most important of these limiting factors is the bank's liquidity ratio. This is the relationship between those assets of the bank which are in money or in securities which can very quickly be turned into money (the liquid assets), and the total balances which the customers of the bank have on their banking accounts (described in the bank's balance sheet as 'Current, deposit and other accounts'). The bank must always keep a certain minimum percentage of its assets in a liquid form to be sure of being able to meet any possible demands on it, and it must bear this in mind when lending money, so creating debts (or claims or assets) which may not be particularly liquid.

Furthermore, a general expansion of credit, which will

show up in the system as a whole, is subject to the overall control of the central bank. It cannot rest on the decisions of any individual bank.

Bank lending may be inflationary in its operation if the total supply of money is increased without any corresponding increase in the supply of goods and services on which the money can be spent.

This will be the case where money is lent for 'consumer spending', as where a private individual borrows money to buy a colour television set. Although the manufacture of the set provides employment and incomes for the workers concerned, after that the end product is the satisfaction and pleasure of the private individual and his family, from which no one else derives any benefit.

But if a bank lends money to a farmer to buy agricultural machinery, the lending is not inflationary, for the loan is a step in a process which will eventually result, assuming that the machinery is properly used, in increased crops. This will be to the benefit of the community generally. When the crops are sold, the loan will be repaid out of the proceeds. Then the money is returned to the bank and ceases to exist. The banks not only create money, they destroy it too.

Revision Test 1

Put ticks in what you think are the right boxes.

(1) Metal coins are homogeneous. Does this mean they are
    (a) easy to mint? ☐
    (b) all of the same type? ☐
    (c) easily portable? ☐

(2) Which of these is money?
    (a) an early convertible banknote ☐
    (b) a cheque ☐
    (c) a 5op piece ☐
    (d) a modern inconvertible banknote ☐

(3) Is a banknote
   (a) a receipt ☐
   (b) written proof of a link with gold ☐
   (c) a promissory note ☐

(4) Token coins
   (a) have milled edges to prevent 'clipping' ☐
   (b) are free from the risk of forgery ☐
   (c) have metallic content equal to face value ☐

(5) Inflation is shown by
   (a) good coins driving out the bad ☐
   (b) a run on the bank ☐
   (c) a rise in general prices ☐

(6) A coin which has intrinsic value
   (a) is worth near its face value ☐
   (b) can only be paid into a bank ☐
   (c) is worth nothing ☐

(7) Between 1821 and 1914 the country was
   (a) on the Gold Bullion Standard ☐
   (b) on the Gold Standard ☐
   (c) on the Silver Standard ☐

(8) Which of these statements are true?
   (a) money must be generally acceptable as resistant to inflation ☐
   (b) token coinage is used in advanced and civilized communities ☐
   (c) if prices go up, this really means that the value of money is falling ☐
   (d) the form which money takes is all-important for sustaining confidence in the currency ☐

Check your selections with the answers on p. 395
Take one mark for each correct answer.
Each Revision Test totals 10 marks.

Questions for discussion

1. List some commodities that have been used as money. What qualities led to their selection as a form of money, and in what ways were some better able than others to perform the function of money?

2. Trace the development of paper money in Britain from the goldsmith's receipt to the Bank of England note.

3. In what circumstances might barter reappear today?

The central bank

Establishment of the central bank

The first and most important function of a central bank is to accept responsibility for advising the government on the making of the country's financial policy, and then to see that it is carried out. The government must decide how much money there shall be in the country at a given time, and the central bank must take steps to increase or decrease the supply accordingly.

This was by no means clear when the Bank of England was founded in 1694. The specific reason then for its formation was to provide money for the government during the war of the Grand Alliance against France (1689–97). Wars had become too expensive to be financed out of current taxation.

The Royal Charter of Incorporation was granted in the first instance for eleven years, but only three years later an Act provided for an increase in the Bank's capital and extended the charter until 1711, after which date it was periodically renewed. In 1709 the Bank was constituted the only joint-stock bank in England. Its business at first was the receiving of money on deposit, the discounting of approved bills of exchange, and the lending of money against satisfactory security.

At first this lending was nearly all to the government, and gradually the Bank came to perform other services on behalf of the government, and so to become regarded as 'banker to the government'. Thus it undertook on the government's behalf the circulation of exchequer bills, which were simply promissory notes of the government, first issued in 1696, and constituting the floating debt of the country for the next century and a half. They were the forerunners of the present treasury bills. In 1718 subscriptions for government loans were for the first time received at the Bank and thereafter it undertook the management of the issue of government securities. In 1751 it took over the administration of the government accounts and the National Debt.

There had been many crises in these early years. Only three years after its incorporation the Bank had to suspend payment because of a shortage of silver and gold which made it impossible for the Bank to honour its notes in metal. It seems likely that the metal had disappeared because it was being melted down and exported. This showed a profit over using the coins as currency in this country, because the foreign exchanges had moved against London.

This was an early recorded instance of the phenomenon of inflation, and the reason was probably an over-issue of notes by the new Bank. The Bank survived the crisis by paying a part on each note and promising by endorsement on the note to pay the rest later, by calling up the balance of its subscribed capital, and by borrowing from abroad.

In 1720 it was in danger of becoming involved in the South Sea Bubble, but again survived. In 1734 its business was transferred from the Grocers' Hall to a site in Threadneedle Street.

In 1780 the Gordon Riots occurred. These had a religious basis and were directed by Protestants against Roman Catholics. Sixty thousand people marched through the streets to Westminster on 2nd June and there was a great deal of disorder. There was further rioting on the 4th when the Bank of England was attacked and some of the prisons were

broken into. In the end the riots had to be put down by force.
The Bank had not been altogether unprotected, for a company of foot guards were on duty on the premises. Ever since
then a picket of Grenadier or Coldstream Guards has mounted
guard at the Bank each night. The practice was discontinued
only in 1973 on the grounds of unnecessary expense and dis-
location to London's traffic.

The Bank began to issue notes for £10 and £15 in 1759,
notes for £5 in 1793, and notes for £1 and £2 in 1797. Before
1759 it appears that the lowest amount of note issued was £20.

In 1797 there was another crisis because of an excessive
demand for specie (gold and silver coins and bullion) and the
Bank was authorized by an Order in Council not to pay metal
for notes presented to it. Later in the same year a Restriction
Act was passed confirming the order. In 1810 the House of
Commons received a report on the high price of bullion and
the state of the country's currency. In 1816 the Bank was
authorized to increase its capital to £14½ million, at which
figure it stood until nationalization in 1946. In 1819 the Bank
Restriction Act was further continued. On 1st May 1821, the
Bank began to pay its notes in gold.

The Gold Standard had arrived.

At this time there were more than five hundred banks in
England. Because of the prohibition of any joint stock bank
other than the Bank of England, and because of the monopoly
held by the Bank of the issue of notes in London, most of
these banks were country banks, limited to not more than six
partners. The result was that most of these banks had inadequate resources. Sometimes they issued notes too freely.
This was the main cause of a crisis in 1825 when the Bank
again passed through a very severe time. We are told that
the credit of the Bank was saved by the providential 'finding
of a box containing some £1 notes'.

Whatever really happened, the credit of the Bank was still
good and its notes respected. In the country areas there was
general suspicion of the notes of many country banks.
Accordingly the Bank of England was empowered to open

country branches for the purpose of restoring confidence by issuing its notes in the country.

Branches were duly opened at Gloucester, Swansea and Manchester. The present day branches of the Bank are to be found at Birmingham, Bristol, Leeds, Liverpool, Manchester, Newcastle, Southampton and at the Law Courts in London.

In 1826 an Act was passed permitting joint-stock banks with note-issuing powers to be set up outside a radius of sixty-five miles from London. Another Act in 1833 permitted joint-stock banks without note-issuing powers to be set up within the sixty-five mile radius.

The Bank of England's monopoly of joint-stock banking was over. Its monopoly of note issuing was about to begin.

The Bank Charter Act, 1844

It is difficult for us today to realize the instability of the banking structure at this time. In the first quarter of the nineteenth century nearly three hundred country banks went bankrupt. This instability was attributed to the over-issue of notes, and a demand for reform led to the passing of the Bank Charter Act, the object of which was to control the issue of notes and so to control inflation and thus restore confidence. It was the damage to confidence in the notes of these many small banks which led to the periodical runs on the banks. These crises obliged the banks in question to draw on their balances with London Banks, who in turn were obliged to draw on the Bank of England.

The Bank of England was the ultimate source of cash in the monetary system.

The Bank Charter Act gave the Bank of England a monopoly of note issue within a radius of three miles from the City of London, provided that no new bank thereafter was to be allowed to issue notes, that the note issue of existing banks was to be limited, and that the right to issue notes was to be given up by any bank deciding to amalgamate with another. The last amalgamation of a note issuing bank took place in 1921. The Treasury issued £1 and 10s notes until 1928, but thereafter the Bank of England was the sole note issuing authority in England and Wales.

The Act also provided that the Bank might continue its existing issue of £14,000,000 in notes not backed by gold, but that all notes issued in excess of this figure were to be fully covered by gold. The issue not covered by gold was called the fiduciary issue. This was to be covered by securities.

So that the issuing of notes could be more closely checked the Bank was to publish a weekly balance sheet (the Bank Return), and was to be divided into two departments – the Issue Department and the Banking Department. One of the earliest returns made after the Act is shown in simplified form.

ISSUE DEPARTMENT

	£ millions		£ millions
Notes issued	28	Government debt	11
		Other securities	3
		Gold coin and bullion	13
		Silver bullion	1
	—		—
	28		28
	=		=

BANKING DEPARTMENT

	£ millions		£ millions
Capital	14	Government securities	14
Rest	3	Other securities	8
Public deposits	4	Notes	8
Other deposits	9	Gold and silver coin	1
Bills	1		
	—		—
	31		31
	=		=

The fiduciary issue can be seen at a glance from the Issue Department's figures. The total of the fiduciary issue was allowed to increase by two-thirds of the amount of any note-issuing powers given up by other banks. In the Banking Department the 'Capital' is that of the Bank's stockholders.

The item 'Rest' is the Bank's reserve, accumulated out of undisclosed profits and never allowed to fall below three million pounds. 'Public deposits' is the balance in the government's account. When taxes are collected, for example, they are paid into this account. 'Other deposits' included the money left at the Bank by other bankers and by the Bank's private customers.

The Bank was originally intended to carry on the two roles of central note-issuing banker and fully competitive commercial banker, but the last hundred years have shown that the central bank functions are all-important and that the Bank ought to concentrate on them. Its activities as a commercial bank have been curtailed and it now undertakes only a very small amount of private business and will not normally accept new private accounts.

In passing the Bank Charter Act parliament thought it was establishing control over inflation by strictly limiting the supply of money at its source.

The quantity theory of money was understood – the more money which is issued, the less it is worth. Prices will go up (really the value of money going down) and there will be inflation.

What was not understood by parliament was that bank deposits were also money. The Bank Charter Act gave no control over them. During the years which followed the passing of the Act the total quantity of money available increased as did Britain's trade. For bank deposits – a third type of money besides bank notes and coin – were being used to carry on the bulk of the expanding Victorian commerce.

Parliament had understood that there would be times when an exceptional demand for banknotes could be expected, for example, at Christmas. Then people would draw out money from the banks and spend it. This money would pass into the hands of shopkeepers and traders who would in due course pay it back into their banking accounts. So the demand would be temporary.

Therefore there was an arrangement to suspend the Bank

Charter Act so that more notes might be printed and issued when necessary, without the extra backing in gold. In time of war it would not be possible to find gold to back all the extra notes that would have to be printed to finance the government's expenditure in prosecuting a war.

The Act was suspended during crises in 1847, 1857 and 1866. In each case an extra issue of notes was successful in restoring confidence and the crisis passed away. Power was again given to suspend the Act on the outbreak of war in 1914, but it was not used. Instead, the need for more notes was met by an issue of £1 and 10s notes by the treasury. Gold coins were withdrawn from circulation.

In 1928 the treasury issue was amalgamated with that of the Bank of England, which had continued to issue notes for multiples of £5. At this time the fiduciary issue, which between 1844 and 1921 had increased only from £14,000,000 to £20,000,000, had reached the figure of £260,000,000, a measurement of the post-war inflation. This tendency was to increase and gather momentum. In 1952, after another war, the figure was £1,450,000,000 and in 1978 it was £8,550,000,000.

Control of the fiduciary issue is placed, by the Currency and Bank Notes Act, 1954, in the hands of the Treasury, with the proviso that any upward change lasting for more than two years has to be confirmed by parliament. The banknotes of the Scottish and Northern Irish banks are issued under licence of the Treasury.

In the twentieth century the work and responsibilities of the Bank have been considerably increased by the growth in government expenditure, by the management of the currency following the suspension of the Gold Standard in 1931, and by the introduction of exchange control in 1939.

The Bank was nationalized by the Bank of England Act, 1946, the existing stockholders being compensated by the receipt of government stock. That Act included the clearest possible indication that the government was to make itself henceforth solely responsible for the country's monetary policy.

Section IV of the Act provided that the Treasury may from time to time give such directions to the Bank as, after consultation with the Governor of the Bank, they think necessary in the public interest. The Bank, in turn, is empowered to make requests of, and issue directives to, the clearing bankers and other financial institutions.

Present day functions

As the central bank of the United Kingdom, the Bank of England:

(1) Implements the monetary policy of the government
(2) Acts as banker to the government:
 – administers exchange control
 – manages the Exchange Equalization Account
 – keeps the government's banking accounts
 – handles the government's treasury bill issues
 – acts as registrar of government and nationalized industry stocks
 – is the note-issuing authority
(3) Acts as banker to the deposit banks.
(4) Acts as lender of last resort to the discount houses.
(5) Has about 90 accounts for overseas central banks and for such bodies as the International Monetary Fund and the International Bank for Reconstruction and Development (the World Bank).
(6) Has a small number of private customers.

The functions of the central bank include the duty of controlling the amount of money there is in the country. Money consists of banknotes, coin and bank deposits, the last very much the most important. Fresh money is created by the banks when they lend. All this we know.

Control of banknotes and coin is already in the hands of the Treasury (under parliament), working through the Bank; control of bank deposits and the natural consequence of this, the encouragement or discouragement of lending, remain to be discussed.

Before we do this, let us take a look at a modern Bank Return:

BANK OF ENGLAND

Wednesday the 8th day of September 1976

ISSUE DEPARTMENT

	£		£
Notes Issued:		Government Debt	11 015 100
In Circulation	6689 732 528	Other Govt.	
In Banking		Securities	6090 669 398
Department	10 267 472	Other Securities	598 315 502
	6700 000 000		6700 000 000

BANKING DEPARTMENT

	£		£
Capital	14 553 000	Govt. Securities	1585 904 840
Public Deposits –		Advances and Other	
including Exchequer,		Accounts	225 938 125
National Loans Fund,		Premises, Equipment	
National Debt Com-		and other Securities	83 826 011
missioners and		Notes	10 267 472
Dividend Accounts	17 237 163	Coin	239 720
Special Deposits	1037 170 000		
Bankers' Deposits	321 091 440		
Reserves and Other			
Accounts	516 124 565		
	1906 176 168		1906 176 168

Dated the 9th day of September 1976

D. H. F. SOMERSET, Deputy Chief Cashier

The layout is not so very much different from that far off Return of 1844, but how the figures have changed! That old 'Government Debt' on the assets side of the Issue Department is still there. It represents the original loan made to the government by the founders of the Bank in 1694, plus some later loans. The fiduciary issue is now £6,700 million, up by more than four-fifths on 1971. On the liabilities side of the Banking Department the government accounts ('Public Deposits') are now specified in part. 'Bankers' Deposits' shows the total of the money kept at the Bank of England by the deposit banks. Special deposits we will come to in a moment.

The assets side is more or less self explanatory. 'Government Securities' shows those securities held which are other than those held against the fiduciary issue. All the note issue is now fiduciary.

'Premises, Equipment and Other Securities' is a rather unlikely amalgamation, the reason for which is that the Bank does not wish, for reasons which seem good to it, to reveal the exact total of 'Other Securities'. 'Advances and Other Accounts' includes discounts.

Open market operations

The Bank of England traditionally exercised control over the cash reserves of the deposit banks by open market operations, by manipulation of the Bank Rate, and, from 1960 onwards, by the imposition of special deposits. The first of these concerned the cash ratios of the deposit banks.

The banks must at all times be ready and able to honour their customers' withdrawals on demand. To be able to do this, the banks must maintain adequate amounts of cash in their tills at all their branches and head offices. They do know that in normal times it will never happen that all their customers come in at one and the same time to demand repayment, and therefore that a proportion of their deposits will be sufficient, if the proportion is wisely chosen. Too small a proportion means that the banks are risking running out of ready cash – a disgrace that it would take them some time to live down – while too large a proportion means that profits are being lost. The idle money in the tills could have been lent to trustworthy borrowers at interest.

The banks had found by experience that a prudent ratio to keep was 8 per cent. Formerly the leading banks agreed amongst themselves to maintain their cash ratios at this figure. The balances at the Bank of England (described in the Bank Return as Bankers' Deposits) were (and still are) used for paying for, or receiving payment for, notes and coin supplied by the Bank of England or returned to it; making payment to the exchequer; or making daily adjustments with the other banks on the credit and debit clearings. But they are also accounts from which the banks can obtain fresh funds very rapidly, so those balances are as good as cash.

If the Bank of England desired to reduce bank deposits it might sell government securities in the open market. The cheques in payment would be drawn on commercial banks. The deposits of the commercial banks fell when the cheques were presented and paid. The figure of Bankers' Deposits in the Bank of England fell and the cash ratio was affected. The percentage dropped below 8 per cent. To restore the cash ratio to its customary figure the banks had to reduce their deposits until they again represented twelve and a half times their cash figure. They did this by reducing existing advances and refusing to grant new ones. Or they could sell some of their investments, thus replenishing their stock of cash.

The opposite result was achieved if the Bank of England bought securities in the open market.

It is rather a clumsy method, and to be effective the operations had to be on a very large scale.

The cash ratio is not now maintained at 8 per cent, as will be seen later, nor is it now regarded as a measure of Bank of England control.

Bank Rate

The Bank formerly influenced interest rates through a change in the Bank Rate, for the clearing banks' rates for deposits and advances were linked with Bank Rate and moved with it. All other short-term rates were also strongly influenced by it. Thus a rise in the Bank Rate made borrowing more expensive and tended to discourage it. In this way the supply of bank credit was reduced.

Of recent years some rethinking has been done about the effectiveness of Bank Rate. The slump conditions in the 1930s caused the Bank Rate to be reduced to 2 per cent, partly in the hope that industrial and commercial borrowers, finding money cheap, would be encouraged to borrow and would use the money to expand their business. This did not happen and the Bank Rate remained at 2 per cent for nearly twenty years (except for a brief period at the outset of the second world war). It seemed that when businessmen lacked confidence and were not willing to invest, even 2 per cent was not cheap enough to make them change their minds.

On the other hand, when the economy is expanding, there is full employment, order books are full, and confidence is unlimited, even a very high rate of interest seems to be accepted by borrowers who can still borrow and make a profit. But dear money will hit the small people in the country, for example, young folk wanting to get married and buy a house on mortgage. There will be political repercussions which are bound to be respected by a government which is dependent on a majority of public approval if it wishes to remain in power.

The government is also bound to preserve equilibrium in the foreign exchanges. The value of the pound sterling in terms of other countries' currencies must not vary too dramatically or there will be adverse results for our international trade. If the value of sterling begins to drop overseas investors here will tend to take their capital out of the country before its value drops any more. There will be many sellers of sterling and few buyers. This will result in a still greater fall in the value of sterling. This tendency can be reversed by raising the interest rates in this country so that foreign capital flows back to take advantage of the good rates. For a time there will be many buyers of sterling and few sellers, so that the exchange value of the pound will rise again.

But although high interest rates have supported sterling in the foreign exchange market they have brought hardship to some people in this country. House mortgages have become more expensive. It is dearer to buy a car on hire purchase.

The conclusion from this is that on a number of occasions Bank Rate was raised to force corresponding short-term money rates higher than they would have been if domestic conditions had been the only factor to be considered.

Special deposits

As banks are institutions dedicated to making a profit they seek to relend some of the money which has been deposited with them. They cannot lend it all, even if this were wise, because they have to keep some money in their tills, and some is in the pipeline of the clearing system. None of this money earns any interest. The rest of the banks' deposits are lent in varying proportions to the government, the discount houses, other financial institutions, and to other customers of the bank, whether companies, firms or individuals.

In making these advances the banks must keep in mind that the obtaining of a high rate of interest is not the only consideration. If it were the banks would lend as little as possible to the government and to the discount market (where the risk of loss is non-existent and so the interest rate is comparatively low), but would lend as much as possible to their customers (where the risk of loss, and so the interest rate, is higher). They must also remember that if they are obliged to realize some of their assets (instead of holding them to maturity) there is a risk of loss on sale.

A more important consideration is the length of time for which lending is granted. Money at call or short notice can be regained at once or quickly. These advances are liquid. Money lent to other customers of the bank may take some time to get back. These advances are not very liquid.

But the bank always has to have enough liquid resources to meet its commitments. The saying is, those who borrow short must not lend long. The bank 'borrows' from its customers and may have to repay at any moment. As with the cash ratio (which is concerned with cash: now we are talking about liquid assets) only a proportion of deposits need be kept in liquid form. The proportion which was approved by the Bank of England from 1963 onwards was 28 per cent (as a minimum). This was a ratio of liquid assets to total deposits. It was called the liquidity ratio.

Special deposits were introduced in 1960. They were to supplement and ultimately replace the Bank of England's quantitative and qualitative controls over the clearing banks. A quantitative control meant that each individual bank was asked not to lend more than a certain quantity of money. These requests were made at various times between 1950 and 1970. They took various forms. In 1955 the banks were asked to restrict loans to 90 per cent of what they had been before. In 1957 they were asked to keep their advances to no more than they had been the year before. In 1958 all controls were lifted. In 1960 they were again imposed.

These contradictory orders were the result of the monetary policy of the government of the day. This became known as the stop–go period. Industry would be encouraged to expand by borrowing, and then expansion would be halted by a drying up of credit.

Qualitative controls were directions to the banks on priorities to be observed when lending. At times when money was tight the private borrower could get nothing. Advances were allowed only to priority borrowers who were essential to the government's policies, such as exporters, builders of hospitals and houses, farmers and those engaged in some branch of national defence.

Although these directives were duly followed by the banks, it was recognized that they were in many ways harmful. Although banks might be in a good liquid position, they could not lend. The quantitative control hampered the banks' freedom of action and prevented them from competing with each other for new business.

The system of special deposits was designed to control credit by reducing the banks' liquid assets. The call would be, usually, for 1 per cent of the banks' deposits to be transferred to the Bank of England. It was held there on a separate account which did not qualify for inclusion in the computation of total liquid assets. In this way the banks' ability to lend was cut down because they had to preserve their liquidity ratio. Interest was paid on special deposits at treasury bill rate.

Special deposits did not at first apply to other lending bodies such as merchant and overseas banks, and insurance companies, although hire purchase finance companies had been closely regulated from 1950 onwards. Consequently many business organizations found little difficulty in arranging loans for their needs, albeit at a rather more expensive rate of interest. These attempts at control were thus largely ineffective and it was realized that the government should aim to control the general liquidity of the economy. The deposit banks were the biggest but not the only lenders in the system. Determined borrowers could obtain money elsewhere, and fringe operators (not always as stable or responsible as the big lending banks) could flourish. To avoid losing ground in the competitive scramble, the clearing banks acquired subsidiaries, e.g. finance houses or the London offices of overseas subsidiaries, through whom they could operate without being subject to controls.

Competition and Credit Control

The Bank of England was not unaware of the shortcomings of its systems of credit control, nor did it think that the various agreements among the deposit banks to restrict competition of certain kinds between them was good for the efficiency of the national banking system. (Until 1971 the London clearing banks had an agreed common cash ratio of 8 per cent; a uniform rate of interest – 2 per cent under Bank

Rate – for customers' deposits subject to seven days' notice
of withdrawal; and a uniform rate of interest on overdrafts
to high-class company borrowers.)

Therefore it produced in May 1971 a document called
Competition and Credit Control, setting out a new system which
would allow freer competition between the banks, while at
the same time allowing the authorities to exercise a comprehensive control over the national credit. All banks were to be
included in the scheme, the merchant and overseas banks
along with the clearing banks.

Some measure of competition was also to be introduced
into the discount houses' bidding for treasury bills.

Some modifications were made to the original proposals
as a result of discussions with the banks and the money
market, but they were not of a major kind, and the basic
policy points were put into operation as from September
1971.

These were:

(1) Quantitative directives to the banks would end.
(2) Banks and discount houses would abandon their
mutual agreements on various rates so as to allow for
freer competition and thus greater efficiency.
(3) Bank overdraft and loan rates were no longer to be
linked with Bank Rate, but each bank would calculate them by reference to its own 'base' rate, which it
would vary as it wished.
(4) Instead of keeping a liquidity ratio of 28 per cent banks
would maintain day by day a uniform minimum
reserve asset ratio of $12\frac{1}{2}$ per cent of its 'eligible
liabilities'.

Eligible liabilities is a new name for deposits. They
are called liabilities because the banks are liable to have
to repay them to their customers. They are described
as eligible because they have been chosen as suitable
by the Bank of England in a definition which begins:
'Eligible liabilities are defined as the (short-term)

sterling deposits of the banking system as a whole'
and then goes on to make certain qualifications.

(5) The liquid assets required have also been redefined, and
also described as eligible to show that they are approved
by the Bank of England. They include the banks'
balances with the Bank (but no longer the cash in their
tills), treasury bills, and money at call with the London
Money Market. These are, roughly speaking, those
assets which the Bank will always be willing to convert
into cash, on demand.

The purpose of a reserve ratio is to ensure that the
banking system will be influenced reasonably quickly
by the operation of the central bank's instruments of
policy. Therefore the central bank must have some
measure of control over the total quantity of the reserve
assets. The selection of the assets by the Bank of
England therefore represents those instruments which
the Bank is willing to turn into cash, either through
the agency of the discount houses, or directly, without
unduly upsetting the existing market practices. (For a
full list of eligible liabilities and reserve assets see the
glossary, at pages 390 and 393.)

(6) Reserve assets, and special deposits, would be calculated as percentages of eligible liabilities.

(7) London clearing banks would be required to keep
about $1\frac{1}{2}$ per cent of their eligible liabilities in cash with
the Bank of England. This forms a credit balance which
is big enough to absorb the day-to-day fluctuations
and so ensures that the banks' accounts never become
overdrawn. This cash would earn no interest.

A similar scheme, with a reserve asset ratio of 10
per cent, was applied to deposit-taking finance houses.

Working of the new system

In introducing Competition and Credit Control the authorities
hoped to establish a properly planned system of control over

the increase in the money stock. The government, for its part, must place a high priority on:

- a progressive rate of national economic growth (no more stop and go);
- the maintenance of full employment;
- a reasonable stability of the currency on the foreign exchanges;
- the restraint of inflation.

These are the aims of any modern civilized community.

It was intended that taking all these factors into account the government would plan ahead to see how much the country wanted to spend on desirable things like defence, education, public services, and then to calculate how much of this expense would be covered by national savings and investment in government securities, and by taxation. If the country continued to expand economically a continually increasing supply of money would be required, but unless a corresponding increase in goods took place there would be inflation. Again, if we failed to sell as much of our goods abroad, as we had to buy from abroad, then there would be an adverse trade balance which would tend to weaken sterling on the foreign exchanges.

By doing their best to estimate all these unknown factors, and hoping that there would be no exceptional factors such as prolonged labour troubles, coal or oil production difficulties, or unexpected rises in the costs of raw materials abroad, the government would decide on a rate of money growth and the Bank of England would then control the supply of money to match the rate of money growth arrived at.

Control would now be exercised over the whole of the country's credit structure, not merely on the lending banks. The stock of money is the money which people have in their pockets or at the bank, or can get, the money they are able to spend if they want. It is control of bank deposits which is required rather than the control of bank advances. If the stock of money is too high the rate of tax can be raised, or people can be persuaded to save more of their income by making government securities more attractive (e.g. by raising the return on National Savings Certificates).

Bank lending is still a way of creating new deposits, so it must still be controlled, but this will be done by the manipulation of interest rates. Where lending is expanding too rapidly it must be checked by a very high interest level.

The weapon of special deposits can still be used to soak up excessive liquidity in the banks' holdings of reserve assets. These deposits, withdrawn from the banks' liquid resources, necessarily cut down the amounts they are able to lend while still maintaining their reserve asset ratio.

The Bank can still push up short-term interest rates by money market operations. It can still buy or sell government securities. But in the latter respect its former policy of invariable support for gilts (i.e. it would always buy such government securities as were on offer) has been changed. The Bank will not now buy gilts from the banks if it thinks that the result will be to replenish to an undesirable extent the banks' supplies of ready cash.

The use of these instruments of policy – operations in the gilt-edged market, the reserve assets ratio, and special deposits – will give the Bank a sufficient control over the liquidity of the banking system, through which it can influence the structure of interest rates.

At the time of the introduction of the new system bank liquidity was good, interest rates were not excessively high, and there was no bar on lending. The banks at once engaged in a competitive struggle to gain new deposits so that they could lend more and more. They were not now restricted to money paid in to banking accounts – they could bid for money on the parallel money markets, in particular on the inter-bank sterling market. The banks also competed in devising new services.

One hope was quickly justified – there was free competition in getting and lending money. But the new base rates varied very little as between banks, and then only for a few days at a time.

Minimum Lending Rate

The Bank of England still had one more change to make. It was announced in October 1972 that Bank Rate would be superseded by a new rate linked by a direct formula to market rates. The new rate was called the minimum rate for lending to the money market. It would be based on the average rate of discount for treasury bills at the weekly tender, plus $\frac{1}{2}$ per cent and rounded off to the $\frac{1}{4}$ per cent above.

Of course, the role of Bank Rate had been severely modified by the new credit control policy. It had itself become less an instrument of monetary policy and more a technical lending rate of last resort in the money market. In introducing the change the Chancellor said that it was inappropriate that the rate should be subject to the rigidities that had governed the movement of Bank Rate in the past. What was needed was a rate which could respond more flexibly to the changing conditions of the money market and one whose week-to-week movements were not interpreted as signalling major shifts to monetary policy. But the formula did not exclude the possibility of a special change in the new rate when it was felt necessary to give a lead to interest rates, and this was done in November 1973 when the Minimum Lending Rate was raised to 13 per cent, the link with the treasury bill rate being broken momentarily.*

During 1972 and 1973 the economy went through a difficult time, and wages, incomes and prices were subject to control in the interests of restraining inflation. World prices of raw materials rose markedly and the pound was floated to avoid having formally to devalue it. Thus it was free to respond to the forces of supply and demand, and gradually lost value.

The policy of Competition and Credit Control now came under criticism of a type which had been foreseen. Since its introduction money had become scarce and dear, and Minimum Lending Rate rose to a peak of 13 per cent. Although

* See p. 396.

bank base rates were no longer linked with this successor to Bank Rate, they rose just as if they were. The reason given by the banks was that if they did not raise their base rates, those large companies which had more or less permanent overdraft limits with them would borrow as much as they could and could re-lend this money at a profit on the parallel money markets. Indeed the banks could find themselves borrowing money which they had themselves lent at a cheaper rate of interest. (Such a process is called arbitrage.) In the end this profit-taking was defeated by the banks' decision to lend to these large organizations (e.g. local authorities, finance houses and other banks) only at a rate linked with money market rates, instead of a rate linked to a base rate.

During its upward progress any base rate eventually reached a point where the deposit rate moving up with it challenged building societies for investors' deposits, and new savings were diverted from building societies to bank deposits. The building societies raised their rates to investors, so mortgage rates had to go up; and anything which touched housing was a political matter. The Chancellor intervened to place a limit on deposit rate of $9\frac{1}{2}$ per cent for sums under ten thousand pounds. This limit continued until March 1975.

Such high interest rates were a necessary part of the new system. They were to restrain all but the most efficient borrowers. They were necessary to support the pound on the exchanges. The alternative was to go back to the old system of quantitative control, which nobody wanted. This was narrowly avoided towards the end of 1973. The economic and political conditions demanded much more stringent restraint on demand. Cuts in government spending and some tax increases were announced. Hire purchase controls and similar restraints on bank lending, including the use of credit cards, were reintroduced. To avoid a return to lending ceilings, the authorities introduced in December a new system of non-interest-bearing special deposits related to increases in the banks' interest-bearing eligible liabilities. Banks were to be penalized by the imposition of such special deposits if the

growth in their interest-bearing liabilities exceeded 8 per cent
in the first half of 1974 (the 'corset'). The banks would in
future have to maintain a close short-term control over the
growth of their deposits which paid interest, for if any bank
exceeded the permitted rate of growth by 1 per cent or less, it
would have to make special deposits with the Bank of
England at 5 per cent of the excess; if the excess was 1 – 3 per
cent the rate was to be 25 per cent, while for any higher
excess it would 50 per cent.

The corset was renewed for a further six months on progressively easier terms for the banks, and was finally discontinued in March, 1975. Its effect had been to impose quantitative controls without actually calling them that. Thus the
system of Competition and Credit Control was preserved, at
any rate in name, by a clever artifice.

The qualitative controls, which oblige the banks to restrict
lending to personal borrowers and to the property and financial sectors of industry, and to favour industrial investment
and exports, remained in force. The Bank reserved the
right to reimpose the corset at any time, using a new base.
Only a handful of small banks exceeded the limits and only one
incurred the maximum obligation to redeposit up to 50 per
cent of excess funds with the Bank of England.

This was really because the corset was introduced only
after the real boom in bank lending had passed its peak. For
this reason the limits imposed on the banks did not bite
harshly and the full effects of the scheme were not realized.
The main argument against it is that it impedes competition
between banks by linking each institution's growth to a base
arbitrarily fixed at one point in time.

The clearing banks have, on the whole, found the system of
Competition and Credit Control an improvement. They were
released from the disadvantage of being controlled while their
competitors were not. They quickly regained much of the
ground they had lost.

The conservatively fixed 8 per cent cash ratio dropped to
something between five and six after the inter-bank agreement

lapsed. This released more funds to be lent, while still enabling the banks to feel confident that they could honour all their customers' cheques on demand over their counters. The ratio between advances and deposits, customarily kept around 50 per cent or a little higher, leapt up into the 70s. An increased level of competition between the banks resulted in the appearance of many new services.

The banks certainly took full advantage of the new lending opportunities, making unusually high profits in doing so when interest rates were so high. This exposed the banks to some adverse public criticism and led indirectly to a review of banking charges (see p. 292). A further criticism concerned the amount of money lent to the property market. The government had allowed the money supply to increase sharply so that there might be adequate funds to finance replacement of capital assets and reinvestment generally by industry.

Unfortunately the industrial borrowers did not come forward – the property developers did. There were at that time no qualitative controls in force, and so the foundation was laid for a boom in the property market, a bubble which burst in 1974 when the stock market collapsed.

The aftermath of Competition and Credit Control

Even so long after the introduction of Competition and Credit Control in September 1971, it is extremely difficult to distinguish between its direct effects, and therefore its success or otherwise, and other factors which caused dramatic changes in the course of the UK economy. In the five years 1971–6 the UK and other major countries moved from recession to boom and back to the deepest recession since the 1930s; the international monetary system broke down and floating exchange rates replaced the stability of the Bretton Woods agreement that had prevailed for some 26 years; at its peak, inflation in the UK reached an annual rate of nearly 30 per cent; and one single event, the quadruplication of oil prices was responsible for a deterioration of £2,500 million in the UK balance of payments.

Competition and Credit Control, it must be remembered, was introduced at a time almost unique in recent UK economic history – the conjunction of low international interest rates, a strong balance of payments, and an economy in need of a stimulus. Added to this was a growing belief, particularly in political circles, that competitive free market forces made for greater efficiency in the allocation and use of resources. The basis of the proposals was, in the words of the Governor of the Bank of England, to introduce a system under which 'the allocation of credit is primarily determined by its cost'. He also added that the extent of pressure the Bank of England would be able to exert on interest rates by the new weapons might be affected by, for example, the financial position of the central government or the current sensitivity of foreign-exchange flows to short-term rates in London. However, he saw no limitations on the authorities' ability to neutralize excess liquidity or to bring about sufficiently strong upward pressure on bank lending rates.

The removal of 'ceiling' and quantitative controls on bank lending, which had inhibited interest-rate competition by the clearing banks for more than a decade, was a necessary requisite for a competitive market just as much as the abandonment by the clearing banks of their interest-rate agreements and the automatic links with Bank Rate. For clearly there had been no point in the clearing banks competing for deposit resources while they were prevented from using them profitably. Under the new arrangements, they were on very much the terms as all other institutions 'listed' by the Bank of England as falling within the banking sector, in respect of the uniform $12\frac{1}{2}$ per cent minimum reserve asset ratio to be maintained against eligible liabilities and control by special deposits. Cash held in bank tills did not, however, count as a reserve asset, and balances at the Bank of England, which the clearing banks agreed to maintain at a level of $1\frac{1}{2}$ per cent of eligible liabilities, while qualifying as a reserve asset, did not earn interest. Nevertheless, for all practical purposes, the clearing banks were, for the first time, able to compete on equal terms with the other 200-odd 'listed' banks for deposit resources both in sterling and foreign currencies. To meet the demand for advances they were able to issue negotiable certificates of deposit or bid for funds directly, rather than through the subsidiaries which had not been subject to the earlier cash and liquidity ratio controls imposed upon the parent banks, and whose existence now needed to be justified by some new or expanded market role.

Putting some 200 'listed' banks, including well over 100 foreign banks operating in the UK, on an equal footing for credit control purposes had wider implications, some of which became apparent only at a much later stage. The immediate effects were a rapid expansion of the discount market, as the major market for reserve assets and the secondary market for negotiable certificates of deposit, and the inter-bank market, as a means of profitably employing short-term funds and a source of liquidity, not least to the burgeoning secondary, or fringe, banks. As interest rates rose, corporate treasurers became increasingly sophisticated in placing short-term funds or in finding alternative sources of short-term finance – sometimes with little regard to the risks not entirely outweighed by interest-rate differentials. Where the Bank of England had not discriminated, they saw no need to do so either.

Expansion of deposits and lending (See Tables 1 and 2)

Most categories of banks entered the era of Competition and Credit Control with reserve asset ratios comfortably above the $12\frac{1}{2}$ per cent minimum – for the banks as a whole the ratio averaged 15·9 per cent, with the London clearing banks at 16·5 per cent and Foreign banks and affiliates as high as 24·0 per cent. The stage was set for meeting the pent-up demand for advances, particularly from the personal and other sectors on which the earlier restrictions had borne most heavily. And the demand materialized, aided by the reduction within the first two months of the clearing banks' base rates from 5 to 4½ per cent. Bank lending and deposit liabilities increased rapidly, and although the clearing banks took advantage of their ability to compete for funds in the interbank market, their expansion was based to a much greater extent on the issue of negotiable sterling certificates of deposit.

TABLE 1

All banks in the UK: Deposit liabilities

		Sterling			Other currencies		
		Total	of which Deposits by UK banks	CDs	Total	of which Deposits by UK banks	CDs
1971	Oct. 20	20,686	2,004	1,863	24,270	5,988	1,781
	Dec. 8	22,047	2,200	2,242	24,809	5,996	1,924
1972	Dec. 13	30,772	4,573	4,926	34,661	8,631	3,072
1973	Dec. 12	41,125	7,694	5,983	54,364	13,755	4,429
1974	Dec. 11	43,723	8,582	4,318	65,761	15,511	5,088
1975	Dec. 10	43,941	7,415	2,979	85,152	19,022	6,509
1976	July 21	46,457	7,929	3,311	101,392	21,379	8,335

Source: Bank of England Quarterly Bulletin.

TABLE 2

London clearing banks: Deposit liabilities

£m

		Sterling			Other currencies		
		Total	of which Deposits by UK banks	CDs	Total	of which Deposits by UK banks	CDs
1971	Oct. 20	11,191	183	83	291	79	—
	Dec. 8	11,735	309	203	460	147	—
1972	Dec. 13	14,923	592	1,292	1,264	363	40
1973	Dec. 12	19,613	1,317	2,006	2,019	551	74
1974	Dec. 11	22,160	1,084	1,416	3,351	721	156
1975	Dec. 10	22,533	695	598	4,018	824	368
1976	July 21	23,785	858	991	4,534	1,028	294

Source: Bank of England Quarterly Bulletin.

International considerations first impinged upon the operation of Competition and Credit Control in June 1972 when, in the very unsettled international monetary conditions of that month, a sharp and severe run developed on sterling which was halted by the decision to float. The run, however, placed a heavy strain on bank liquidity, and the Bank of England gave assistance to the clearing banks through a sale and repurchase agreement over 15 days involving £400 million of gilt-edged securities with over one year to maturity. Effectively, the terms amounted to a loan against the securities at $6\frac{1}{2}$ per cent and established a precedent of direct recourse by the clearing banks to the Bank of England, as lender of last resort, instead of through the traditional link of the discount market. Severe pressure on short-term interest rates was therefore avoided, with the crisis entailing a rise in Bank Rate only from 5 to 6 per cent and a similar rise in clearing bank base rates.

With sterling floating, the authorities felt able to regard the continued expansion of credit and its contribution to growth in the domestic economy as still desirable. Nevertheless, the first qualitative directive of August 1972, requesting the banks to moderate their lending to the property and financial sectors, indicated some disquiet about the direction of lending and the calls for special deposits towards the end of that year, about the rate at which it was growing. Despite higher levels of interest rates, bank lending continued to expand rapidly in 1973 requiring further very substantial recourse by banks to the wholesale money markets. Monetary conditions became much tighter in the second half of the year, with the Bank of England's minimum lending rate rising in two stages from $7\frac{1}{2}$ per cent in June to $11\frac{1}{2}$ per cent in July. The clearing banks' base rates followed to reach 11 per cent in August, by which time their seven-day deposit rate, at $9\frac{1}{2}$ per cent, had become competitive with building society investment rates. The warning, given in the 1971 consultative document, that some limit might be placed on bank deposit interest rates to protect savings banks and building societies became a reality.

In September banks were requested not to pay more than
$9\frac{1}{2}$ per cent interest on deposits of less than £10,000 – a
restriction that remained in force until February 1975.

November 1973 saw another sharp upward turn in interest
rates to counter inflation and external pressures on sterling.
In addition to calling for special deposits, the Bank of England, exercising its prerogative of giving a definite lead to
rates whenever necessary, over-ruled the formula, raised its
minimum lending rate from $11\frac{1}{4}$ to 13 per cent and requested
the banks to raise their base rates to the same level. As part of
the counter-inflation policy banks were, however, obliged for
the next twelve months, to forgo interest on that part of their
special deposits which related to non-interest bearing eligible
liabilities – essentially their current accounts – offsetting the
additional benefit derived from these current account resources from the rise in interest rates.

Stronger curbs and recession

High and volatile interest rates were already beginning to
produce problems for the clearing banks. Occasions arose
when their lending rates lagged below market rates and it
became possible for major borrowers who were entitled to
overdrafts to finance their normal business activities at the
'blue chip' rate of base rate plus 1 per cent, to draw on these
facilities and place the funds at higher rates in the money
market. Some misuse was prevented by linking lending rates
to market rates, but there is little doubt that at their height
these 'arbitrage operations' reached sizeable proportions,
causing difficulties to the banks in their asset and liability
management and frustrating the authorities in their attempts to control the growth in the money supply. Even
allowing for these distortions, it became clear towards the
end of 1973 that money supply, and particularly the interest-
bearing part of it, was still growing at an unacceptably high
rate and that sterner monetary measures would be necessary.

The December 1973 package, as well as re-emphasizing the

need for restraint in lending to the personal, property, and financial sectors and backing up consumer credit restraint with restrictions on credit card usage and the reimposition of hire-purchase controls, introduced the 'corset' as a means of directly constraining the growth in banks' wholesale deposits and therefore their lending.

The essence of the 'corset', or the supplementary special deposits scheme, to give it its official title, was that to the extent that the interest-bearing eligible liabilities of an individual bank grew in excess of a specified rate, the bank would be obliged to place additional non-interest-bearing Special Deposits with the Bank of England, with the rate of such special deposits rising progressively in relation to the excessive growth in interest-bearing eligible liabilities. It was also indicated by the Bank of England that the banks were not expected to circumvent the measures by a general increase in their lending rates. Banks, therefore, exceeded the specified rate of growth in interest-bearing eligible liabilities at progressively penal costs which they were, of course, perfectly at liberty to bear if the circumstances so warranted.

The scheme, renewed with some slight modifications for two further six-month periods in April and November 1974, represented a major departure from the spirit of Competition and Credit Control. However, some success can be claimed for it as an instrument of monetary policy. For although there was considerable demand for bank finance from industry suffering a liquidity squeeze from the effects of short-time working early in 1974 during the miners' strike and inflationary increases in fuel, stock, and labour costs, the rate of growth in bank lending was restrained reasonably well within the specified limits. Some non-clearing banks were obliged to place supplementary deposits around the middle of the year, and although the clearing banks were able to avoid these penalties, the scheme undoubtedly influenced their attitude towards the growth and the direction of their additional lending.*

With the onset towards the end of 1974 of the recession,

See p. 396. *

which deepened throughout 1975, demand for bank finance became increasingly sluggish and the need for the banks to seek additional deposit resources from the wholesale sterling money markets was considerably reduced. The supplementary special deposit scheme, which had become inoperative, was suspended in February 1975 – although it remains available for reactivation in case of need – and the $9\frac{1}{2}$ per cent ceiling on seven-day deposit interest was removed as the drop in interest rates had removed the need for its protective role. Apart from further qualitative directives emphasizing priorities for bank lending, monetary policy during the next year or so was relatively relaxed.

In the meantime, however, there had been other important developments obliging the banks to take a more cautious line in their lending policies and to strengthen their financial structures.

The secondary banking crisis and other strains

During the 1960s the strict lending controls over the main banking system had encouraged the growth of a number of fringe institutions varying widely in size and in the banking-type business which they undertook. Unhampered by the controls, they were able to flourish in the developing whole-sale money markets; charging higher interest rates needed for profitable growth, particularly to finance property development. They benefited from the increased resources available in the inter-bank market after the introduction of competition and credit control and continued to expand. However, the sharp rise in interest rates in the second half of 1973, the collapse of the property market, beset by a rent freeze and prospects of a heavy development gains tax, and a generally wider economic climate, left some weak positions exposed.

The failure of one secondary bank brought into question the liquidity of others, leading to a withdrawal of funds from many of the secondary banking companies. To protect depositors and to prevent a further spread of mistrust, the

Bank of England and the clearing banks joined together in a rescue operation – the life boat – to provide support which eventually reached a peak of some £1,200 million. Although it was originally hoped that such support would be required for only a few months, it soon became clear that the problems would take much longer to resolve. Most of these arose from the fall in property values and the difficulties of the property companies to which the secondary banks had lent long-term funds on the basis of short-term deposits. Other banks suffered too from the fall in property prices, not only those who had lent direct to property companies, but also those relying heavily upon property as security for advances in the normal course of business. The situation was further aggravated by the collapse of the stock market as the prospects for industrial and commercial companies became increasingly bleak, and fears arose of world recession in the wake of the oil crisis. Adding to these problems were the repercussions of banking failures overseas, through losses in the more volatile foreign-exchange markets of floating exchange rates.

Although conditions subsequently improved and the worst fears proved unfounded, the shocks were considerable and are likely to have longer-term effects on the banking system. Closer attention has been given to bank capital and liquidity adequacy and risk assessment by the banks themselves and by the Bank of England, which, in 1975, formally affirmed its responsibility for the regulation and supervision of UK banks and took steps to make such regulation and supervision effective. The Bank of England is soon to be armed with legal authority to license and supervise banks and other deposit-making institutions in a new statutory system which distinguishes between recognized (exempt) banks and licensed deposit-taking institutions and lays down appropriate criteria for the regulation and control of both categories.*

See p. 397. *

Conclusions and assessment

It would be surprising indeed if a new system, so radical in its changes as competition and credit control, had not required modifications at a fairly early stage. Some of these have been touched upon which could be interpeted as within the spirit of the original document – the frequent qualitative directives and even the ceiling on interest payable upon seven-day deposits of less than £10,000 of which the banks were fore-warned. There were others – the July 1973 modified arrange-ments for the discount houses, aimed at eliminating dis-tortions in the gilt-edged market, and the, as yet untried, agreement of March 1973 for a system differentiating between liabilities to residents and non-residents in calls for special deposits. The major amendment, the supplementary special deposit scheme, was too close to the former 'ceiling' control to be regarded as anything but a retrograde step, but, given the circumstances of the time, it was an ingenious compromise and about the best that could have been ex-pected. With this now in abeyance, the original structure remains remarkably intact.

So far as Competition is concerned, it can certainly claim to be successful – perhaps too successful, for the authorities must certainly have under-estimated the pent-up demand to be satisfied and, as the money markets expanded and interest rates rose, the mobility of short-term funds in response to small interest-rate differentials. This mobility, based on al-most perfect knowledge of the market, now calls for sophisti-cated liability and asset management by the banks and makes it extremely difficult for bank base and deposit rates to remain out of line for any length of time.

With the benefit of hindsight it is now clear that the ex-pansion of credit in 1972 and 1973 was far too rapid and that later problems of inflation can be attributed to its excessive growth. But this can hardly be blamed upon the banks, who were acting in the way they were intended to in grasping the opportunities presented and providing the stimulus that enabled the economy to achieve record growth. It is also questionable whether interest rates could have been effective in influencing the demand for credit or directing it to efficient users. Circumstances changed too rapidly to establish this. Interest rates were not, in fact, left to be determined by free market forces and, given the social and political pressures domestically and the external considerations which a government cannot ignore, even with a floating exchange rate, it is inconceivable that they should be. As to the direction of credit, it is a common criticism of Competition and Credit Control that it helped to divert resources from 'good' users, such as manufacturing industry and exports, to 'bad' users, particularly property, financial transactions, and personal lending. The statistics (Table 3) confirm that there were indeed substantial increases in lending to those 'non-priority' sectors, but it would be difficult to argue (at least on the figures for the London clearing banks) that this involved a misallocation of financial resources. Advances to manufacturing industry and other production rose by even greater amounts, and there was no suggestion that they had been deprived of needed funds.

There can be no doubt that Competition and Credit Control brought great benefits to the clearing banks and, more indirectly, to the banking system as a whole. Expanded deposits and lending and higher interest rates produced higher profits, the greater part of which, after taxation, was ploughed back to strengthen their capital structures. Even the massive provisions for losses which they found necessary to make in 1974 and 1975 against support and other lending, were able to be comfortably absorbed from operating profits maintained to an increasing extent by earnings from international operations. Given the ability to compete for non-resident sterling and currency deposits, the clearing banks had rapidly expanded their international banking activities and established themselves among the world's leading international banks.

In the home market, the clearing banks' ability to compete

TABLE 3. *Analysis of advances by banks in the UK (£m)*

	London clearing banks				All banks in Great Britain			
	Nov. 1971	Nov. 1972	Nov. 1973	Nov. 1974	Nov. 1971	Nov. 1972	Nov.† 1973	Nov.† 1974
Manufacturing	2,274	3,184	4,138	5,987	3,670	4,771	6,337	9,374
Other Production*	936	1,410	1,898	2,183	1,281	1,861	2,880	3,569
Financial	535	1,208	1,588	1,885	1,555	3,370	6,347	6,961
(of which property companies)	(261)	(642)	(850)	(925)	(498)	(1,154)	(2,320)	(2,802)
Services	1,359	1,810	2,452	3,078	2,204	3,111	5,180	6,960
Personal	1,121	2,130	2,755	2,628	1,404	2,635	4,076	4,037
Total to UK residents	6,225	9,742	12,831	15,761	10,114	15,748	24,820	30,901
Overseas residents	70	89	206	919	6,530	7,802	11,246	14,976
Total	6,294	9,831	13,037	16,680	16,644	23,550	36,066	45,877

* Agriculture, forestry and fishing, mining and quarrying, construction.
† Includes from November 1973 advances by the six large finance houses recognized as banks.
Source: Bank of England Quarterly Bulletin.

in wider fields of finance stimulated innovation in products. Freedom to lend to the personal sector now made sense of credit-card operations and encouraged personal loans and home-improvement loans. The personal customer became more important, not just as a stable depositor or borrower, but as a potential buyer of insurance, unit trust units, investment management services, and a wide variety of other personal services developed by the bank or its subsidiaries and, eventually, to be wooed by competitive terms for current accounts. For the corporate sector, efforts were intensified to provide comprehensive financial services and finance across the whole spectrum. Subsidiaries, their deposit-taking role no longer dominant, had to justify their continued existence by developing new and specialist activities. Some concentrated on eurocurrency business, others on point-of-sale consumer credit, industrial leasing, medium-term finance, or merchant banking; competing vigorously with established institutions in these fields.

Within the banks themselves, new skills had to be learned in money-market management, in planning, and in marketing the new range of products. Expansion and diversification opened up new career opportunities and increased promotion prospects.

Competition therefore produced a great many advantages to be set against the deficiencies of Credit Control and, with due allowance for the unprecedented upheavals in the domestic and world economies since Competition and Credit Control was introduced, it is perhaps fair to say that the benefits outweighed the drawbacks.

Revision Test 2

Put ticks in what you think are the right boxes.

(1) Early banking firms were limited to no more than six partners. This was because
   (a) their total capital resources were to be kept on a modest scale as a matter of government policy ☐

(b) if the bank failed it would be easier for depositors to bring a civil action against a small number of debtors ☐

(c) decisions on behalf of the bank needing the signatures of all partners could be taken more quickly ☐

(2) The object of the Bank Charter Act was
(a) to nationalize the Bank of England ☐
(b) to control the issue of bank notes ☐
(c) to force the Bank to present its accounts more clearly ☐

(3) At the present time the fiduciary issue is
(a) fully covered by gold ☐
(b) partly covered by gold ☐
(c) fully covered by securities ☐
(d) not covered at all ☐

(4) Which of these statements is true?
The Bank of England
(a) is the sole note-issuing authority in the British Isles ☐
(b) is a fully competitive commercial banker ☐
(c) keeps accounts for overseas central banks ☐
(d) is not allowed to have any branches ☐

(5) The item 'Public Deposits' in the Bank Return refers to
(a) money which has been temporarily taken away from the deposit banks to reduce their liquidity ☐
(b) money deposited by the government ☐
(c) balances maintained by the deposit banks to make daily adjustments between themselves ☐

(6) When the Bank of England wants to borrow money over a short term it issues treasury bills. These are tendered for by
(a) the discount houses ☐

(b) the clearing banks ☐
(c) the Treasury ☐

(7) The ratio between a deposit bank's total deposits and its total advances is called
(a) the cash ratio ☐
(b) the reserve asset ratio ☐
(c) the lending ratio ☐

(8) If the authorities want to support the pound sterling on the foreign exchanges they will
(a) raise the Minimum Lending Rate ☐
(b) issue more banknotes ☐
(c) make a call for special deposits ☐

(9) One result of Competition and Credit Control was
(a) the end of wasteful competition between the clearing banks ☐
(b) the end of restrictive controls over hire purchase companies ☐
(c) the end of restrictive agreements amongst the clearing banks ☐

(10) The Minimum Lending Rate is calculated by reference to
(a) the average overdraft rate charged by banks to first-class company borrowers ☐
(b) the average rate of discount on treasury bills ☐
(c) the average interest rate offered to investors by building societies ☐

Check your solutions with the answers on p. 395
Take one mark for each correct answer.
Each Revision Test totals 10 marks.

Questions for discussion

1. Banks in the UK are required to hold certain reserve assets in proportion to their eligible liabilities. Define reserve

assets and eligible liabilities. What role does the reserve asset ratio play in official control of bank credit?

2. What were the reasons for the introduction of Competition and Credit Control?

3. Why was the Bank Rate superseded by Minimum Lending Rate?

3

Other banks

Deposit banks

The first 'bankers' in this country were, as we know, the goldsmiths, who by issuing transferable receipts on the security of gold deposited with them paved the way for the development of rudimentary current accounts, bill discounting, and cheque and loan facilities.

The Bank of England at first enjoyed a monopoly in the London area, but this began to be eaten away when an Act of 1826 allowed joint-stock banks with note-issuing powers to be set up outside a radius of sixty-five miles from London. Seven years later another Act allowed joint-stock banks to be established inside the sixty-five mile circle, although they were not allowed to issue notes.

A joint-stock company is simply a public company whose capital consists of money received in exchange for shares in the business of the company. The shares are transferable and so any share holder can get his money back at any time by selling his holding to another person.

The Bank Charter Act in 1844 restricted the power of banks to issue notes and intended in that way to control the supply of money. However, the growing use of the cheque made the restriction on note issue a factor of ever-lessening

WESTMINSTER BANK LIMITED

GENEALOGICAL TREE

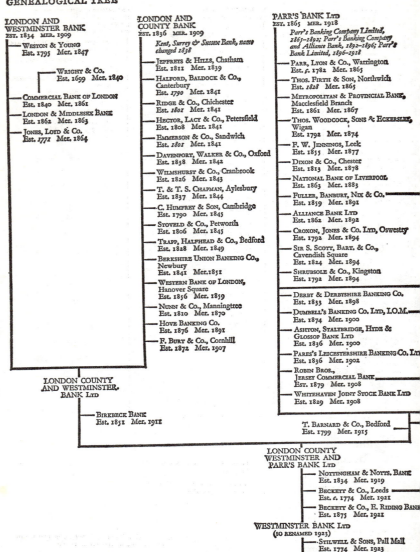

LONDON AND WESTMINSTER BANK
Est. 1834 Mer. 1909

— WESTON & YOUNG
Est. 1795 Mer. 1847

— WRIGHT & CO.
Est. 1699 Mer. 1840

— COMMERCIAL BANK OF LONDON
Est. 1840 Mer. 1861

— LONDON & MIDDLESEX BANK
Est. 1862 Mer. 1863

— JONES, LOYD & CO.
Est. 1771 Mer. 1864

LONDON AND COUNTY BANK
Est. 1836 Mer. 1909

Kent, Surrey & Sussex Bank, name changed 1838

— JEFFREYS & HILLS, Chatham
Est. 1811 Mer. 1839

— HALFORD, BALDOCK & CO.,
Canterbury
Est. 1790 Mer. 1841

— RIDGE & CO., Chichester
Est. 1801 Mer. 1841

— HECTOR, LACY & CO., Petersfield
Est. 1808 Mer. 1841

— EMMERSON & CO., Sandwich
Est. 1801 Mer. 1841

— DAVENPORT, WALKER & CO., Oxford
Est. 1838 Mer. 1842

— WILMSHURST & CO., Cranbrook
Est. 1826 Mer. 1843

— T. & T. S. CHAPMAN, Aylesbury
Est. 1837 Mer. 1844

— C. HUMFREY & SON, Cambridge
Est. 1790 Mer. 1845

— STOVELD & CO., Petworth
Est. 1806 Mer. 1845

— TRAPP, HALFHEAD & CO., Bedford
Est. 1828 Mer. 1849

— BERKSHIRE UNION BANKING CO.,
Newbury
Est. 1841 Mer. 1851

— WESTERN BANK OF LONDON,
Hanover Square
Est. 1856 Mer. 1859

— NUNN & CO., Manningtree
Est. 1810 Mer. 1870

— HOVE BANKING CO.
Est. 1876 Mer. 1891

— F. BURT & CO., Cornhill
Est. 1872 Mer. 1907

PARR'S BANK LTD
Est. 1865 Mer. 1918

Parr's Banking Company Limited, 1865–1892; Parr's Banking Company and Alliance Bank, 1892–1896; Parr's Bank Limited, 1896–1918

— PARR, LYON & CO., Warrington
Est. c. 1782 Mer. 1865

— THOS. FIRTH & SON, Northwich
Est. 1828 Mer. 1865

— METROPOLITAN & PROVINCIAL BANK,
Macclesfield Branch
Est. 1861 Mer. 1867

— THOS. WOODCOCK, SONS & ECKERSLEY,
Wigan
Est. 1792 Mer. 1874

— F. W. JENNINGS, Leek
Est. 1855 Mer. 1877

— DIXON & CO., Chester
Est. 1813 Mer. 1878

— NATIONAL BANK OF LIVERPOOL
Est. 1863 Mer. 1883

— FULLER, BANBURY, NIX & CO.
Est. 1859 Mer. 1891

— ALLIANCE BANK LTD
Est. 1862 Mer. 1892

— CROXON, JONES & CO. LTD, Oswestry
Est. 1792 Mer. 1894

— SIR S. SCOTT, BART. & CO.,
Cavendish Square
Est. 1824 Mer. 1894

— SHRUBSOLE & CO., Kingston
Est. 1792 Mer. 1894

— DERBY & DERBYSHIRE BANKING CO.
Est. 1833 Mer. 1898

— DUMBELL'S BANKING CO. LTD, I.O.M.
Est. 1874 Mer. 1900

— ASHTON, STALYBRIDGE, HYDE &
GLOSSOP BANK LTD
Est. 1836 Mer. 1900

— PARES'S LEICESTERSHIRE BANKING CO. LTD
Est. 1836 Mer. 1902

— ROBIN BROS.,
JERSEY COMMERCIAL BANK
Est. 1879 Mer. 1908

— WHITEHAVEN JOINT STOCK BANK LTD
Est. 1829 Mer. 1908

LONDON COUNTY AND WESTMINSTER BANK LTD

— BIRKBECK BANK
Est. 1851 Mer. 1911

— T. BARNARD & CO., Bedford
Est. 1799 Mer. 1915

LONDON COUNTY WESTMINSTER AND PARR'S BANK LTD

— NOTTINGHAM & NOTTS. BANK
Est. 1834 Mer. 1919

— BECKETT & CO., Leeds
Est. c. 1774 Mer. 1921

— BECKETT & CO., E. RIDING BANK
Est. 1875 Mer. 1921

WESTMINSTER BANK LTD
(SO RENAMED 1923)

— STILWELL & SONS, Pall Mall
Est. 1774 Mer. 1923

— GUERNSEY COMMERCIAL BANK
Est. 1835 Mer. 1924

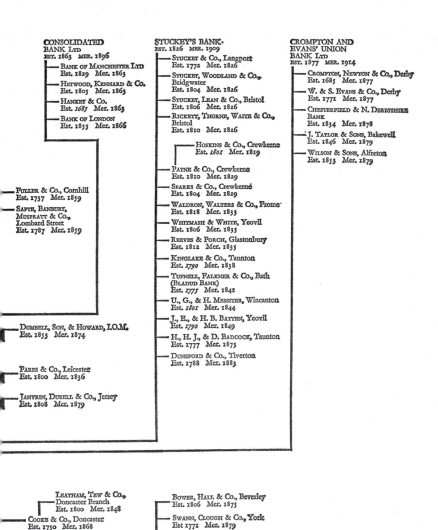

CONSOLIDATED BANK LTD
EST. 1863   MER. 1896

- BANK OF MANCHESTER LTD
  Est. 1829   Mer. 1863
- HEYWOOD, KENNARD & Co.
  Est. 1805   Mer. 1863
- HANKEY & Co.
  Est. 1685   Mer. 1863
- BANK OF LONDON
  Est. 1855   Mer. 1866

- FULLER & Co., Cornhill
  Est. 1737   Mer. 1859
- SAPTE, BANBURY, MUSPRATT & Co.,
  Lombard Street
  Est. 1787   Mer. 1859

- DUMBELL, SON, & HOWARD, I.O.M.
  Est. 1853   Mer. 1874

- PARES & Co., Leicester
  Est. 1800   Mer. 1836

- JANVRIN, DURELL & Co., Jersey
  Est. 1808   Mer. 1879

STUCKEY'S BANK.
EST. 1826   MER. 1909

- STUCKEY & Co., Langport
  Est. 1772   Mer. 1826
- STUCKEY, WOODLAND & Co.,
  Bridgwater
  Est. 1804   Mer. 1826
- STUCKEY, LEAN & Co., Bristol
  Est. 1806   Mer. 1826
- RICKETT, THORNE, WAITE & Co.,
  Bristol
  Est. 1810   Mer. 1826

  - HOSKINS & Co., Crewkerne
    Est. 1801   Mer. 1819

- PAYNE & Co., Crewkerne
  Est. 1810   Mer. 1829
- SPARKS & Co., Crewkerne
  Est. 1804   Mer. 1829
- WALDRON, WALTERS & Co., Frome
  Est. 1818   Mer. 1833
- WHITMASH & WHITE, Yeovil
  Est. 1806   Mer. 1835
- REEVES & PORCH, Glastonbury
  Est. 1812   Mer. 1835
- KINGLAKE & Co., Taunton
  Est. 1790   Mer. 1838
- TUFNELL, FALKNER & Co., Bath
  (BLADUD BANK)
  Est. 1775   Mer. 1841
- U., G., & H. MESSITER, Wincanton
  Est. 1801   Mer. 1844
- J., R., & H. B. BATTEN, Yeovil
  Est. 1790   Mer. 1849
- H., H. J., & D. BADCOCK, Taunton
  Est. 1777   Mer. 1873
- DUNSFORD & Co., Tiverton
  Est. 1788   Mer. 1883

CROMPTON AND EVANS' UNION BANK LTD
EST. 1877   MER. 1914

- CROMPTON, NEWTON & Co., Derby
  Est. 1685   Mer. 1877
- W. & S. EVANS & Co., Derby
  Est. 1771   Mer. 1877
- CHESTERFIELD & N. DERBYSHIRE BANK
  Est. 1834   Mer. 1878
- J. TAYLOR & SONS, Bakewell
  Est. 1846   Mer. 1879
- WILSON & SONS, Alfreton
  Est. 1853   Mer. 1879

- LEATHAM, TEW & Co.,
  Doncaster Branch
  Est. 1800   Mer. 1848
- COOKE & Co., Doncaster
  Est. 1750   Mer. 1868

- BOWER, HALL & Co., Beverley
  Est. 1806   Mer. 1875
- SWANN, CLOUGH & Co., York
  Est 1771   Mer. 1879

N.B. Dates of establishment in italics indicate only that
the bank was in existence at that time.

importance. The forerunners of the big banks today were by now already established. The London and Westminster Bank opened for business in 1834 with two branches, one in the City, and one at Westminster. Barclays had been in existence as a private company with an office in Lombard Street since 1694. Lloyds Bank started in a Birmingham partnership of 1765. Birmingham was also the birthplace of the Midland Bank, where the Birmingham and Midland Bank was founded in 1836. The National Provincial Bank was founded by a timber merchant in Gloucester in 1834.

Such were the modest beginnings of the giant banking groups of today. The principle of limited liability was first established by an Act of 1855 and extended by the Companies Act of 1862 to banks. From then on the formation of large joint stock banks was unhindered, and a process of amalgamation and expansion progressively swallowed up the smaller banking firms as the big groups sought to achieve a nation-wide coverage. It was a question of looking at the map, seeing the blank spaces where there were no branches, and then trying to buy up, or amalgamate with a bank well represented in that area.

The scale of the amalgamations is suggested by a genealogical tree devised to show the history of the former Westminster Bank Ltd (see pages 68 and 69).

It was not until the time between the wars that banks really started to open their own new branches on any scale. By this time there were the 'Big Five' (Barclays Bank Ltd, Lloyds Bank Ltd, Midland Bank Ltd, National Provincial Bank Ltd, and Westminster Bank Ltd) and the 'Little Six' (Coutts & Co., District Bank Ltd, Glyn Mills & Co., Martins Bank Ltd, National Bank Ltd, and Williams Deacon's Bank Ltd).

In 1968 a further round of amalgamations took place. Westminster Bank Ltd, and National Provincial Bank Ltd (which already owned District Bank Ltd, and Coutts & Co.) formed the National Westminster Bank Ltd. A merger proposed about the same time would have brought together Barclays Bank Ltd, Lloyds Bank Ltd, and Martins Bank Ltd, but permission for this was refused by the Monopolies Commission on the grounds that such an enterprise would or might tend to operate against the public interest. It would have been too big. It would have stifled a lot of the competition and, while good for the producer or supplier, would have been to the detriment of the consumer. However, Barclays Bank Ltd was permitted to absorb Martins Bank Ltd.

In 1970 Williams and Glyns Bank Ltd was formed from Glyn Mills & Co., National Bank Ltd, and Williams Deacon's Bank Ltd.

These great changes left very large groups with comprehensive branch networks in undisputed control of banking in England and Wales. Similar changes were taking place in Scotland and Northern Ireland. The groupings are now as follows:

England and Wales

Barclays Bank Ltd
Lloyds Bank Ltd
Midland Bank Ltd
National Westminster Bank Ltd
Williams and Glyns Bank Ltd

(Coutts & Co., a subsidiary of National Westminster Bank Ltd, has not been absorbed, and continues to trade under its own name.)

Scotland

Bank of Scotland
Royal Bank of Scotland Ltd
Clydesdale Bank Ltd

(Barclays Bank Ltd has an interest in the Bank of Scotland. The Clydesdale Bank is a subsidiary of Midland Bank Ltd. The Royal Bank of Scotland is owned by the National and Commercial Banking Group Ltd, which also owns Williams and Glyns Bank Ltd.)

Northern Ireland

Ulster Bank Ltd (a subsidiary of National Westminster Bank Ltd)

Northern Bank Ltd (a subsidiary of Midland Bank Ltd)

and various branches of Eire banks.

If we add to these the following:

Co-operative Bank (CWS Ltd)

C. Hoare & Co.

Isle of Man Bank Ltd (a subsidiary of National Westminster Bank, Ltd)

Lewis's Bank Ltd (a subsidiary of Lloyds Bank Ltd)

Scottish Co-operative Wholesale Society Ltd Bankers

Yorkshire Bank Ltd (jointly owned by four deposit banks)

– we shall have a list of the deposit banks, as so classified by the Bank of England.

By contrast with the inter-war period, which was one of near stagnation by present day standards, the 1950s marked the beginnings of new approaches and new methods. Gradually at first, and then more quickly, the next two decades saw a period of constant development and expansion. In this period the big banks entered, usually through subsidiaries, into the field of hire-purchase, merchant banking, unit trusts, factoring, export finance, insurance, investment management, and many other activities, while on the domestic side developing their computer services and on the international side joining overseas banking groups and opening their own branches all over the world.

Competition and Credit Control has without doubt been good for the banks, whatever its effects in other directions, and the new climate which encourages the provision of all services which a customer can require, also gives a greater and more varied choice of interesting work than ever before to bank staff. Associated with this is the chance of more rapid promotion for the right sort of young men and women.

The traditional lending role of the deposit banks has been to provide working capital for business, or to make available bridging loans pending the provision of more permanent capital from other sources. Recently the banks have shown greater willingness to lend for longer periods, for example, to help finance ship building and to provide finance for the export of capital goods. This attitude is a response to the new ability to borrow on the parallel money markets. If they were still wholly dependent on customers' deposits they would still have to remember that those who borrow short must not lend long.

Clearing banks

The clearing banks are those banks which are members of the Committee of London Clearing Bankers, and therefore have a seat in the Clearing House. These are, Barclays Bank, Coutts & Co., Lloyds Bank, Midland Bank, National Westminster Bank and William & Glyns Bank. The Bank of England, the Co-operative Bank and the Central Trustee Savings Bank also participate in the clearings.

Those banks without a seat in the Clearing House get their cheques cleared by a bank which has, acting as an agent.

The volume of cheques handled by the deposit banks is very considerable. The average monthly value of cheques, drafts and bills passing through the clearing system in 1975 was 149,564 million.

The origin of the Clearing House was somewhere in the 1770s, when the clerks of the private bankers of those days met each other daily to exchange cheques on their various banks and to settle up. An inn in Lombard Street came to be a convenient place for this because refreshment and exchange could proceed simultaneously.

The Clearing House is still in Lombard Street, and is now a limited company, whose members are the clearing banks.

Clearing is the process whereby the amount of a cheque is transferred from the drawer's bank to the payee's bank. When the drawer draws the cheque and sends it to the payee he will usually cross the cheque for greater security. When the payee gets the cheque and sees that it is crossed he knows that he cannot go to the drawer's bank and cash the cheque over the counter, but must pay the crossed cheque into his account at his bank (the collecting bank).

His bank will credit his account on the same day as he pays the cheque in, but his bank has not at that time got the money for the cheque because the cheque has to be sent to the drawer's bank to be paid and debited to the drawer's account. This will take at least three days, and five if a weekend intervenes. During that time the money is on the payee's account as 'uncleared effects' and the payee should not try to draw it out without special permission. If he does he may find that his cheque is returned unpaid with the answer 'Effects not cleared'. His bank wants to be sure that the drawer is good for the amount before it parts with the money.

The General Clearing

Millions of drawers are drawing cheques every day and millions of payees are paying the cheques into their banks. Every day each bank in the country gets a bundle of cheques in this way, some drawn on other banks, and some drawn on other branches of the same collecting bank, some even drawn on other accounts at the same branch bank. These latter do not have to go through the Clearing House, but can be debited to the drawer's account straight away (or returned to the payee 'unpaid' and his account debited). The rest of the cheques are sorted into bundles according to the banks they are drawn on and posted at the end of the day to the clearing office in London of the collecting bank (the 'Out' clearing).

This takes up the first day.

At the clearing office the cheques on the other branches of the collecting bank are taken out. They do not have to go through the Clearing House. They can be sorted at the clearing office into various bundles for the branches and mailed to them for payment (or return as unpaids).

The cheques which are left are sorted into bundles for the other banks and put into trays, labelled with the name of the bank to which each tray is to go. A list or docket giving a total of the amounts of the cheques in each tray is put into the tray along with the cheques. The trays are loaded on to a small electric van and taken to the Clearing House, where they are left in racks to be collected by similar vans and taken to each of the other clearing banks. In return trays containing cheques drawn on the presenting bank, which have been paid in at branches all over the country of the other banks, are picked up and carried back to the presenting bank's clearing office. Each clearing office lists the cheques received to compare the total with the total of the docket, to make sure it is correct. Then the cheques are sorted into branches electronically, and mailed to the branches concerned.

This takes up the second day.

The paying branches receive the cheques on the morning of the third day (the 'In' clearing) and inspect them for genuineness of signature and to see that they are otherwise in good order. If any have to be returned unpaid for any reason they are mailed direct to the collecting bank on the same day as they are received. An unpaid claim form debiting the collecting bank is passed through the General Clearing and ultimately finds its way to the collecting bank which will have sent the returned cheque back to its customer and debited his account with it.

The members of the Clearing House clear their own cheques and the cheques drawn on the banks for whom they act as clearing agents. The exchange of cheques in the General Clearing takes place in the morning and deliveries there can be made only between 9 a.m. and 11.30 a.m.

When the clearing banks have agreed all the totals each

will find that it either owes each other bank on balance, or is owed. A daily settlement is held for the items exchanged on the previous working day and balances owing are paid by a transfer from one bank's account to another in the books of the Bank of England. Any cheques wrongly sorted have to be returned to the presenting banks the same day and are entered separately on the daily settlement sheet.

The Clearing House is therefore well described as a place for exchange, and a place for settlement. By its time- and labour-saving system any number of cheques can be paid for by a simple transfer voucher.

The Town Clearing

Excluded from the General Clearing are articles of £5,000 and over drawn on and paid into the banks and branches in the Town Clearing. There are about one hundred 'town' branches of the clearing banks, all within the City of London and therefore near to the Clearing House premises. By using this clearing large cheques can be paid in up to 3 p.m., and still be cleared or returned unpaid the same day. The numbers are naturally only a fraction of those in the General Clearing and this allows the actual work of listing to be done in the Clearing House itself. From 3 p.m. onwards each bank keeps a representative at a certain table to receive cheques drawn on his bank as they are brought in by messenger. At 3.45 p.m. the reception of cheques ceases, and they are listed and totalled. They are taken back to the paying branches where they constitute a second in-clearing. Any unpaids or wrongly delivereds must be returned to the Clearing House by 4.30 p.m. on the same day, whence they are dispatched to the collecting branches.

The Credit Clearing

The system of clearing was extended to credits in 1960. It dealt with credit transfers and standing order payments. Credit transfers were lists of accounts to be credited, with a simple cheque for the total, handed in by a customer at his branch. He had also to prepare individual credit slips showing the name and address of the recipient's bank with a note of the remitter's name. The bank then sent the credits on to the right branches. These payments used to be called traders' credits, and were originally devised as an alternative for the customer who had been sending individual credits with cheques through the post. They were much used for salary payments at the end of the month.

When the National Giro was established the banks renamed these credit transfers 'Bank Giro', to offset the new competition, slightly redesigning the forms. Bank Giro also covered a new service, that of direct debiting.

Standing orders are instructions given to the bank by a customer to make regular payments thereafter of a fixed amount at certain times.

All these devices are brought together under the description of money transfer services. Non-customers may use branch banks to pay in for such things as rates, gas or electricity payments, and these all swell the numbers of items in the transfer service.

All these credit vouchers are sorted into bundles for each bank, totalled, and handed over to the representative of the receiving bank in the Clearing House Exchange Room between 9 a.m. and 10.30 a.m. each working day. A docket giving the total is attached to each bundle, for checking by the receiving bank. Wrongly delivered items must be returned before 9.30 a.m. the next day, because at that time the totals of the previous day's credit clearing are agreed at the Clearing House by the representatives of the banks concerned and the totals are carried forward on to the daily settlement sheet.

The Bankers' Automated Clearing Services are part of the Credit Clearing. The computer processes magnetic tapes, containing details of standing orders, Bank Giro credits, payroll credits and direct debits, prepared and sent to the Clearing House by the clearing banks and by company customers who have their own computers.

In 1975 a total of 962,719,000 articles were cleared through the Debit Clearing to a total value of £1,794,767 million. These figures included bills, cheques, etc. for which settlement was made at the Bankers' Clearing House, but not those passed through the banks' internal clearings, which are not published.

138,181,000 articles were cleared through the Credit Clearing to a total value of £22,089 million. These figures exclude inter-bank clearings through Bankers Automated Clearing Services Ltd and all inter-branch clearings.

The merchant banks

Merchant bankers carry on a great variety of business, and each tends to specialize in certain activities or in transactions with particular countries. Some activities, however, are basic to all of them. These are deposit banking, underwriting, and the management of clients' funds.

A list of merchant bankers would total about fifty names and of these, seventeen are members of both the Accepting Houses Committee and the Issuing Houses Association.

We shall see something of the origins of the accepting houses, where merchants trading in particular commodities such as wool or cotton acquired a comprehensive knowledge of the world markets relevant to their trading, and became so well known that they began to be asked to accept bills of exchange, to make them more readily saleable. This backing of bills became very profitable. The practice assisted in the development of London as the financial centre of the world. In turn this attracted representatives of foreign merchanting and financial houses to London, where the opportunities for advancement were greater. These men brought with them detailed knowledge of the trading resources and customs of their native countries, and the expertise which has always been the supreme virtue of the merchant banks was developed. These men were remarkable for initiative and shrewd ability to develop new financial methods to meet growing demands; they contributed much to the industrial and financial pre-eminence of the United Kingdom at the peak of its power and influence in the nineteenth century.

The work of the accepting houses made the bill on London so well trusted that it passed readily from hand to hand and became the nearest thing there was to an international currency. The acceptance business continued to flourish until the world recession in the 1930s, but long before that the merchant bankers, with their ability to raise large sums of money, had found another remunerative outlet for their skills. Between 1870 and 1914 London was the chief centre for the raising of long-term loans for imperial and foreign governments, and for companies engaged in the major enterprises of building ports and railways, installing street lighting, water mains, irrigation and sewerage, and constructing tramways, in foreign countries.

Money, mostly raised through the efforts of merchant banks, poured out of Britain into the Americas, the British Empire, and European and Asian countries. The merchant banks with their specialized links with particular countries – Hambros with Scandinavia, Schroeder's with Peru, Barings with Russia, Rothschilds with central Europe, Morgans with Chile – were the obvious first choice for making these financial arrangements. The Issuing Houses acted as intermediaries between those seeking capital, and those able to provide it. The Issuing Houses Association was formed in 1945 to represent the interests of the merchant banks and other institutions acting as issuing houses. There are 58 members, 17 of whom are the members of the Accepting Houses Committee, which confers upon them the facility of discounting commercial bills at the Bank of England at the finest rates. Every member has direct access to the Bank on any matter at any time.

Underwriting

The issuing houses sponsoring capital issues on behalf of their customers first satisfy themselves that the amount required can be raised on conditions which are acceptable to investors, and at a price at which the issue may be expected to be fully subscribed. They then make themselves responsible for taking up any of the issue which has not been taken up by others. They do not carry the whole of this underwriting risk themselves, but make arrangements with a wide circle of institutional investors, such as insurance companies, to share the risk; that is, they sub-underwrite the issue. The sub-underwriters undertake, for a commission, to subscribe for stock if public subscriptions fall short of the total issue. The issuing house, however, retains as the principal underwriter the ultimate responsibility for finding the money, as it has undertaken to do.

New issues may be for public companies already having a quotation on the Stock Exchange, or they may be for private companies 'going public'. Securities may be made available to the public either by means of an offer for sale by the issuing house, or by an issue by the company. In the case of an offer for sale the issuing house buys the whole of the issue for cash from the company and itself offers them to the public. In the case of an issue by the company the issuing house undertakes to find subscribers in full for the whole issue. New issues may also be 'placed', that is, sold privately to a limited number of investors, usually the big institutions, but in these cases a proportion of the securities is allocated to the market to be available to the general public. Still another alternative is for the new issues to be made available by the company to existing share-holders only, by rights issues or by open offer.

A rights issue gives the shareholder a right to take up and pay for some of the new issue in proportion to the number of shares which he already holds.

An open offer gives the shareholder a right to take up any amount of the new issue, irrespective of the number of shares which he already holds. Such an offer is rare.

The issuing house agrees the timing of the issue with the Bank of England (it would not do for several big issues all to come on the market at the same time) and where a quotation is to be granted it handles the negotiations with the Quotations Committee of the Stock Exchange, ascertaining the requirements of the Committee and producing the evidence which will be required as to the standing and reliability of the company. The advice of issuing houses is also available over a wide range of company problems, from the complete reorganization of the company to the best way in which to present the company's annual accounts.

By 'deposit banking' the merchant banks did not mean the same thing as did the clearing banks. The depositors of the merchant banks were mostly non-residents, and the currency held by the merchant banks was partly foreign currency, for large amounts only. This naturally led to the creation of a foreign exchange business.

The issue of long term loans led naturally to the appointment of the merchant bank as paying agent. In this capacity the bank kept registers of shareholders and debenture holders for companies, acted as paying agents for their dividends and debenture issues, and arranged for the investment of funds and safe custody of securities for accounts of clients in Britain and abroad.

Fund management

The decline of the commercial bill as a means of financing foreign trade led the merchant banks to take a greater interest in domestic matters. Until the first world war, while deposit banking and underwriting were expanding, the management of clients' funds was in its infancy. Some private individuals were asking the merchant banks to look after their securities – mostly government and foreign bonds – but the volume of this business was very small. After the war it was a question of building up the country's economy again, and industrial reorganization and reconstruction schemes, often supported by the government, gave the merchant banks the opportunity to associate themselves closely with industry and commerce by helping to raise capital and advising on financial matters generally. At the same time they were taking over the management of the investments of an increasing number of bodies and private individuals, working out ways to beat inflation and to reduce tax payable, and devising methods, such as the unit trust, whereby the small investor could share in a wide range of investments and have the benefit of specialized, expert management.

During the period after the second world war when the United Kingdom's exchange control restrictions were being relaxed only gradually, it became feasible to offer exporters a complete service, from financing the operation to ensuring compliance with the exchange controls, and seeing to the due departure of the goods at the right time, properly insured. Indeed in both insurance broking and in ship broking the merchant banks were at home. Any problems in either of the fields, connected with the finance of trade, could be readily solved.

By 1958 the reserves of gold and securities in the country were in a stronger position and full convertibility was granted at the end of the year. This meant that traders in goods and services between this country and another could make or receive payments in their own currencies at a rate of exchange fixed within narrow limits. Convertibility is associated with an absence of exchange restrictions and can be sustained only by countries with satisfactory balances of payments. All major industrial countries now permitted almost full freedom of movement of capital between non-residents, and the merchant banks once more looked principally to the international scene. The rapid expansion of the Euro-currency markets brought an increasing amount of foreign currencies into the merchant banks' deposits, and the character of the merchant banking business shifted towards wholesale rather than retail banking, that is, they tended to deal more with other financial institutions than with domestic customers. There was a great increase in mergers and amalgamations as British companies prepared to move into the international field and ever larger funds were raised for them in the overseas and international markets. For foreign borrowers issues in Euro-currencies were sponsored and foreign funds managed. In competition with the deposit banks, now increasingly inter-ested in traditional merchant bank activities, the merchant banks developed unit and investment trusts to new levels and gained a large share in the rapidly expanding pension funds.

A revival in the acceptance business, principally conducted in sterling, had made it quite important again, and while it is still largely supported by the merchant banks' deposit funds an increasing proportion of the funds comes from other banks and financial institutions. Since Competition and Credit Control the Bank of England has stated that it no longer has any objection to the resources of merchant banks being acquired by, or shared with, any other bank or financial group whether domestic or foreign.

It seems, therefore, that the paths of deposit banks and merchant banks are converging. Under the spur of com-petition the latter have acquired interests in hire purchase, leasing and factoring finance, usually through organizations specializing in this form of trade. At the same time they play an important part in the international short term capital market, continue their specialist activities in the foreign exchange markets, act as gold and bullion traders, match the needs of lenders and borrowers in the parallel money mar-kets, and mastermind mergers and takeovers. They remain the dominant force in underwriting and large company finance activities.

In recent years they have expanded into European centres and several have acquired interests in continental banks and participate in international hire purchase finance organizations.

British overseas and other banks

London is the headquarters of a number of British overseas banks which were originally set up in the days of the British Empire in the nineteenth century to provide banking facilities for settlers and traders in the colonies. At first, therefore, they opened branches in the main centres throughout the country, offering deposit services and lending for trade on the pattern of the banks at home. In doing this they naturally built up a specialized knowledge of the financial and trading conditions in their area.

The rapidly changing conditions after the second world war posed special problems for these banks. In some countries, particularly in Africa, the new national consciousness of developing countries naturally resented the financial dominance of foreign banks and sought to rid itself of it as soon as possible. Great numbers of their staffs came to Britain over the years to learn the business and to gain the qualification of the Institute of Bankers before returning home to pursue a career in a local bank. As the new countries gathered strength and experience closer local control was to be expected. In some cases this amounted to outright nationalization. Exchange regulations, monetary policies designed to attract foreign currencies, and taxation affected the ability of these banks to switch their funds freely from one overseas centre to another, while their links with London were loosened.

The development of new opportunities for business from 1950 onwards, the emergence of big international companies requiring advice and long term finance for exports and for economic growth, found the British overseas banks ill-equipped to meet the sort of competition which developed. It became apparent to them that their existing banking business, developed on conventional models (which was in any case now being challenged by local banks) was no longer enough. They had to be able to provide a broad range of international banking services.

This was done by strengthening the base in London, either by taking over a merchant bank or by amalgamation with other concerns who could open the door to the new money markets in London, and by setting up subsidiaries to offer long term finance to be made available to the developing countries.

In recent years these banks have successfully adapted to the new conditions, building up their foreign currency deposits and increasing their participation in the money markets. Together with about twenty Commonwealth banks – Canadian and Australian banks having offices in London (but with their headquarters abroad), the British Overseas Banks are members of the British Overseas and Commonwealth Bankers Association. Since Competition and Credit Control they are subject to the same requirements, as far as their London offices are concerned, of reserve asset ratios and special deposits, as are the deposit banks.

Foreign banks

Foreign banks of course have their headquarters in their own countries, but those we are concerned with here have a branch in London, some of them more than one. The two wars checked their growth here for some time, and many shut down on the outbreak, to reopen after the peace. Foreign banks bring competition for the home banks, but they also bring new business to London and provide a quick intelligence service as to conditions in their own countries. They came to London because London was the world's premier financial centre and they needed access to sterling resources and to London's facilities – particularly insurance and shipping – for the benefit of their own customers. They were engaged in financing international trade, mainly through the acceptance business, and in raising loans for overseas borrowers. They found it convenient to keep large working balances in London.

With the coming of convertibility the foreign banks, like everyone else, acquired freedom to participate in the exchanges and to move capital about the world. They began also to build up some domestic lending. The great bulk of their deposits were in foreign currencies as a result of their participation in the Euro-currency markets. Thus they are now a central part of London's foreign exchange market.

The largest group is formed by the American banks, who opened branches in London in considerable numbers when the Euro-dollar market developed. Indeed, foreign banks have been successful in obtaining the greater part of the Euro-dollar business.

But their principal business is to offer a full international range of banking services to customers requiring finance and advice on international operations, preceded perhaps by market research and reports on possible buyers or sellers.

They give many of the services provided by merchant and deposit banks – credit cards, factoring, travel service.

To meet this competition a number of British banks have in recent years participated with foreign banks, in large banking groups, formed especially to compete in international markets. At this time there are more than twenty of these groups, many of which are either associates with, or subsidiaries of, London clearing or Scottish banks.

The British overseas, Commonwealth and Foreign banks provide a means by which funds for investment can be switched rapidly to any place in the world. Because they hold considerable amounts of sterling and other currencies they are substantial investors in money market assets, in short term bonds, and in longer-dated government securities.

The National Giro

The National Giro was established by the Post Office in 1968. Factors reinforcing the setting up of the National Giro were the need to modernize the remittance services of the Post Office (postal and money orders), and the substantial increase in recent years of the sort of transactions for which a giro system is particularly appropriate; the payment of rates and bills by instalments, hire purchase and mail order remittances, and payments for the renting of consumer durables.

All accounts in the National Giro are maintained at the National Giro Centre at Bootle, near Liverpool. Payments are made between one account and another by sending transfer instructions authorizing instant payment, thus cutting out any need to 'clear' a voucher with the built-in delay which such a system necessarily imposes. The 'branches' of the National Giro are the post offices of the country, at which cash transactions in or out may be made. After a transfer has been made the centre sends a notification to both transferor and transferee, including in the latter case a note of the name of the remitter. There is a system for standing orders between Giro accounts to cover regular transfers of fixed amounts.

Withdrawals are by Girocheque. The account holder has to nominate on his application form the addresses of two post offices which he will use. He can then take the Girocheque, his Giro card for identification purposes, and his withdrawal record form to a nominated post office, where he can withdraw up to £50 every other working day. If he wants more than that he has to make out the Girocheque and send it to the Centre where his account is immediately debited. The Girocheque is then returned to him for cashing as before.

Provision is made for working the Giro system in with the clearing bank system. A person having a Giro account wishing to pay money to a person not having a Giro account may send a Girocheque to the centre which authenticates it and forwards it to the payee, who may then cash it at any post office. Alternatively, the drawer may cross the Girocheque and send it directly to the payee, who may then clear it through his bank. A person not having a Giro account wishing to pay money to someone who has may pay in for the account at a post office. Giro has special arrangements with Cooks, whereby sterling or U.S. dollar travel cheques and foreign currency can be supplied.

Giro provides a credit card, the Giro Gold Card, restricted to those who are paid through Giro.

Giro has the advantage that most account holders can pay most of their bills free of any transmission charge. All the public corporations have National Giro accounts and so 'phone, gas, electricity bills, etc. can be paid at the post office. Another advantage is that withdrawals can be made at normal shopping hours six days a week. Again, Giro provides a detailed statement showing the names of the people to whom the account-holder has paid money.

Personal loans and overdrafts are now allowed, and a diversification of services is taking place, to enable the National Giro to compete more effectively for the profitable business of handling government and local authority payments and bidding for the accounts of corporate customers and nationalized industries. Personal loans of up to £2,500 are now offered to customers of at least one year's standing who have their earnings paid direct into their accounts. Applications are dealt with by post, and decisions are made within a few days. There will be no interviews. The interest is 10 per cent flat, equivalent to about 19¾ per cent true rate per year. A £50 cheque card has been introduced which will guarantee on-the-spot payments by Girocheque and also allow card-holders to cash cheques at any of the 21,000 Post Offices. Cards are available only to account holders who have their pay or other regular deposits paid into Giro Accounts.

From July 1976 account holders holding a guarantee card no longer have their cheques automatically returned if they overdraw by a small amount for a short period. No interest is charged on the amount overdrawn, but there is a service charge of 25p if the account goes more than £5 into the red. The Post Office (Banking Services) Act 1976, which authorized these and other changes designed to put Giro on a firmer financial footing as its competition with the banking industry of the private sector is intensified, also provided for the writing off of half of the Post Office Giro losses to date (some £16·7 million). It is believed that Giro can service the re maining debt.

It is perhaps apt to remark here that ordinary banks have to pay off their own losses without relying on the public to make them good, and that for this purpose they prudently build up very big reserves. Eventually Giro hopes to pay interest on money deposited with it but as the banking business develops it is intended that the Giro should become subject to the same monetary controls as other banks.*

Money shops

One big drawback to the service provided by the clearing banks is the restricted hours during which they are open to the public. Of course the staff do not leave when the bank closes: they have to summarize and agree the work of the day. But the public compare bank hours with shop hours, to the detriment of the banks. Also the banks are closed on Saturdays. Bank staffs were late in gaining a five-day week, and now that unions have been established in the industry there is no hope in the forseeable future of any change.

These facts led to the establishment from 1970 onwards of what have been described as money shops. These are operated by finance companies and some American banks, in offices in the High Streets of many towns in London and the provinces, designed to be comfortable, informal, and to appeal primarily to the private individual. The accent is on lending and not all of them provide current account facilities, although some do; but attention is given to the provision of personal, home improvement and mortgage loans, life and general insurance facilities, investment advice, and savings accounts. There were probably getting on for one hundred of these money shops by 1976. One great advantage which they offer is that they are open from 9 to 5 or 5.30 six days a week. One big American bank alone has a couple of dozen money shops and a dozen 'financial and sales' offices.

Similar to them are the money shops in chain stores, open when the store is open – the 'in-store banks'. Of these the most numerous are those of the Co-operative Bank, which in 1976 set up nine 'handybanks' in the Birmingham area and hopes that within two years there will be 500 of these banking points in Co-operative stores around the country. Such a handybank gives facilities for cashing cheques, depositing

See p. 398. *

money, ordering travel cheques, etc., and it is open all day Saturday.

At the same time several hundred 'Cash-a-cheque Points' have been operating in smaller Co-operative stores, in the Midlands, and their number is expected to grow to 3,000 throughout the country.

However, it has not all been an uninterrupted story of success. The banks in department stores operated by London and County Bank were closed on the demise of that institution, and the First National Finance Corporation has withdrawn its three railbanks. The plan to enter retail banking with a network of forty banks in mainline railway stations has been permanently shelved.*

Revision Test 3

Put ticks in what you think are the right boxes.

(1) The traditional lending role of the deposit banks has been
    (a) to finance long term the purchase of dwelling houses □
    (b) to provide working capital for business concerns □
    (c) to invest in property

(2) 'Clearing a cheque' means
    (a) guaranteeing that the cheque is good □
    (b) paying the cheque at the branch on which it is drawn □
    (c) passing the cheque through the Clearing House □

(3) The Town Clearing is for
    (a) cheques of £5,000 and over drawn on certain London branches □
    (b) cheques of £5,000 and over drawn on certain London and provincial branches □
    (c) any cheques of £5,000 and over □

(4) The Credit Clearing is for
    (a) Credit Card Accounts □

* See p. 398.

    (b) Bank Giro transfers ☐
    (c) Girocheques ☐

(5) Underwriting is
    (a) guaranteeing that a new issue of shares will be
        fully subscribed ☐
    (b) signing a legal document transferring shares ☐
    (c) putting one's name to a promissory note ☐

(6) A new issue is 'placed' when
    (a) it is advertised in the press ☐
    (b) it is given a quotation on the Stock Exchange ☐
    (c) it is sold privately to a limited number of inves-
        tors ☐

(7) Which has its headquarters in London?
    (a) a British overseas bank ☐
    (b) a Commonwealth bank ☐
    (c) Giro ☐

(8) A 'consortium' is
    (a) a decision on monetary policy by the Treasury ☐
    (b) a group of financial institutions ☐
    (c) a savings scheme for small savers ☐

(9) Which is true?
    (a) Girocheques can be cleared through the bank-
        ing system ☐
    (b) Clearing bank cheques can be cleared through
        the Giro centre ☐
    (c) Bank Giro transfers can be cleared through the
        Giro centre ☐

(10) Money shops are
    (a) moneylenders ☐
    (b) banks concentrating on personal services ☐
    (c) mail order organizations ☐

Check your solutions with the answers on p. 395.
Take one mark for each correct answer.
Each Revision Test totals 10 marks.

Questions for discussion

1. Which enactments, or developments, would you regard as the major milestones in British banking history? Give reasons for your selection.

2. A person sends a crossed order cheque through the post to the payee. Trace the history of the cheque until it is finally paid.

3. What are the sources of funds available to the deposit banks and what factors will determine the degree to which a bank will resort to one rather than another?

4

The London
Money
Market

The importance of the City of London as a world centre for international financial circles has been built up by a long tradition of innovation, flexibility, and above all, integrity. The financial institutions which have grown up over the centuries are collectively known as the London Money Market. In general terms, this is composed of dealers in money and credit who either have money to lend, or want to borrow money.

The Bank of England, which borrows large sums in the Money Market by its weekly issues of treasury bills by tender, is closely connected with, and indeed part of the Market, as also are the various London bankers, who as we have already seen, engage in many varied functions, of which participation in the Money Market is but one.

Besides the Bank of England and the deposit banks, the Market consists of the discount houses and the accepting houses.

The accepting houses

Bills drawn for a term usually specify three months but may also, of course, be for other periods, according to the time estimated to be necessary for the goods to reach their destination, be resold, and for the proceeds to become available to meet the due dates of the bills. These periods of time became customary for certain places, thus a usance bill was one drawn at a term governed by the custom in the trade, for example three months' date for bills on Paris, ninety days' date for bills on Lisbon, thirty days' sight for bills on Bombay.

We shall see how banks accepted the bills of the merchants to provide a more widely known name in support of the bills. The merchant banks who are prominent in acceptance credit assist in financing a considerable part of world trade, dealing with the bills of both exporters and importers.

Thus an importer who has to pay for the goods he has bought may accept the bill drawn on him by the exporter abroad, but the acceptance will be more readily dealt with when it reaches the exporter if it has been accepted, not by a merchant in a relatively small way of business, but by a firm of international repute.

The accepting house pays the bill when it becomes due in London, remitting the appropriate currency to the exporter abroad. The importer pays the accepting house the sterling equivalent of the amount of the bill, plus a commission for the service.

An exporter who receives money for his goods sent abroad may stipulate with the buyer that the bill which he will draw shall be accepted, not by the importer, but by a merchant bank in London. If this is agreeable to the importer, the exporter will draw his bill on the bank, have it accepted, and then either have it discounted, negotiate it, or keep it until the due date. The importer will remit the currency equivalent of the sterling bill, plus the commission, to the bank.

Alternatively, the exporter who manufactures the goods and then sells them abroad may finance the whole transaction from start to finish by drawing a bill on the acceptance house as soon as the contract with the foreign buyer has been signed, having it accepted, discounting it, and with the proceeds buying the raw materials which he needs to satisfy the contract. Because the name of the accepting house is on the bill, it will be readily discountable, whereas it would not have been on the name of the drawer alone. As before, the foreign buyer must remit the funds in payment to the acceptance house by the due date.

The merchant banks mostly had their origins in immigrants from Europe and now they have extensive international contacts. Some have affiliated companies overseas; most have banking correspondents in various parts of the world. Their links are particularly close with the European countries and with the United States.

Bills of exchange are accepted by any one bank of a large group of deposit or merchant banks, but the description 'accepting house' more properly applies to the seventeen members of the Accepting Houses committee. The chief qualifications for membership of the committee are:

(1) that a substantial part of the business of each house shall consist of accepting bills to finance the trade of others,
(2) that the bills when accepted can command the finest rates on the discount market, and
(3) that the acceptances are freely taken by way of re-discount at the Bank of England.

This last qualification is one which implies long experience and an unquestionable financial standing. To retain this standing an accepting house has continually to satisfy the Bank of England that it has adequate capital and liquidity.

A bill of exchange drawn on and accepted by an accepting house or British bank with an unquestioned financial standing is known as a prime bank bill. Prime bank bills are readily saleable in the London market at a good price. The banks buy them as first-class liquid assets, and will accept them as security against their loans to the discount houses. The discount houses themselves are willing to hold them, again because they are first-class liquid assets, but also because if need be they can be readily re-discounted with, or used as security for a loan from, the Bank of England.

Thus an accepting house, when accepting a bill, confers on

the drawer of the bill (and on anyone who discounts it for him) the certainty of being able to get sterling in exchange for it from any bank or discount house in London.

The accepting houses also keep accounts for customers, including foreign banks who keep balances with them. In recent times they have been willing to enter into medium- and long-term commitments, either alone or with others, to finance major projects. They have been instrumental in setting up groups of deposit banks and other institutions, such as insurance companies, or of home banks and foreign banks, to meet demands for really large sums. Such groups are called consortia. (See also merchant banks, p. 78.)

The discount houses

When a banker discounts an acceptance, he buys it outright for a sum less than its face value. The difference is the discount, which is in effect the interest charged for the loan until the due date of the bill. A bill is usually, though not always, discounted after it has been accepted.

If a merchant has drawn a bill at three months on a buyer abroad, and has had the accepted bill returned, he may find that there are, say, two months and twenty-two days left before the bill is due for payment. If the merchant wants the money immediately, as is often the case, he will wish to discount the bill.

For this there must be two good names, usually those of the drawer and acceptor. Each, by putting his name on the bill, has guaranteed that the bill will be paid on the due date. This very much reduces the risk of loss to a bank which buys the bill, for in the event of dishonour they have two reputable names to fall back on, either one of which should be sufficient. We have seen how any of the accepting houses will always be taken as one of the necessary two good names.

As an example, suppose an acceptance at three months for £8,000 is due for payment on 30th June. The drawer takes it in to a discounting bank on 8th April, so that, as suggested above, the acceptance has two months and twenty-two days to run. This is calculated in days. There are twenty-two days left in April (9th–30th inclusive), thirty-one days in May, and thirty days in June, a total of eighty-three days. The discount rate will normally be the same as the bank's overdraft rate, for this discounting transaction is money lent against the security of the bill.

If the discount rate is 10 per cent, the discount will be:

$$£\frac{8,000 \times 10 \times 83}{100 \times 365} = £181·92$$

The merchant will be paid £7,818·08 by the discounting bank. The latter may keep the bill until maturity, to present then to the acceptor and receive payment in full. In this case the discounting bank will make a profit of the amount of the discount, for this is the difference between the sum he gave for the acceptance when he discounted it, and what he gets for it when he presents it for payment. Or the acceptance may be re-sold, that is, re-discounted to another banker or financial institution.

When such a bill, bought on the London Market, is sold by a discount house, the latter endorses it and so adds its name to the two good names already there, thereby assuming responsibility for the payment of the bill at maturity in the event of default. The rate of re-discount will include a small commission, say $\frac{1}{8}$ per cent to pay for the services rendered and to recognize the liability of the discount house evidenced by its endorsement. This has added to the value of the bill as security. The Bank of England when buying such bills always requires one of the good names to be a British acceptor of the bill.

Dealing in commercial bills is a highly specialized business. It requires up-to-date information concerning the credit worthiness of thousands of customers in many trades, some in countries overseas. A good commercial bill is one that is self-liquidating on a short term basis. It is called a first class bill, or first class paper. Those who discount such bills are often called bill brokers.

When the Bill on London became something approaching an international currency, the discount houses were an essential part of the system for dealing in such bills: in the process they built up their unrivalled knowledge of the names on the bills. When the Bill on London declined in importance as a result of the first world war, the discount houses became associated with the handling of treasury bills, which were assuming ever-increasing importance as a method of borrowing by the government. Recently they have begun to act as dealers in sterling and dollar certificates of deposit, as brokers and principals in the parallel and foreign exchange markets and as jobbers in the gilt-edged market.

Perhaps their most important function from the banks' point of view is their willingness to borrow money from the banks at call or at short notice, thus enabling the banks to adjust their liquidity positions whenever required. Such borrowing is always secured and certain of repayment as soon as demanded.

There are eleven discount houses, each one a public company, owned and operated quite independently of any other financial institutions. These houses together form the London Discount Market Association. This has been described as an organization to provide the best possible secured return on overnight money. The discount houses make their money by absorbing surplus funds from the banking system and investing it, mainly short-term, in a mixture of government and commercial paper. The market is at the centre of short-term money dealings.

All the houses take part in the weekly tender for treasury bills. These are notes with a term of ninety-one days, issued by the Treasury with the backing of the government. They are similar to commercial bills in that they are issued at a discount and fall due at certain intervals. They represent money borrowed by the government and form part of the country's floating debt.

Each week, except when the government does not wish to borrow in this way, a notice is put in the London Gazette

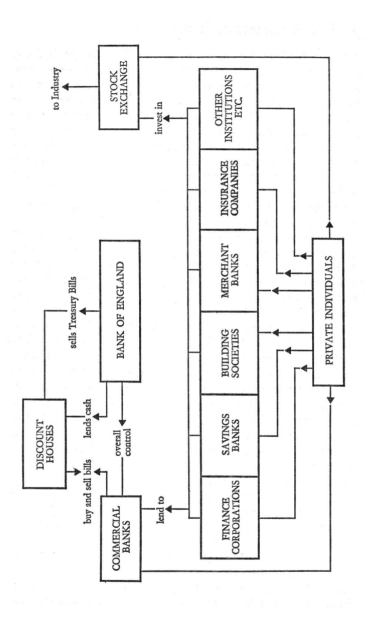

inviting tenders, or offers, to be received at the Bank of England each Friday, the bills being issued the following week. The bills carry no interest and that, of course, is why they are issued at a discount. Thus if a tenderer (lender) offered £49,000 for a £50,000 treasury bill, and his tender was accepted, he would pay £49,000 now and receive a bill payable in ninety-one days' time for £50,000. If he kept it for the full term and then surrendered it he would have made a profit of £1,000, and the treasury bill rate would be 8 per cent. If he sells it during its currency he will calculate the selling price according to the number of days the bill still has to run, at treasury bill rate.

The discount houses used to tender for the bills as a syndicate, each house bidding for a proportion of the total tender, at a price previously agreed amongst themselves, in relation to its capital resources. Since Competition and Credit Control, however, each house is free to tender at a price decided by itself alone. In making the tenders the houses are in competition with other tenderers such as foreign banks and nationalized industries. British Clearing banks do not tender directly, but buy any bills they may want from the brokers. In this way the London banks can choose bills of the maturity which they want, planning ahead so that the money will become available just at the time they will need it. Treasury bills are a part of the banks' liquid assets and so influence their power to create credit.

Treasury bills are issued in amounts from £5,000 to £250,000. No tender may be for an amount less than £50,000, but a proportion only of the tender may be accepted. The total amount of Treasury bills issued each week varies according to the amount of money the government wishes to borrow, and treasury bill rate varies with the general level of interest rates on money.

Another way in which the government borrows is by the issue of bonds. Government bonds are documents whereby the government binds itself to pay a certain sum at a certain time. When the issue of bonds is made the government announces the rate of interest which it is offering, and the year during which it will repay the capital. Sometimes the repayment year will be expressed as a spread, say 1988–92. This gives the government a choice, so that repayment can be made at the time most favourable for the government. For instance, if the rate of interest on the particular issue is $7\frac{1}{2}$ per cent, but by 1988 the general rate of interest has fallen to 5 per cent, the government may be expected to repay as soon as possible, to get rid of the duty of paying what is by then a high rate of interest. If interest rates rise, the opposite result will ensue.

Bonds are bought and sold during their currency like stocks and shares, and their prices can be found daily in any paper with a financial page, under the heading British Funds. They may be there divided into short-dated bonds (those repayable within five years), medium-dated (five to fifteen years), and long-dated (over fifteen years).

The discount houses deal in short-dated government bonds providing a market in them which is very welcome to the government. The Bank of England encouraged the discount houses to develop this market, by telling them that such short-dated bonds would be acceptable as security by the Bank when the discount houses wanted to borrow there. The facility was particularly useful to the government during the second world war, when the discount houses took up large amounts of short-dated national war bonds, issued periodically by the government to raise money to continue the financing of the war.

It was the discount houses who were instrumental in setting up what came to be called the secondary markets for dollar certificates of deposit, and then sterling certificates of deposits. These will be described later.

To maintain all these activities the discount houses need a great deal of capital. They buy and sell, or keep 'in stock' good commercial bills of exchange, treasury bills, and short-dated government bonds. They also hold bills and bonds issued by local authorities and public corporations, and sterling and dollar certificates of deposit.

The discount houses borrow 'at call' and at short notice from banks. 'At call' means that the money is repayable to the lending bank immediately it calls for it. The banks are pleased to have this outlet for their surplus funds, which otherwise might be earning no interest. The borrowers are undoubted and the money will be promptly returned when wanted.

The discount houses have to consider their position daily, for each day will see acceptances which they hold maturing due (money in) while other acceptances have been bought by them (money out). Similarly they will have bought and sold various securities to various people during the day, and finally they will come up with either a surplus for the day, or a deficit.

If it is a deficit they must borrow, at least overnight, to put their books straight. They can try at all the head offices of the big banks and will usually be able to borrow from at least one of them.

When money is in short supply, however, not only may they not be able to borrow, but one or more of the banks may call back an existing loan, thus making matters worse. In such a case the houses are always sure of being able to borrow, against acceptable security, from the Bank of England. They leave the Bank until last, however, because it is more expensive than the clearing banks. The Bank of England 'Minimum Lending Rate' is the rate at which the Bank will lend to undoubted borrowers.

The discount houses certainly come into this category, but it remains true that the Bank's Minimum Lending Rate is higher than the rate which the clearing banks would have charged.

The Bank of England is the 'lender of last resort'. When discount houses have to borrow from the Bank the 'market has been forced into the Bank'. Discount houses are the only institutions to which the Bank of England lends money at last resort, but to them the Bank will lend up to any necessary amount. This is because of the special importance of the discount houses to the Bank of England. The houses specialize in taking funds from the banks, which they must be ready to repay on demand or at very short notice. The Bank of England has become the lender of last resort to make sure that the discount houses are always able to repay the banks when asked to do so. This is a way of protecting the entire banking system, and a way of feeding into the system whatever funds are required. The Bank will provide this support only on penal terms, but nevertheless everyone knows that it will give this assistance whenever it is required, and this knowledge gives stability to the financial system of the country. The discount houses smooth out irregularities in the flow of money, and provide an agency through which the central bank acts to influence short-term interest rates.

The Euro-currency markets

Exchange control restrictions in all countries can but hamper trade, and not a little part of the expertise of the banks has been to keep up to date with them and to know how to minimize their effects as far as possible.

Banking accounts are described as resident or non-resident. The balances on non-resident accounts belong to people living abroad. From the 1950s onwards markets developed in the foreign currency deposits of non-residents. (If any residents had amounts of foreign currency in this country they were required by law to offer them to the Bank of England for sale.) As the war receded, so exchange control restrictions slackened.

In 1958 convertibility was granted to non-resident holders of sterling (this meant that thereafter such funds were free to move from abroad into the various London short-term money markets and out again in response to the level of interest rates at home and abroad).

The term Euro-currency was used to describe these deposits of currency, mainly dollars, but also Dutch guilders, German deutschmarks (D. marks for short), Swiss francs, and British sterling, which were held by people who did not live in the country whose currency it was, and who kept them in a third country. For example, a bank in France which received dollars from Spain (or any other country except the United States) would have some Euro-dollars. They could lend these dollars out at a good rate of interest to anyone anxious to borrow in that currency. Many of our big companies, wanting to expand abroad, but unable to get the loans they needed in this country, could borrow abroad instead. It must be emphasized that the dollars throughout remain in the United States. Thus the Spanish owner exemplified above deposited dollars with a French bank. The latter perhaps deposited these dollars with a Swiss bank, who might lend them to a client. The French bank's US dollar account held with one US bank was credited with the dollars and then debited as the dollars were redeposited with the Swiss bank, whose dollar account, with the same or another US bank was in turn credited; and so on. Throughout these operations the total amount of foreign-owned dollar deposits in the United States remains unchanged, although there is a kind of 'chain of ownership' between the Spanish depositor and the US bank. It is the control over the dollar deposit which changes, and this naturally affects the use to which the dollars are put. This chain of ownership is composed of lenders and borrowers. When the French bank deposited the dollars with the Swiss bank they did not send them a packet of actual dollar notes, but effected the transfer from their agent bank in the United States to the agent bank of the Swiss bank in the same country. In the same way German D. marks remain physically in Germany, Swiss francs in Switzerland, and so on.

Euro-dollars were the main currency of this international market. They came from people in European countries who could get a better interest rate from banks in Western Europe than they could by sending them to banks in the USA, which were limited by their own laws as to the interest on deposits which they were able to pay, and the reserves to be held against them. These laws did not apply with such severity to dollars accepted by American banks outside America, and this was one reason why many American banks opened branches abroad, particularly in London. There they were able to take dollar deposits on the Euro-market to send back to their head offices, who could then relend them profitably in the United States, where from 1959 onwards credit was becoming increasingly difficult to obtain. American companies were therefore anxious to seek dollar loans from sources outside America. More and more American companies operating on the Continent and in this country also helped the Euro-market by investing their profits in it, instead of sending them back to America, where the rate of interest to be gained was not so high. These deposits were then available for eventual use in overseas expansion programmes. There was a ready market for Euro-currencies, particularly for dollars. The demand came from the American banks as already mentioned, continental industrial firms, and continental banks. The latter could use Euro-dollars to lend to dealers and brokers in America.

The main market in Europe for these currencies is in London. In this country local authorities, hire-purchase concerns, and finance houses, all of whom have had a large expansion in their activities and have consequently wanted to borrow more and more money, have been able to satisfy their requirements in the Euro-currency market. The merchant banks, the discount houses, and the British overseas and foreign banks are prominent in these exchanges. A bank offered foreign currency either relends the amount in the same currency in which it is offered, or relends the amount in whichever other currency proves to be most advantageous at the time, covering the risk of exchange loss by a forward operation.

These transactions have been traditionally short term, but until late 1974 there was a willingness to lend for longer periods. A number of long-term loans, mostly in dollars, have been arranged for the benefit of American corporations and European public authorities.

Dollar certificates of deposit

Certificates of deposit were introduced in the United States in 1961 and were so successful that similar dollar certificates were issued by New York banks on the London market five years later. The certificate is evidence of a deposit with a bank repayable on a fixed date. It is a fully negotiable bearer document transferable by delivery and therefore passes readily from hand to hand. The rate of interest being paid is competitive, and therefore varies from time to time.

A substantial market developed in these certificates, in which the discount houses obtained permission to deal, and certain British and Continental banks also began to issue them. The dollars are obtained from the Euro-market.

The certificates appeal to short-term holders of dollars who would like to invest a sum of dollars which is not large enough to be of interest to the Euro-dollar market, or who do not know for certain how long they will need to hold them. By investing them in dollar certificates of deposit they are certain to get the dollars back immediately they have need of them, and in the meantime they enjoy a good rate of interest. To ensure the marketability of the certificates there needs to be what is called a 'secondary' market, that is, somewhere where the holder of the certificate can sell it if he wants to. This secondary market is provided by the discount houses.

Certificates are issued in multiples of $1,000, minimum $25,000, for maturities of 30, 60, 90, 120, 150, 180 days, 12 months, and several years.

The inter-bank sterling market

In addition to the Euro-currency market a separate market in sterling has arisen to satisfy the placing and taking of sterling deposits between London banks. Its development was accelerated in 1964 when sterling was weak in terms of other currencies, and therefore foreign banks were reluctant to hold sterling in London in case it depreciated still further.

At the same time British banks were anxious to lend, local authority loans in particular at that time offering good lending opportunities in terms of a high interest rate, coupled with a high degree of safety.

Domestic lending, limited by the amount of money deposited by customers of the banks, began to be less limited when further supplies of sterling could be obtained from the inter-bank sterling market. To be sure, the rates charged were more expensive than those obtaining in the conventional money market, but the expense could be recovered in the rate charged to the borrower.

The inter-bank market is now very active. Banks still compete within the United Kingdom for retail deposits (see p. 247, but they are no longer completely dependent on them.

All transactions on the market are unsecured. They are predominantly short term, the largest amount of dealing being for overnight funds, although it is possible to obtain rates for periods of up to one year. The market is run by brokers who arrange the transactions between banks and discount houses, who also participate in this market, and earn commission on completed deals; but there is some negotiation directly between principals. The big banks use the brokers because only the latter can make the necessary number of telephone calls to arrange the transactions quickly enough. It is advisable to get large sums of money placed before the word gets round the market and the rate moves against the individual operator.

Sterling certificates of deposit

Negotiable sterling certificates of deposit were a logical follow-up to their dollar counterpart. As with the dollar certificates of deposit, the sterling certificates are fully negotiable bearer documents, evidencing a sterling deposit with the issuing bank, which is transferable by delivery. They are issued for a minimum period of three months up to a maximum period of five years.

The minimum denomination of a certificate is £50,000 and the maximum is £500,000. They are issued by the clearing banks and by other London banks. Their attraction, as with the dollar certificates, is that they assure the lender of instant liquidity by giving him a readily-negotiable certificate.

The existence of an efficient secondary market on which depositors can recover their money before the maturity date if they need it, is of course an essential factor in the issuing of certificates of deposit by bankers. The main dealers in the secondary markets for both types of certificates of deposit are the discount houses.

Revision Test 4

Put ticks in what you think are the right boxes.

(1) A usance bill is one
    (a) payable at sight ☐
    (b) at a term fixed by custom ☐
    (c) drawn abroad but payable in this country ☐

(2) A prime bank bill is one
    (a) accepted payable at a bank ☐
    (b) issued by the Bank of England ☐
    (c) drawn on, and accepted by, an accepting house ☐

(3) Discount is
    (a) interest charged for an advance ☐
    (b) a period of time allowed to an acceptor before a bill is presented for payment ☐
    (c) the rate at which treasury bills pass from hand to hand ☐

(4) Treasury bills
    (a) bear interest at minimum lending rate ☐
    (b) bear no interest ☐
    (c) are issued at a discount ☐

(5) In a financial newspaper the heading 'British Funds' refers to

(a) the total amount of British bank deposits ☐
(b) local authority issues ☐
(c) government bonds ☐

(6) Borrowing 'at call' means
   (a) the borrower must make personal application ☐
   (b) the lender must lend for a minimum of seven days ☐
   (c) the borrower must repay immediately he is asked to ☐

(7) The 'minimum lending rate' is
   (a) the rate at which the Bank of England will lend to a discount house ☐
   (b) the cheapest interest rate charged by London banks for loans of £10,000 or over ☐
   (c) the rate charged by the accepting house for accepting a bill ☐

(8) Which of these is Euro-currency?
   (a) Dollars held in New York by a British resident ☐
   (b) Sterling held in France by a Swiss resident ☐
   (c) Swiss francs held in Germany by a German resident ☐

(9) Sterling certificates of deposit
   (a) are issued by local authorities ☐
   (b) are repayable on demand ☐
   (c) are fully negotiable instruments ☐

Check your solutions with the answers on p. 395
Take one mark for each correct answer.
Each Revision Test totals 10 marks.

Questions for discussion

1. Describe how the government may borrow funds through the Money Market.

2. Describe the activities of the discount houses.

3. What is the Euro-currency market?

5

Other markets and financial institutions

The most important markets remaining are those in stocks and shares, in insurance and in gold. After describing these we will go on to look at the finance houses and finance corporations.

The Stock Exchange

The London Stock Exchange is an integral part of the financial machinery of the City of London. There is no precise record of its beginnings, but we know that nearly three hundred years ago dealers called 'stockjobbers' conducted business in their main market place in the City, the Royal Exchange. By 1698, four years after the founding of the Bank of England, the stockjobbers had become so numerous, and so noisy, that the other merchants of the Royal Exchange encouraged them to find another home.

The best they could do was the open street in nearby Change Alley. On cold and wet days they used to repair to coffee houses and do business with each other in them. One house in particular, Jonathan's, became their main centre for some years to come.

This was a period of expanding commerce and adventure overseas. In India and on the west coast of Africa merchant adventurers were establishing themselves. The famous Hudson's Bay Company, founded in 1669, was building up its influence in Canada and establishing trading posts in the northern territories. Gradually the number of companies grew, as more and more people formed themselves into groups to find the money for new trading expeditions. Joint-stock companies began to replace one-man concerns and partnerships as internal and overseas trade expanded rapidly and larger opportunities needed greater resources of capital.

In the joint-stock company, each investor became entitled to a share in the trading profits, in accordance with the number of shares which he held. Such investors could sell their shares to other investors wishing to buy, thus recovering their money without the necessity of withdrawing their capital from the company. These purchases and sales were arranged in Jonathan's coffee house, or in one of the other coffee houses, or in Change Alley.

In bank stock and in government loans a considerable volume of business built up following the founding of the Bank of England and the establishment of the National Debt. The first foreign government loan, for Austria, was floated in 1706. Thereafter followed a boom period, with optimistic speculation leading to reckless risk taking. The South Sea Company was incorporated by act of parliament in 1710 and was given a monopoly of trade in the Pacific Ocean. Unfortunately Spain placed restrictions on the trade with Spanish colonies in South America, so that it never really prospered.

The company was also engaged in various financial dealings at home. In particular the directors of the company had worked out a scheme for taking over most of the National Debt from the government. Parliament was persuaded to agree to this, although there was strong opposition. The price of South Sea stock rose dramatically and people rushed to buy shares, recklessly investing their life savings. When the share value reached ten times the nominal value people began to realize that the shares were not worth nearly as much as their quoted value, and confidence suddenly evaporated. There was a rush to sell and prices dropped catastrophically. Thousands of people were ruined.

The affair was known as the South Sea Bubble. It caused rioting in the streets and the suicide of a minister. It took some time for public credit to be restored. The nation had had its first lesson in the economics of share trading.

Eventually business increased so much that the accommodation at Jonathan's and in the Change Alley was inadequate. The first 'Stock Exchange' was opened in 1773 in a building on the corner of Threadneedle Street and Sweetings Alley. The French wars brought about a large increase in government borrowing and in speculation generally. A still larger building was needed. In 1801 a move was made to Capel Court, near to the Bank of England.

The nineteenth century was a stable period of continuous growth. In the first half of the century the expanding business was in loans for foreign governments. As the industrial revolution took hold the railways were built while overseas trade multiplied. Joint stock banking companies appeared from 1826 onwards, and in 1862 the first Companies Act gave a tremendous fillip to trade by introducing the idea of limited liability. The century closed with the South African mining boom in 1895.

Since the move to Capel Court the Stock Exchange has twice been rebuilt, in 1953-4 and in 1971-3. The present building is a twenty-six storey tower rising three hundred and twenty feet from the ground. A modern communications system has been installed and a closed circuit television system with twenty-two channels of information about prices, controlled by a computer, has been introduced.

The purpose of the Stock Exchange is to provide an efficient market for the purchase and sale of securities. It plays an important part in the provision of new capital for industry. It is administered and managed by the Council of the Stock Exchange, an unpaid body elected by the general body of Stock Exchange members. The Council exercises full authority over the election of new member firms and on matters of business conduct. It makes the rules which govern market dealings, determines the rate of commission, and settles all disputes falling under its jurisdiction.

Various committees are formed from the members of the Council: perhaps the most important is the Quotations Committee which considers applications from companies for quotations on the Stock Exchange, takes decisions to suspend dealings in securities where irregularities are suspected, and if need be, recommends the removal of companies from the list. A recognized code of acceptable conduct has been established. This includes a set of rules to govern the procedure for take-over bids, which arise when one company wishes to take over another, or to gain control of it. If the bidding company aims at total ownership it must acquire every share of the other. The offer may be directly to the other company's shareholders, or there may be an agreement between the boards of the two companies.

The consideration offered may be cash, or shares in the bidding company, or a combination of both. The preliminary negotiations must be kept a secret, or the price of the shares of the company to be acquired will rise, sometimes quite steeply. There is therefore a temptation for people in the know to take a private profit in advance of any official announcement. The majority of take-over bids have performed a useful service to the community in forcing a realistic assessment of company assets. This has tended to result in a greater benefit being passed on to shareholders by way of dividends. Nevertheless, some abuses have taken place and in 1959 a working party, composed of representatives of the Stock Exchange Council, the Acceptance and Issuing Houses, the clearing banks, and other bodies, was set up at the request of the Bank of England. The result was the Take-over Code, a set of regulations for the guidance of companies engaged in negotiations.

Protection for investors is also provided by a compensation fund, set up to guard against losses through the default of any one of the more than two hundred firms which form the membership of the Stock Exchange. If any member is unable to meet his liabilities, his failure is announced in the House after three blows with a mallet have been struck upon the rostrum of the House. The defaulter is thus said to be 'hammered', and has his name posted on a board showing those who are expelled from the House. Any loss to that member's clients is then met from the compensation fund, which is guaranteed by all members.

Over the years the Stock Exchange has seemed to some of the electorate to represent part of the system whereby the idle rich grind the faces of the workers. Nothing could be further from the truth, for the Council has continuously been concerned with the protection of investors and the keynote of all dealings has been integrity. Nevertheless the occasional unfortunate episode has invariably received a bad press and often the Stock Exchange has suffered through some company scandal with which it had nothing whatever to do. In recent years, therefore, the Council has been increasingly concerned with creating a wider understanding of its functions among the general public. This has become particularly important because it is evident that share ownership is becoming more widely spread. Holdings by individuals are increasing in number while diminishing in average size. One might say that the capitalistic symbol of participation in company management is gradually spreading outward and downward amongst our society. The Council has therefore used its influence to see that adequate information about the way in which companies are run is given to the shareholders. Under the Companies Act, 1967, for example, fuller information than in earlier years has been required from companies seeking a quotation. More information about the remuneration of directors has now to be made available for shareholders, who may therefore be better prepared to raise issues at company general meetings. More financial information is required to accompany balance sheets.

These measures all show a concern for the small investor.

Method of dealing

The grouping of stocks and shares, or 'markets', is into gilt-edged (Government securities and some others of comparable standing); banks and insurance; shipping; foreign government bonds; American and Canadian shares; breweries; commercial and industrial; iron, coal and steel; financial, land and property; investment trusts; rubber and tea plantations; oil; South African mines; Rhodesian, Canadian, Australian and miscellaneous mines; West African mines; and cables and transport.

The members of the Stock Exchange who deal in these stocks and shares are divided into two categories, jobbers and brokers. Jobbers are dealers who specialize in certain kinds of stocks, and they make their money on the deals which they are able to arrange between two brokers. They are trading on their own account and do not deal directly with the public. They do not receive commission or fees but earn their income, in competition with each other, on the 'turn' or difference between the price they buy shares at and the price they re-sell them for.

The Stock Exchange is not divided up physically into the separate markets, but jobbers trading in the same market are usually to be found near each other on the same 'pitch' each day, so that brokers know where to find them. When asked for a quotation the jobber does not know whether it is to buy, or to sell. Accordingly he 'makes' two prices, one – the 'bid' price – for buying at, and one – the 'offered' price – for selling at. For example, a jobber may quote a price of 100–102p. This means he will buy the particular shares at 100p each, or sell them at 102p.

Jobbers are guided in making prices by their experience and by any information about the particular shares which they may have, but mostly on the weight of buying and selling which they encounter. Prices naturally vary according to supply and demand. If there are more brokers anxious to sell than there are to buy, the jobber will reduce his prices until the buyers are attracted. If there are more buying brokers than there are sellers, he will put his prices up until the sellers are attracted.

In a large and active market, such as gilt-edged stocks, the jobbers can make very narrow quotations because they have a considerable turnover (there will not be very much difference between their buying and selling prices). Where the market is more restricted, enquiries tend to be fewer, and the margin between the jobber's quotations wider.

Brokers are agents for the public who want to buy or sell shares. They have to get the best possible terms for their clients, and are remunerated by a scale of commission called 'brokerage'. This is fixed by the Council, according to the size and type of transaction. Brokers also offer advice to clients on possible investments.

When they have an instruction to buy, or sell, they look for the jobber who will be the best buyer or the cheapest seller. If the broker wishes to deal right away, the jobber is bound by the prices he has quoted provided that the transaction is for a 'marketable' amount. A verbal agreement completes the bargain between the broker and jobber. The broker sends a contract note to his client and attends to all the paperwork involved in the transfer of stocks and shares from seller to buyer. The contract note gives details of the stock bought and sold, the price, and the date of the settling day when the price is due to be paid.

Settlement of bargains in gilt-edged securities is 'for cash'; payment is expected from the client as soon as he receives the contract note, which should normally be the business day following the date of the bargain.

Settlement for all other securities is 'for the account': the account runs for two weeks (sometimes three) and then all bargains made and still outstanding are paid for. Delivery of the securities and payment for them takes place, as far as possible, on a single 'settlement day' or 'account day', and this is the second Tuesday following the end of the account.

During the account some of the business will be speculative

in its nature. 'Bears' are investors who have reason to believe that the price of a certain stock or share will go down. A 'bear' therefore sells the holding, although he does not actually possess it, relying on the fact that he can buy it back, at a cheaper price, before the end of the account, and thus show a profit.

'Bulls' are investors who believe that the price of a certain stock or share will go up. A 'bull' buys the holding now, at the day's price, although he hopes that he will never actually have to pay for it. Between the date of purchase now, and settlement day, he expects the price to rise so that he can sell then at a profit, and be paid the difference. (Both sets of operators must allow for the commission and stamp duty they will have to pay.)

The securities dealt in on the Stock Exchange are mostly 'registered' stocks or shares. A transfer from one person to another is made by completion of a stock transfer form, signed by the transferor. This is sent, together with the registered certificate which shows the holding in the transferor's name, to the registrar of the company in which the stock or shares are. The company keeps the register, or list, of shares which it has issued, with the names of the persons to whom the shares were issued.

The purpose of the stock transfer form is to bring about the change on the register. The transferor's name has to be deleted, and that of the new owner – the transferee – recorded. The old registered certificate is discharged or cancelled and filed away, and a new certificate is issued to the new owner of the stock or shares.

With bearer securities ownership can be transferred by mere delivery. There is here a much greater risk of loss through accident or fraud, and greater care has to be taken over the safe-keeping of these securities. Bearer securities are of diminishing importance nowadays, but they have always been popular on the continent, and this fact partly accounts for their continuing existence.

The Stock Exchange publishes official daily and monthly

lists containing quotations for all the securities in which it deals. In the range of securities, and in the size of its membership, the Stock Exchange is the largest in the world. Its trading is world wide.

In March 1973 the Stock Exchanges of Great Britain and Ireland became one. The new organization is called simply 'The Stock Exchange'. It brings together the separate markets which previously existed in cities and towns throughout the British Isles. The main trading floor and central administration will be in London. The Council of the Stock Exchange will meet in London. Trading floors will remain in being in Glasgow, Liverpool, Manchester, Birmingham, Bristol, Cardiff, Dublin and Belfast.

A two-way business is also conducted with stock exchanges abroad in centres such as Singapore, Calcutta, Montreal, New York, Paris, Tokyo, Vienna, Frankfurt, Brussels and Amsterdam.

Lloyd's

The name is used firstly to describe a market in insurance where practically any insurable risk can be covered, and secondly to refer to a society, incorporated under Act of Parliament in 1871 and known as the Corporation of Lloyds, which provides the premises, shipping information services, administrative staff and other facilities by which the market is able to carry on its business.

As with the Stock Exchange, the seeds of the insurance market are to be found in the coffee houses of the seventeenth century. There were no insurance companies then, as we understand the term today, but there were people called underwriters, so called because they wrote their names under the wording on insurance policies, which provided cover on a limited and personal basis for merchants' undertakings. These were almost wholly concerned with ship voyages and cargoes.

One particular coffee house became associated with the

insurance business. This was Lloyd's Coffee House, situated near the river Thames and thus usually filled with merchants connected with the sea, ships' captains and mates, and the merchants who specialized in underwriting marine risks. As time went by it became generally recognized that Lloyd's Coffee House was the place to go to if you wanted cover.

The exact year which saw the start of this association is not known, but certainly the coffee house was in existence in 1688. Edward Lloyd was not himself an insurer, nor ever became one, but he was a man who knew how to encourage business profitable to himself and he helpfully provided his customers with writing materials and then with shipping information brought from the waterfront by runners. In 1696 he took the next logical step of publishing a news sheet called Lloyd's News, but he got into trouble with this and it had a short life. Still, the idea was good and it was to be resurrected later by others. Lloyd died in 1713 with no inkling of the international fame and prestige which was one day to be associated with his name.

In 1769 there was a move to another coffee house in Pope's Head Alley. This is believed to have been due to a gambling element among the customers of Lloyd's Coffee House, which was, of course, quite bad for the reputation of men seeking to provide responsible insurance cover. The 'New Lloyd's Coffee House' was much the same as the old, but without the gamblers. The early London coffee houses were centres of political debate and literature as well as of commerce, and there must have been an advantage in having a house exclusively devoted to the insurance business. As business increased the new coffee house quickly became too small, and in 1774 there was another move, this time to rooms in the Royal Exchange.

In subsequent years there were other moves in search of adequate space, but in 1957 the present site of the market was opened in Lime Street with a bridge at first floor level communicating with earlier premises in Leadenhall Street.

The act of parliament which incorporated Lloyd's was

passed in 1871. Lloyd's had then been in existence in one form or another for nearly two centuries, but the growing scope and complexity of the business it undertook made it desirable for the organization to be placed on a legal footing. This incorporated the principles which until then had been accepted by underwriters on a voluntary basis. It also gave a committee elected by the members of the market powers to endorse the rules setting out those principles. The corporation does not itself accept insurance or assume any liability for insurance business transacted by its members.

Underwriters and brokers

Lloyd's is now an international market for almost any type of insurance. Ships, aircraft, cargoes, oil rigs, personal accident and third party liability, civil engineering projects, houses and buildings are a few examples of the risks covered. Some of the sums involved are truly impressive. A modern jet aircraft, valued at £10,000,000, carrying up to 500 passengers, each insured against loss of life or injury, amounts to a formidable potential total. The value of a giant oil tanker must today approach £20,000,000, and in the event of its loss there might well be claims for pollution in addition to the replacement cost of the vessel. Every step forward in technology, such as Concorde, demands the formulation of new policies to meet new circumstances.

These enormously increased values have naturally brought about a change in the old system whereby each underwriter personally transacted his own insurance business. Today, there are more than seven thousand underwriting members of Lloyd's who are formed into syndicates, which are represented at Lloyd's by underwriting agents. When a syndicate underwriter accepts (or 'writes') a risk he can do so for a very much larger amount than if he were acting on his own behalf alone.

There are four main sectors of the market – marine, non-marine, aviation and motor. The underwriters for syndicates sit with their staffs in the Underwriting Room at 'boxes', pew-like desks which, together with liveried staff called 'waiters', recall the origins of the business. They cannot be approached directly by members of the public, but only by brokers approved by the Committee of Lloyd's and known as Lloyd's brokers. This measure is based on practical considerations, for it requires specialized knowledge to find the appropriate underwriter and to place the business at the most advantageous terms and rates. Lloyd's brokers are thus an essential link in the chain between the assured and Lloyd's underwriters. The broker represents his client and if he cannot deal satisfactorily with the underwriters he can place the business with other insurance companies.

The method used is for the broker to begin the procedure by preparing a document called a 'slip'. This describes the risk to be covered and gives all details which might be required. The broker then shows this slip to one or more underwriters and asks them to quote a rate of premium for the insurance. He may also contact an insurance company and get a quotation from them.

When the broker is satisfied that he has obtained the best quotation he will go back to the underwriter who gave it and ask him to accept the contract by initialling the slip. The underwriter will not usually accept the whole of the risk if the sum is a large one, but will initial the slip for a percentage of the risk. The broker must then approach other underwriters in order to complete the coverage of the risk. Each will accept for a certain percentage. When the risk is fully covered the slip goes to the Signing Office, where the policies are checked against the information on the slips, signed on behalf of the syndicates, and sealed with the seal of Lloyd's Policy Signing Office. The Office also provides the underwriters with all the details of their underwriting transactions.

Once a slip bears the initials of underwriters the brokers know that a justified claim will be honoured, even though time has not permitted the issue of the policy. If there should be a claim the broker arranges the settlement, collects the money from the underwriters, and pays it over to his client. His remuneration is a deduction from the premium payable to the underwriters, and he receives no other remuneration from the person insured.

The security behind a Lloyd's policy

Members of Lloyd's may be men or women of any nationality.

Applications for membership have to be recommended by existing underwriting members. Applicants have to prove that they have substantial assets and must satisfy the Committee of their integrity. On election, which is by ballot of the Committee, a member pays an entrance fee and makes a deposit in cash or approved securities, according to the volume of business which he or she intends to underwrite. As an example, a member not previously connected with Lloyd's who provides security of £15,000 may do business involving premiums totalling up to £100,000 in any year.

Every underwriting member trades with unlimited liability, that is, he is liable in respect of his insurance obligations to the full extent of everything which he has, including his private fortune.

All premiums have to be paid into Premium Trust Funds under Deeds of Trust approved by the Department of Trade. Claims, expenses, and ascertained profits only may be paid out of these funds.

Each member must furnish a guarantee policy each year, based on his premium income, which policy must be subscribed by other members according to conditions set out by the Committee.

Each member contributes by means of a levy on premium income to a Central Fund. This Fund is held to meet possible underwriting liabilities of any member who is found to be unable to meet his underwriting commitments. The Fund is for the protection of those whom the underwriter has assured. The underwriter himself is still fully responsible for his debts and obligations.

The underwriting accounts of each member are subjected once a year to a strict audit. It is a searching examination into the affairs of every individual member, conducted according to rules approved by the Committee and by the Department of Trade. It is carried out by a panel of auditors, again approved by the Committee. It seeks to establish that the member's assets are sufficient to meet his liabilities. The Committee can require that unless reserves are increased, the member must stop underwriting.

Lloyd's, therefore, offers to those seeking insurance, not only such protection as the law demands, but also the security of vast assets administered under rules which are a guarantee that a valid claim will be met.

Lloyd's intelligence system

Lloyd's has always been closely connected with the sea. Its early business was almost wholly concerned with marine insurance, and it was not until the 1880s that other forms of insurance were pioneered – burglary cover, block cover for jewellers, and insurance for loss of profits due to fire were examples. The first aviation insurance was written in 1911, two years after Bleriot flew across the English Channel.

Nevertheless the bulk of the business is still marine in its nature and Lloyd's has accordingly developed a world-wide shipping intelligence centre.

The Committee maintains a world-wide system of agents and sub-agents who are constantly sending news of shipping movements and other information relating to their own ports, towns and areas.

The enormous volume of information received from these agents and from radio stations, ship owners and other sources, is arranged together and distributed to newspapers, radio and television services, and throughout the marine and commercial communities in general. Edited, printed and published at Lloyd's, *Lloyd's List* is London's oldest daily newspaper, a descendant of the original Lloyd's News of the coffee house.

It contains shipping, insurance, air, and general commercial news, together with reports of the latest shipping movements received, and casualty reports – ships and cargoes damaged or sunk.

Lloyd's Shipping Index contains an alphabetical list of 16,000 merchant vessels giving details of each vessel, its current journey and latest position as known at Lloyds. It is the only publication of its kind in the world, requiring some 5,000 corrections daily in order to keep the information up to date. Copies are flown to New York on the same day of publication.

Other publications include *Lloyd's Weekly Casualty Lists*, *Lloyd's Law Reports*, *Cargo by Air* – a monthly publication giving details of scheduled flights from the United Kingdom and Europe – and *Lloyd's Loading List*, an alphabetical list of ports throughout the world, showing vessels loading for these ports from United Kingdom and continental ports.

A far cry indeed from the system of news brought back to the coffee house by runners from the waterfront!

The Intelligence Department at Lloyd's is open day and night throughout the year to receive, arrange and distribute this information to subscribers throughout the world. These subscribers include newspapers, the BBC, the big banks, ship owners, salvage companies, towage companies, and insurance companies. The Department will initiate a broadcast to all shipping, seeking information when a vessel is overdue.

Details of marine and aviation casualties and reports of non-marine losses such as fires, floods and robberies are posted on the Casualty Boards in the Underwriting Room at intervals throughout the day. Marine casualties are shown on yellow sheets and by tradition are written by hand; non-marine casualties are typed on pink sheets and aviation casualties on blue.

The Casualty Book in the centre of the Underwriting Room contains names of vessels which have become or are likely to become total losses. This information enables Lloyd's underwriters to be kept informed of vessels which have sustained serious damage and in which they may have an insured interest.

Above the rostrum hangs the Lutine Bell, which is for many of the public a symbol of Lloyd's. It was salvaged from H.M.S. Lutine, a frigate which sank off the coast of Holland in 1799 while carrying a cargo of gold and silver insured at Lloyd's and valued at over a million pounds.

It is not known when the bell was first hung in the Underwriting Room, but it is thought to have been in the late 1890s when Lloyd's was in the Royal Exchange. There is a widespread belief that the bell is rung for a major disaster, or each time a ship sinks. This is not true. The sounding of the bell originally meant that an announcement was to follow giving firm news of a vessel previously reported missing. But because most ships nowadays are equipped with radio and rarely disappear without trace, the bell is more frequently used for ceremonial occasions. It signifies that an important announcement is about to be made to the market. It is struck once to indicate bad news, and twice for good news.

Lloyd's, it can be seen, is an organization of many different kinds. It is a corporation; a society of underwriters covering risks from a film star's legs to a jumbo jet; an international market; printers and publishers of shipping publications; and the world centre of marine intelligence. As a business institution it is unique.

The London Gold Market

Goldsmiths and brokers in the City of London have dealt in gold for many hundreds of years, but the necessity for a daily gold market did not arise until after the first world war. Before that war the country was for some seventy years on a full gold standard and there was no need for a daily market. Anyone, resident or non-resident, could obtain gold bullion from the Bank of England on tendering banknotes or gold sovereigns to the required amount. Similarly, anyone could deliver bullion to the Bank and receive payment. There were, therefore, permanent facilities for buying and selling gold.

On the outbreak of the 1914–18 war the Gold Standard was suspended, and the Bank of England bought all gold on offer, at a fixed price. After the war the demand for gold for non-monetary purposes became very heavy, and the Bank of England agreed that new gold could be sold to the highest bidder and re-exported subject to licence. This was the start of the London Gold Market, with its daily meeting to fix the price. The first meeting took place in the autumn of 1919. In 1925 the country returned to a gold bullion standard and for the six years this lasted the Bank of England bought and sold at fixed prices. This limited the scope of the market, but the daily meetings continued.

After the gold bullion standard had been abandoned the market had a most active period, which lasted right up to the outbreak of the second world war. Speculative operations increased rapidly as the political and economic situation in Europe got worse and the flood of refugee capital from the continent seeking gold for security further increased the turnover of the market.

The London Gold Market remained closed from the outbreak of war until 1954, during which time any transactions in gold were effected at official prices published by the Bank of England. The market was reopened in March, 1954 and rapidly recovered its former position as the world's main bullion centre, handling about four-fifths of the gold coming on to the free markets. Dealings were permitted only against dollars and registered sterling until the end of 1958, when gold dealings were permitted under exchange control regulations against external sterling and any other convertible foreign currencies. ('Registered sterling' was sterling registered for use in payment for gold purchased in London.)

The gold market consists of five firms dealing in gold bullion. One of the members melts, refines, processes and assays gold. The five firms meet together twice on each working day for the fixing of the London gold price. It tries to absorb all new production or any other gold which may be offered at the fixing. Operations on the market are not confined to gold changing hands at the official fixing. A fair amount of business is done outside the fixings at varying prices. The market has to be seen against the background of world gold price movements.

Between 1961 and March 1968 the Bank of England acted on behalf of the government as an agent for the 'gold pool' set up by the central banks of Europe and the United States to maintain an orderly market and to try to smooth out unnecessary fluctuations in the price of gold.

All demands for gold, whether official or private, were satisfied on the free markets of the world. However, speculation in gold became so heavy that early in 1968 it became a threat to the international monetary system. Accordingly it was decided to separate the official need for gold reserves from other needs. The central banks participating in the gold pool agreed to suspend its operations, and agreed also not to supply gold to the free market, nor to buy from it; nor to sell gold to any monetary authority to replace gold sold by that authority to the market.

Thus came into being the 'two-tier' gold price. Gold was now bought and sold between monetary authorities at the fixed price of $35 per ounce, the official exchange rate between gold and the United States dollar. This price was revalued in December 1971 to $38 and in February 1973 to $42. The two-tier system was suspended in November, 1973.

The price of gold on the free market is allowed to fluctuate according to the laws of supply and demand. Since April 1968, therefore, the London Gold Market has been functioning without official support or intervention.

Gold coming on to the international markets is newly mined gold which has not been taken into official reserves, together with gold from private sources. The demand is on behalf of overseas customers: residents in Britain are not permitted under exchange control regulations to hold gold bullion, although they may hold gold coins.

In January 1974 Special Drawing Rights, previously defined in terms of gold, were restated on the basis of a 'basket' of currencies following the Nairobi recommendation of the Committee of Twenty. (Special Drawing Rights are a new type of international currency devised in 1969 to try to assist world trade. They are lines of credit opened for countries by the International Monetary Fund, to help them in settling their overseas debts, with the intent that temporary difficulties from payments deficits might be bridged over.) At Zeist in Holland in April 1974 the EEC Finance Ministers agreed to allow the exchange of gold between the nine member countries at free market-related prices. At Martinique in December 1974 the presidents of the United States and France made a joint declaration that any country should be free to revalue its gold reserves at market levels – a course followed by France in February 1975.

A major influence in the market during the latter part of 1974 was the impending liberalization of gold trading in the United States, and substantial quantities of gold were moved to New York and other centres to meet the anticipated public demand. The US Treasury disposed in 1975 of 1,250,000 ounces at market-related prices in two auctions, but there was no great rush to buy and no further auctions have been held. Early in September 1975 it was agreed that the Articles of the International Monetary Fund should be amended, to allow the Fund to sell one third of its surplus gold holdings. One sixth of this IMF gold was to be returned to member countries at the old official price and in the proportions in which they subscribed in gold to the IMF quotas, and one sixth was to be sold either to the central banks or in the market. These sales are to be spread over four years, and the proceeds, over and above the old official price, are to be paid into a trust fund for distribution to the less-developed countries.

The first two auctions were held on June 2nd and July 15th, 1976, their effect being to depress the value of gold. The first auction realized a profit of about 85 dollars per ounce on the old official price at which the gold was valued in the

Fund's books, the second only 80 dollars. This has to be compared with the price of gold at the time of September 1975 – about 150 dollars per ounce – when the decision to sell off the surplus gold was taken at the annual meeting of the IMF in Washington. The decision itself triggered off a steep fall in the value of gold, and buyers now fear the prospect of further auctions adding as much as 30 per cent to the total supply of newly mined gold coming on to the market over the next two years. France, where gold metal accounts for more than half of the country's official reserves, is particularly affected.

Finance houses

'Payment by instalments' is a phrase familiar to most people. Usually three parties are concerned. A sells something to B, who elects to pay by instalments, and signs the necessary paper. A is paid at once by C, a finance company. B repays C over a period, paying interest.

It was after the first world war that cars were first available on instalment, or hire-purchase terms. Hire purchase was subsequently extended to gramophones, radios, and other consumer equipment such as gas and electric cookers, refrigerators, washing machines, etc. Now almost anything can be obtained in this way.

At the time of the world slump in 1930 hire purchase was given as one of the causes. The view then current was that it is wrong to anticipate one's income. If an article is desired, the thing to do is to save up until one can afford it. The only exception was if the article was to be used in a way which would reduce the owner's outgoings. It was all right to buy a motorcycle to go to work on, because this would save train fares. When the motorcycle instalments were all paid, the owner still had the motorcycle as a capital asset, and the savings in outgoings would continue.

Nevertheless, hire purchase survived and expanded. Since the end of the last war there has been a steady annual increase in the figure representing hire-purchase debt. Legislation was passed to protect the consumer and credit sale agreements were invented.

In a hire-purchase agreement the contract is one of hire. The property in the article sold does not pass to the hirer until the last payment is made. Thus it was possible for the finance company, until restricted by legislation, to repossess the article at any time up to the final payment.

With a credit sale agreement (sometimes known as an instalment trading agreement) there is no right of recovery by the finance company, because the contract is one of sale. The ownership of the article passes immediately to the purchaser, although he does not pay the full price immediately, but by instalments at interest.

In recent years there has been an increasing tendency for industry to turn to the finance houses for assistance with machinery and plant. New schemes have been devised, such as the leasing of plant and equipment. Some items, such as some copying machines, cannot be bought at all, only leased. A maintenance obligation may be assumed by the manufacturer by agreement with the finance company and the lessor. The finance company may be a subsidiary of the manufacturing company.

Leasing is the hiring of an asset for the duration of its economic life. The asset is initially purchased by the finance company and then leased to the user, who has no option to purchase. The idea is not, of course, a new one: companies and individuals have rented premises for their business operations, houses and flats are rented to live in, television sets are rented from radio dealers. Since 1960 leasing operations by finance houses have expanded rapidly: the system is suitable for large and costly assets such as computers, aircraft, containers and container ships, and specialized and expensive plant and equipment.

Leasing is an alternative to purchase of an asset by instalment credit or through the aid of a mortgage or term loan. It has the advantage that it involves no capital outlay, requires no down payment, and may have tax benefits for the user. It does not count as borrowing for the purpose of a company's memorandum and articles of association.

Ownership of the asset remains with the lessor. A finance lease usually stipulates two periods of payment. The first calls for rentals to be paid monthly or quarterly until the cost of the asset and the charge made by the finance company has been paid: this might involve a period of some five years or so. In the second period the lessee continues to use the equipment but pays only a nominal rental.

In the case of sale and lease back a company may raise immediate finance by selling a capital asset, whether property or capital equipment, to a finance company, then leasing it back and continuing to use it as before. The ownership of the asset passes to the lessee, the finance company. The leasing rental will contain an element of the cost of the asset purchased from the lessor company plus an interest charge to cover administrative and service charges. Sale and lease back arrangements are usually found only where the asset to be purchased is worth £15,000 or more. However, smaller figures may be found where a scheme exists for the purchase of houses from retired couples, widows or widowers, subject to an agreement allowing them to continue to live in the house for the rest of their lives at a nominal rental.

Between 1957 and 1960 there was a growing demand for funds by medium-sized businesses, property developers, and others. The finance houses as a result expanded the banking side of their business. The banks realized that their traditional lending would suffer from this competition and accordingly the clearing banks acquired interests in leading finance houses, which in many cases they built up until the finance house became a subsidiary. They would perhaps have done this earlier, had it not been for their feeling that hire-purchase finance was not in the ordinary course of their business. However, the profit element was all-important, and when one bank chairman proclaimed that nearly everyone had to buy their houses by instalments, i.e. on mortgage, so what could be wrong with buying by instalments the things which went in them, hire purchase had become respectable. The sums involved became so considerable that the government had to exercise control from time to time by stipulating minimum initial payments and maximum periods for repayment. These regulations were issued by means of control orders which sought to limit the volume of trade in non-essential items of equipment or luxuries.

Over the present decade important changes have been taking place in consumer credit. The services of the finance houses have been used by an increasing number of companies, retailers and suppliers of consumer durables, motor-cars, and a growing range of services. The habit of buying goods on credit has been acquired by many people in all walks of life instead of being confined to the lower income groups as in earlier years. The banks and the finance houses have therefore been to some extent in competition for this kind of business. There are in Britain hundreds of firms engaged in financing hire purchase transactions. About thirty of the larger and better-known of these are members of the Finance Houses Association, which represents 85 per cent of all finance house business. The Consumer Credit Act passed through parliament in the autumn of 1974. It extended the consumer protection available to borrowers on hire purchase, conditional sale, and credit sale to borrowers by way of personal loan.

Under the new legislation details to be specified include the cash price of the goods or the amount of the loan, the cost of credit, the number and amount of instalments and the total sum payable.

Probably, however, the greatest change is the requirement for true interest rates to be given for all types of transactions. The object of this is not only to tell borrowers how much their credit is really costing them, but to allow them to compare rates under different contracts. Another safeguard written into the Act is a 'second thoughts' period of three days for the borrower to change his mind if he wants. Once he has undertaken the contract he will be entitled to a statutory rebate of charges if he settles the debt before the agreed period.

The finance houses have welcomed the Act, which puts every lender, whether a finance house, a bank, or a registered moneylender, on the same footing. Previously the smaller finance houses were obliged to register under the Money-lenders Act if they wished to make personal loans, which was felt to carry a certain stigma. After the passing of this Act they are free to use whatever type of lending instrument is acceptable to the contracting parties. This could well lead to a further reduction in hire purchase and an increase in personal loans.

Sources of funds

Naturally the proportion of capital and reserves to borrowed funds varies considerably between finance companies, but it is common ground that the greater part of their operating capital is borrowed. There are three main sources of borrowed funds, loans from banks, discounted bills, and deposits, that is, funds borrowed from the public.

When credit has to be restricted, the bank overdrafts of finance houses are among the first to be limited and even reduced. In normal times, however, the clearing banks are usually quite happy to lend against the security of the hire-purchase agreements held by the finance company. These, of course, are continually changing as old agreements run off and new ones are entered upon.

The finance houses also take deposits from accepting houses when the latter have surpluses, usually for quite short periods, and from overseas banks. Such banks hold considerable amounts of sterling and other currencies in connection with the financing of international trade and are substantial investors over a short or medium term.

The second source of borrowing is by way of discount. The finance house draws a bill of exchange which it presents to an accepting house for acceptance. After the bill has been accepted it is offered for discount in the money market. Thus a sum of money is obtained immediately against the need in three or six months' time to put the accepting house in funds to pay the bill on presentment. The accepting house charges a commission for its services.

The third source of borrowing, and much the most important, is by bidding for deposits. The finance companies advertise for deposits from the public and obtain in this way capital which is a collecting together of many individual sums from small savers, deposited for fixed periods up to one year. Money also comes through the parallel money markets, through which companies, financial institutions, and individuals deposit surplus funds with the finance houses for varying periods, sometimes up to six or twelve months.

To get these deposits the finance houses have to compete against banks, building societies, and local authorities, all of whom are in constant need of ever more and more deposits from wherever they can obtain them. As a result the finance houses tend to offer a slightly better rate of interest, although this depends in any individual case on the standing of the finance house, the length of time for which the funds are to be deposited, and the amount. If insufficient funds are attracted, then hire purchase contracts will have to be restricted, and profits will drop.

The working capital of the finance houses may seem rather here today and gone tomorrow, and indeed it is thought that some houses have perhaps as much as one-fifth of their funds at call on seven days' notice. Others have only a very small proportion of their funds deposited at such short periods of notice.

The use made of the funds, however, is also short and constantly changing. A hire purchase contract will be paid off, all being well, in anything from six months to three years, and after the original payment out to the seller has been made, the rest is money coming in all the time at a very good rate of interest. The capital structure is not, therefore, inappropriate. The modern view of hire purchase is that it is a useful way of acquiring a capital asset at an early date, provided always that the purchaser is not over-extending himself by trying to buy too many things at the same time. The success of hire-purchase finance shows that over the last fifty years there has been a rise in the good financial sense and judgement of the public generally, a rise which has gone side by side with a rise in the standard of living. Of course, a check is made in each case from the application form, and in individual cases the finance company will decide not to grant the accommodation. On the whole, though, it is both easier to borrow, and safer to lend, than it used to be.

Finance corporations

Business enterprises wishing to borrow for re-equipment, development, or expansion can borrow from a bank or, if they are big enough, raise the money from the public through the medium of the Stock Exchange by a new capital issue. Banks traditionally provide short-term credit, or temporary capital, while the new issue market provides permanent credit, or long-dated capital.

This seemed to leave some gaps. Enterprises of any size needing to borrow for something between one and five years (intermediate credit) might find that this period was too long for banks, and not long enough for new issue finance.

Small and middling size businesses needing long-term credit might find that they were not important enough for a new issue operation.

Finance for Industry

Finance for Industry (FFI) was formed in November 1973 by the merger of Finance Corporation for Industry (FCI) and the Industrial and Commercial Finance Corporation (ICFC).

FCI was formed in 1945 to provide for industrial concerns, to help them in redevelopment schemes and to assist them to work up to maximum efficiency. This objective was to be achieved by supplementing the activities of other lenders. The aim of the Corporation was to act in the national interest during the post-war reconstruction by providing funds for industry when money could not be wholly raised from ordinary market sources. It has thus restricted its investments to a small number of large companies. It did not provide finance unless the funds required exceeded £200,000 and could not reasonably be borrowed elsewhere.

The share capital of the corporation was provided by the Bank of England, the insurance companies, and investment trusts.

ICFC was also formed in 1945 to provide long-term capital for British-based small- and medium-sized companies which were capable of using additional resources profitably.

It also provided a wide range of financial and specialist services, and had a number of subsidiary companies financing new technical developments; assisting with company mergers and Stock Exchange flotations; providing renting and purchasing services for industrial plant, machinery, and commercial vehicles; and assisting with the finance of British ships. Loans were usually made for 7–20 years. It operates eighteen branches around the country, which to some extent liaise with the regional offices of the clearing banks.

The share capital of this corporation was provided by the principal English and Scottish banks and by the Bank of England.

The new group had potential resources of nearly £500 million, about £300 million of which were absorbed by the existing commitments of ICFC and FCI.

ICFC continued in its former role as a provider of funds for smaller companies.

The role of FCI would, it was thought, be enlarged in three ways: it would become involved in financing large capital projects in the North Sea oil exploration; it would expand its role in Europe by participating in syndicates; and it could become one of the main vehicles for industrial expansion in depressed areas in Britain.

After the reorganization ICFC is willing to consider loans from £5,000 to £1 million, FCI loans from £1 million to £30 million. In each case the period envisaged is between seven and fifteen years.

The merger created a two-tier structure. FFI as a new holding company acquired all the shares in ICFC and FCI, which each remained intact. The institutional investors in FCI were paid out in cash, while the ICFC shareholders became shareholders in FFI with the Bank of England. Since then FFI has raised a further £125 million by a loan stock issue and has had £100 million made available by its share-holders as stand-by facilities.

The new company is concerned in cases where substantial sums of money may be needed for investment before profits can be seen, or with heavy programmes of capital re-equip-ment which must be spread over a number of years unless additional sources of finance can be found. All loans will, however, be made subject to strict criteria of commercial viability. A target of £1,000 million of advances was hoped for. However, high interest rates, low demand for funds, and competition from the clearing banks made for a slow start, and halfway through 1976 only one-fifth of the target figure had been achieved.*

Equity Capital for Industry (ECI) (The Equity Bank)

A fund raised in 1976 from various investing institutions (principally insurance companies and life offices, pension funds and investment trusts) to be invested in fresh equity capital for quoted and unquoted small to medium-sized industrial companies. The new institution met with mixed reactions from those who, it was hoped, would subscribe the capital, the main stumbling block being a doubt that there was a significant gap in the present lending system of finding capital for industry. Funds from banks and financial institu-tions were thought to be usually quite readily available to industry, although there have been criticisms of the major

See p. 399.   *

investing institutions for being too remote from manufacturing industry and too insensitive to its needs.

Eventually the objects and advantages of ECI were stated to be: it would assist those recipients who would normally be too small for major institutions, and who could not turn to other sources of cash for some reason or other, e.g. where a company is unable to make a rights issue because its shares are standing at or below par, or where a company needing equity capital cannot obtain it because it is too highly geared. (Gearing is a relationship between the various classes of capital in a company. If some of the capital comes from loans, then gearing is the relationship between the loan capital and the total capital. The higher the loan capital, the higher is the interest to be paid on it. These sums can come only from trading income.)

About £35 million was raised for these purposes. Contrary to earlier indications, ECI will not take an active role in the management of companies in which it invests.*

Commonwealth Development Finance Company

This company was formed in 1953 to provide financial assistance for development projects within the Commonwealth. Finance has been provided over a wide range of industrial and development projects including chemicals and fertilizers, engineering, forestry, agriculture, and textiles.

The share capital, of this corporation is provided by industrial, commercial, and financial interests jointly with the Bank of England.

Agricultural Mortgage Corporation

This corporation was formed in 1929 to provide facilities whereby farmers could obtain long-term loans at reasonably favourable rates, secured by first mortgages on their farms, for periods of between ten and forty years. Repayments are made by equal half-yearly instalments of capital and interest.

* See p. 399.

To make these loans the corporation needs funds, which it obtains partly from the shareholders and partly from the issue of a debenture stock, secured by a charge on all its property and assets. The government, which is inescapably committed to maintaining a stable and prosperous farming industry, has made the debenture stock additionally attractive to investors by guaranteeing it to the extent of £12 million. In this way a means is provided by which the capital of the private investor can become available for agriculture.

The share capital of this corporation is provided by the clearing banks and the Bank of England.

Revision Test 5

Put ticks in what you think are the right boxes.

(1) The Stock Exchange dealer who quotes buying and selling prices for stocks and shares is called
    (a) an underwriter ☐
    (b) a broker ☐
    (c) a jobber ☐

(2) 'Gilt-edged' is a term used to describe
    (a) shares in gold mines ☐
    (b) government securities ☐
    (c) land and property shares ☐

(3) A man who sells shares which he does not have, in the hope that he can buy them later more cheaply is
    (a) a bear ☐
    (b) a bearer ☐
    (c) a bull ☐

(4) The Official Daily List gives information about
    (a) shipping in UK ports ☐
    (b) stock and share prices ☐
    (c) scheduled flights from the UK ☐

(5) A Lloyd's broker is the agent of

(a) the underwriting syndicate ☐
(b) the assured ☐
(c) an insurance company ☐

(6) The Casualty Board in Lloyd's Underwriting Room gives details of the
(a) members who have been 'hammered' ☐
(b) ships that have been damaged ☐
(c) underwriters who cannot meet their liabilities ☐

(7) The Central Fund at Lloyd's is used
(a) to meet the costs of running the market ☐
(b) to pay any claims which underwriters cannot meet ☐
(c) to take out guarantee policies on members ☐

(8) A television set becomes the property of the purchaser when he pays the last instalment under
(a) a credit sale agreement ☐
(b) a hire purchase agreement ☐
(c) an instalment trading agreement ☐

(9) The London Gold Market is a term used to signify
(a) dealers in gilt-edged securities on the London Stock Exchange ☐
(b) the Bank of England's holding in the 'gold pool' run by central bankers ☐
(c) a number of firms dealing in gold bullion ☐

(10) A directive restricting the terms on which hire purchase is conducted primarily concerns the members of the
(a) Accepting Houses Committee ☐
(b) Finance Houses Association ☐
(c) London Discount Market Association ☐

Check your solutions with the answers on p. 395.
Take one mark for each correct answer.
Each Revision Test totals 10 marks.

Questions for discussion

1. Compare and contrast the measures taken by the Council of the Stock Exchange and the Corporation of Lloyds respectively to safeguard the public against any possible financial instability of their members.

2. Explain how the finance houses obtain the funds which they need for their business.

3. Who are the customers of the finance corporations?

6

The savings
media

National Savings Bank

The National Savings Bank was originally called the Post
Office Savings Bank and under that name was established in
1861. It is now probably the largest organization of its kind
in the world. There are two sorts of account, Ordinary and
Investment. An account may be opened at any post office.
Ordinary accounts are subject to a condition that no more
than £10,000 may be deposited.

Ordinary accounts carry interest, the rate varying from
time to time in accordance with the general money rate level.
Interest is credited on every complete pound, and com-
mences on the first day of the month following the deposit.
Interest is paid yearly on 31st December, being credited to
the account. The first £70 of interest is exempt from income
tax. Deposits and withdrawals must be recorded in the depositor's passbook and may be made at any post office where
savings business is transacted.

Withdrawals on demand are limited to £20, but larger
amounts may be withdrawn at a few days' notice either in cash
at a particular post office, or by crossed warrant payable
through a bank.

National Savings Bank deposits are lodged with the

National Debt Commissioners and are invested in government securities. The government guarantees the repayment of the sums invested, with accrued interest, when required. The interest earned by these investments is set against the interest due to depositors and management expenses.

Investment accounts were introduced in 1966. These accounts carry a rather higher rate of interest than the ordinary accounts. The rate depends on the earnings of deposits when invested by the National Debt Commissioners and is published in the London, Edinburgh and Belfast Gazettes. Investment accounts are subject to one month's notice of withdrawal and all the interest is subject to tax. A £50,000 limit was imposed in July 1977.

Trustee savings banks

Trustee savings banks are regional banks to be found in most of the large towns in this country. They were founded with the idea of promoting thrift and independence in old age, and profit was not originally the objective. They are perhaps more widely known in the North. Each bank serves a particular area, and therefore they do not compete with each other, but in thirty-eight years branch numbers have increased from 680 to 1,655. However, they are in competition mostly with the National Savings Bank and with the building societies, for the funds of small savers.* Most of them originated in the nineteenth century and although their legal constitutions were consolidated in 1954 there are still minor differences in procedure amongst them. They operate under their own boards of (paid) trustees, but are subject to statutory provisions and supervision by the Bank of England.

Trustee savings banks maintain two departments, the Ordinary Department and the Special Investment Department.* A depositor is limited to £10,000 in the Ordinary Department. Savings accounts in the Ordinary Department carry interest at a rate varying from time to time in accordance with the general level of money rates.

See p. 399. *

Withdrawals from savings accounts may be made on demand, without limit. The customer is by no means restricted to his own particular branch for drawings, for if he so desires, and if he notifies the branch accordingly, arrangements exist whereby he can withdraw money through trustee savings banks other than the bank at which his account is held. Income tax relief is applied to the first £70 of interest (£140 in the case of a married couple's joint account).*

Accounts in the Special Investment Department carry a rather higher rate of interest, but are subject to one month's notice of withdrawal. Such interest is subject to tax. The funds in such investment accounts are now invested under the supervision of the Trustee Savings Bank Central Board, in accordance with Treasury determination.

A depositor may not deposit money in more than one trustee savings bank.

The trustee savings banks are clearly working their way towards the provision of a full banking service. A current account service was authorized in 1964 whereby account holders can draw cheques at a small fixed charge, subject to an allowance for a minimum average balance of £50. No interest is paid on current accounts. No overdrafts can be granted,* but some other services are available, not necessarily at all the banks. These include safe custody for valuables, the payment of accounts by standing order, travellers' cheques and foreign exchange, and the sale and purchase of securities through stockbrokers on an agency basis. Dividends from these are automatically credited to the account.

The trustee savings banks administer a unit trust which was set up in 1968, and does not carry a government guarantee. Units are available to both depositors and non-depositors: the minimum initial holding is £250. Subsequent purchases may be made in multiples of £25. Purchases of smaller quantities may be made by means of investment in 'Harvest Bonds', which may be bought in multiples of £50. †

* See p. 400.

On 31 July 1974 it was announced that the government would adopt the recommendation of the Page Committee on National Savings and would allow the trustee savings banks to develop a full range of personal banking services, including personal loans to depositors. They have already made their cheque guarantee card acceptable for cashing cheques in clearing bank branches and have joined the Eurocheque scheme. A new unit trust fund has been launched, with the emphasis on higher-yielding shares. Three life assurance plans are available, two equity-linked monthly savings plans, and a single premium investment plan. Bridging loans will be available for established and credit-worthy customers.

The trustee savings bank movement will be completely reorganized over the next ten years. By the end of 1975 some seventy banks had been restructured into eighteen regional institutions. In 1976 the Birmingham Municipal Savings Bank, with about eighty branches in the Birmingham area, joined the trustee savings bank movement. At the end of the year the bank was offering personal loans and overdrafts to its customers (it has no corporate customers).*

At the end of the transitional period, which will be used largely to build up reserves, the banks will be put on an equal footing with the commercial banks and will be subject to the guidance of the Bank of England.

So that the trustee savings banks can build up the reserves which they will need for their new role, the government is to pay them for the first time the full income from the Fund for the Banks for Savings. The banks will be allowed to phase out their investments in the Fund by gradually running down the Ordinary Department.

The trustee savings banks will become, in effect, mutual organizations run for the benefit of their customers rather than for an outside body of shareholders. They will constitute a considerable competitive rival for the commercial banks as far as private customers are concerned. A pilot scheme on personal loans was launched at eight different TSBs in November 1974. It covered about 200 branches out of the

See p. 400. *

1,500 in the movement. Loans are available to established credit-worthy customers, who can borrow between £150 and £1,500 for between twelve and thirty-six months. The loans are comparable in cost to those offered by the clearing banks. Linked life assurance policies, handled by the TSB Trust Company Ltd, will ensure that the loan is automatically repaid if the borrower should die before its term expires.

The trustee savings banks are linked together through the Trustee Savings Banks Association, of which they are all members.

There is also a statutory body called the Trustee Savings Bank Inspection Committee, which inspects each bank at regular intervals and makes an annual report to parliament.*

National savings securities

The first issue of National Savings Certificates was offered in 1916 under the name of 'War Savings Certificates', the name being changed in 1920. Since then there have been many fresh issues from time to time offering various rates of interest. Interest is by way of accruals to the capital value and is paid out only when the savings certificates are cashed. The current issue is the Fourteenth, offering an effective rate of 7·59 per cent interest over four years. The certificates have always been free of tax and are therefore attractive to the high-tax payer if he is prepared to leave his money in for the whole of the four years. The purchase price of the certificates is £1 per unit and the maximum holding is 3,000 units which may be held in addition to the permitted holdings of the Decimal Issue (1,500 units) and of previous issues. The value, which on maturity after 4 years will be £1·34, will grow as follows:

At the end of year 1 by 6p to £1·06
In year 2 by 2½p for each completed 4 months to £1·13½
In year 3 by 3p for each completed 4 months to £1·22½
In year 4 by 3½p for each completed 4 months
    plus 1p at the year end   £1·34

* See p. 400.

The certificates are available at post offices and banks and are intended for small savers. Gift tokens are available for exchange into certificates, but the familiar National Savings Stamp was gradually phased out over 1975 and 1976. Schemes exist at schools and in offices to encourage the acquisition of the certificates.

The persistent inflation which has existed in recent years has meant that the interest on National Savings Certificates hardly keeps up with the depreciation of the pound. This is quite the opposite result to what was intended, namely, that the savings of the nation, lent to the government, would help to maintain a stable economy and act as an anti-inflationary force.

For the National Savings Retirement Certificate please see p. 148.

British Savings Bonds

Defence Bonds were introduced during the last war as a form of investment, midway between government marketable securities and National Savings Certificates, for the small saver. After the war it was felt that a more appropriate name for a peace-time issue would be National Development Bonds, and these were followed by British Savings Bonds, which were first issued in 1968. They are sold in units of £5 and bear interest at $9\frac{1}{2}$ per cent. They are issued for five years, at the end of which time a bonus of 4 per cent is added. There is a maximum holding of £10,000 on each issue. The interest is paid twice yearly without tax deduction. The holder is then liable for tax. For those paying below the standard rate of tax they are a good investment. Bonds of the current issue may be encashed at one month's notice. Of course to gain the best from them one must leave them uncashed for the whole of the five years, in order to get the terminal bonus.

Holders of Defence Bonds and National Development Bonds which are maturing are generally offered conversion into British Savings Bonds with terms similar to those currently available.

Following the recommendations of the Page Committee's Report on National Savings the Paymaster General on 6th August 1974 announced a new index-linked savings certificate. The link with the cost-of-living index figure should ensure that the certificate-holder is able to protect his capital against inflation. The index-linked facility is limited to pensioners and regular savers only. The pensioners' certificate is available in minimum units of £10 each up to a maximum of £500 to men aged sixty-five and over and women aged sixty and over. The regular savers' scheme is mentioned on p. 151.

The limit of £500 will be reviewed in the light of the working of the scheme. After the certificate has been held for one year its value will be adjusted periodically as from its purchase date in accordance with the general index of retail prices. No interest will be paid, but a terminal bonus will be added if the certificate is held for five years. Neither income tax nor capital gains tax will apply. The certificates will be encashable at short notice. More details were published at the end of January 1975. The Retirement Certificate, as it is named, should enable those of pensionable age to keep a proportion of their savings in line with any subsequent rise in the cost of living. The retirement issue was made available in June 1975 in units of £10 up to a maximum of £700 (£1,400 for a married couple). The value of the holding is adjusted in value each month for any increase in the retail price index in the previous month. A certificate held for the full term of five years matures with a 4 per cent bonus. If a certificate is encashed within the first year only the cash value is repaid; thereafter the holder gets repayments adjusted for any increase in retail price index.

Anyone, retired or not, is entitled to buy the certificates if they are over 65 (men) or 60 (women). A simple declaration of age is all that is needed. Retirement certificates which are inherited by a person below the pensionable age must be cashed in, but if the legatee qualifies for age, he or she can keep the legacy even if he or she already owns the maximum £500 worth in his/her own right.

The National Savings Retirement Issue certificates are not on sale at commercial bank offices.

The clearing banks asked for a 50p commission for every £100 of certificates processed, but the government would offer only 12½p, the commission in force for many years for selling National Savings Certificates, and which the banks had long argued was no longer appropriate in view of the escalation in costs. Talks were terminated inconclusively in May 1975 and have not been reopened since.

Premium Savings Bonds

Investors in these bonds, which are issued in £1 units in multiples of £5, enjoy no interest but are offered the chance of a prize. Premium Savings Bonds are, in fact, a national lottery with security for the investor's money built in. The maximum holding is £3,000 for any individual. A bond must be held for three months before it qualifies for the draw, made by the well-known computer 'Ernie'. From time to time the amounts of prizes are altered, but at the moment (1976) there is a weekly draw for prizes ranging from £25 to £75,000, and a monthly prize of £100,000.

The National Savings Bank, the trustee savings banks, and branches of the commercial banks all provide facilities for the purchase of all these securities and of other government marketable securities also. The administration of the National Savings Bank, National Savings Certificates, Premium Savings Bonds, and Government Bonds and Stock on the National Savings Stock Register is carried out by the Department for National Savings under the Director of Savings, who is responsible to the Treasury. The Department assists and advises the two national committees, composed of voluntary workers, who supervise the collection of savings in England and Wales, and in Scotland. These are respectively the National Savings Committee for England and Wales and the National Savings Committee for Scotland. Below them is a structure of regional and local committees governing the work of 150,000 voluntary workers organizing savings groups in factories, offices, and schools. A similar structure operates in Northern Ireland.

The function of the movement is to educate the public in saving for the benefit of the nation and the individual, and to help the small investor to save through the medium of government securities. In its evidence to the Page Committee, set up to review National Savings, the treasury listed the government's objectives in the savings movement as, amongst others:

(1) The need to assist in financing the government's borrowing by attracting a sufficient flow of funds to it.
(2) The social motive of ensuring that savings facilities are available and that savings habits and personal financial responsibility are encouraged.

Savings Plans: Save As You Earn

This is a government-backed scheme for savings made by regular monthly amounts. It was introduced in 1969 and is administered both by the Department for National Savings and by the trustee savings banks. Savings may be made by deduction from pay (where the employer has agreed to cooperate), by standing order on a bank, the National Giro, or a trustee savings bank.

Known as 'Save As You Earn' (SAYE) it enables all persons over the age of sixteen to save regular monthly amounts of anything between £1 and £20 in deposits with the Department for National Savings.

At the end of five years savings qualify for a bonus, equivalent to fourteen months' savings free of tax (equivalent to an average 12·58 per cent gross yield over the five years).

If the savings are not drawn out, but left in for a further two years, a double bonus equivalent to twenty-eight monthly contributions is added, again free of tax. (This brings the gross interest rate up to 13·03 per cent over the seven years.)

Example £1 per month for 7 years.

	£
Year 1	12
Year 2	12
Year 3	12
Year 4	12
Year 5	12
First bonus	14
Year 6	
Year 7	
Second bonus	28
Total savings	£102

For those who change their minds at some point the rules are that savers who wish to stop payments may withdraw the total sum saved. It must be all or nothing – no partial withdrawals. Tax-free compound interest is paid at the rate of 6 per cent on amounts withdrawn after the first but before the end of the fifth year, or at the rate of 8 per cent where the contributions cease, but the savings are left invested for the remainder of the five years, or where the saver dies before contributions are completed. Savings withdrawn in the first year are repaid in full but without interest.

A separate 'Save As You Earn' scheme (with the same maximum limit) is operated by the building societies. Because of the tax relief a limit of £40 per month is placed on any individual saver. A person wishing to take full advantage of the scheme would therefore have to run two schemes, one with the National Savings Bank (or a Trustee Savings Bank) and one with a building society. This would be a useful idea for a person aged, say 57, due to retire on to half-pay at 65. By taking the full £40 per month while he was earning a good salary he could look forward to a total payment on retirement of £4,080 to supplement his pension.*

Following the recommendations of the Page Report on National Savings the Paymaster General on 6 August 1974 announced a new index-linked scheme for regular savers

See p. 401. *

which would be open to anyone eligible for SAYE. This would replace the SAYE scheme, but would not enable existing SAYE users to convert their original contracts into the new scheme.

The new scheme came into operation in July 1975. Contributions can range between £4 and £20 monthly, and are payable over a period of five years: for another two years without extra contributions there is a bonus. Each monthly payment is increased in value to allow for any increase in the retail price index. Thus after five years the repayment value of the contract will be the total of monthly contributions plus any increase in monthly contributions due to the rise in the cost of living. Leaving the cash untouched for a further two years means a bonus equal to two monthly contributions as well as a further adjustment for the retail price index. If the contract is cancelled in the first year no interest is added to the contributions; thereafter 6 per cent interest payment on top of monthly subscriptions is paid if the contract is stopped at any time before the five-year maturity date.

The principles of SAYE are similar to those of an insurance policy but without the life cover. A similar plan to SAYE but including life cover during the currency of the scheme is run by Williams and Glyn's Bank under the name 'Nest Egg' plan. Here the saver pays anything from £5 a month up by standing order from any bank. After ten years a bonus of twice the monthly payment is added. The bulk of the money is invested, but a proportion of it, dependent upon the age of the saver, goes into a term insurance policy which provides life insurance cover of 180 times the monthly payment (£1,800 for a person investing £10 a month, for example). There is the usual 15 per cent tax relief for standard-rate tax payers.

The money invested earns interest at a rate determined by the bank according to money market conditions. Interest is credited quarterly. For those who change their mind and cancel, one month's premium is deducted in the first year, half-a-month's premium in the second. After that there is no further penalty; the high rate offered is not conditional on the saver completing the full term.

Building societies

Building societies are the major source of funds for the provision of long-term loans (home loans) on the security of houses and land. In this capacity they are non-profit-making bodies and their interest rates are strictly linked with money rates, although they are slower to respond to any change than, say, the banks' base rates. To gather the funds which they lend out, the societies must offer an attractive rate, sufficient to bring in the funds they need. If money is difficult to get, interest rates offered will have to be raised, and this in turn will mean that mortgage rates will also have to go up. This might be bad politically, as was seen in 1973 when the government for a short time subsidized the societies to prevent them from putting up their mortgage rates from $9\frac{1}{2}$ per cent to 10 per cent, and later pegged the banks' deposit rates for deposits under £10,000 to $9\frac{1}{2}$ per cent to prevent the banks attracting depositors' money away from building societies.

Building societies thus have two faces. The first is as a savings medium, the second as a lender. We are here interested in the societies from the savings opportunities point of view. They form an important channel for the investment of small personal savings.

The first building society is said to have been established in Birmingham in 1775. A century later they were to be found in the industrial areas of the country. They were small groups of people, called members, who paid fixed monthly sums, gradually accumulating funds which could then be used to buy land and build houses on it. As the houses slowly became ready for occupation they were allotted to members by ballot or perhaps by payment of a premium. When everyone had eventually acquired a house the society was dissolved. They therefore became known as terminating building societies. They were able in the end to provide the houses, and they did show that regular saving by people working together for mutual benefit could achieve objectives beyond the reach of individuals. But the disadvantage was that members could wait many years for a house. The society did not borrow, and therefore had only the funds which its members paid in.

About 1850 a relaxation of this rigid link between the investing and borrowing aspects of membership permitted the emergence of a new and more efficient type of building society, the permanent building society. Funds were now borrowed, not only from those who were saving for the express purpose of buying a house, but also from those who had savings to invest, but did not wish to take anything out. So the societies were able to make loans to borrowing members so that they could build or purchase a house quite quickly. The members got into their houses much sooner. There was no longer any need to dissolve the society when each of the original members had got his loan.

The development of these societies led to the grant of the right of incorporation under an Act of 1874, and a firm base was secured for the rapid growth which has occurred in more recent times. An Act of 1962, consolidating earlier measures, now imposes conditions affecting the functions, operation, and management of societies, provides for audit and the publication of detailed yearly accounts, restricts borrowing and lending powers, and confers certain privileges, such as the limitation of liability of members. It also regulates the way in which the societies can advertise for funds, and the way in which any surplus funds may be invested.

The Chief Registrar of Friendly Societies is by virtue of his office Registrar of Building Societies. He has powers to investigate the affairs of societies in the interests of depositors or investors and, if he thinks fit, to prohibit particular societies from advertising for additional funds.

Nearly all the bigger societies are members of the Building

Societies Association, which imposes certain conditions of membership, such as the maintenance of minimum liquid resources in cash and securities, and makes recommendations to members on interest rates to be charged to borrowers and offered to investors.

Share accounts

Shares in a building society are not dealt in on the Stock Exchange, but may be withdrawn at par in cash, on giving notice. They carry a rate of interest which is usually fixed by the directors of the society and is varied from time to time in accordance with changes in monetary conditions. The period of notice required for the withdrawal of shares varies according to the rules of the society, usually between one month and six months, although in practice small sums are paid out at once and larger amounts at short notice.

Building society interest is paid free of basic tax because the societies have come to an arrangement with the Inland Revenue to pay the tax at a rate which is supposed to be the average rate which the investors would have paid if they had been taxed on the income instead of the societies.

The amount of share capital in a building society is not fixed, as in a public limited company, but may be regulated in accordance with the amount lent on mortgage.

Shares in an established building society offer a reasonably good rate of interest, coupled with security and the ability to withdraw capital at short notice. They do not, however, offer any protection against inflation.

Some societies offer a slightly higher rate of interest on what are called term shares. To take advantage of this it is necessary for the depositor to leave his money in for a definite length of time, which varies from six months to two years according to the society.

For people who need their income from their building society more frequently than six-monthly some societies run monthly income shares where, as the name implies, interest is paid monthly in return for a condition of one or two months' notice of withdrawal.

Deposit accounts

Building society depositors rank as creditors, and would therefore in the event of the winding-up of the society be able to get their money back before the shareholders. In recognition of this fact the interest is $\frac{1}{4}$ per cent or $\frac{1}{2}$ per cent lower than that paid on share accounts. The big building societies, however, have built up such enormous assets, and are so very strong financially, that it is difficult to see any extra security in their deposit accounts.

Subscription schemes

Regular savings accounts are offered by most societies. Under such schemes a shareholder agrees to save a regular weekly or monthly amount over a period of years. A slightly higher rate of interest is usually paid on these savings provided that there is no interruption to the regularity of the payments. Some societies have introduced a little flexibility by allowing one withdrawal a year, or one withdrawal after two years, others accept only ten payments in a twelve-month. The penalty for any variance from the conditions is a lowering of the special interest rate to that of a share account. A Link-a-Loan scheme guarantees a mortgage for anyone who has saved regularly for two years. However, societies are generally understandably reluctant to guarantee that mortgages will be forthcoming when required, although they naturally look with a favourable eye on a depositor of some standing.

Saving schemes linked with life assurance are ideal for young people saving to buy a house. A regular investment for ten years is stipulated; the minimum monthly saving can be as low as £3. In conjunction with an assurance company life cover is provided at 180 times the monthly payment and this entitles the saver to tax relief. The interest rate on these

fixed-interest saving schemes is very little below that on
SAYE, which has no life cover. After a qualifying period
there is provision for withdrawal without penalty, and at
the termination of the scheme the savings so accumulated
can be used to provide the deposit for a house bought by
mortgage to the society.

Registered provident societies

Registered provident societies take in a group of varied
institutions registered under the Friendly Societies Acts and
other legislation which give them certain privileges, such
as limited liability, and impose upon them various limitations
and obligations.

Friendly societies are mutual insurance societies in which
the members subscribe for provident benefits; in particular,
sickness, death, endowment, and old age benefits, and provisions for widows and orphans. They first appeared in the
sixteenth century as local organizations which had by three
hundred years later developed into centralized bodies with
branches throughout the country. Although the National
Health Service now meets most of the needs for which the
original friendly societies were set up, they still continue to
operate and have diversified to include industrial insurance;
industrial, provident, and building societies; trade unions;
certified loan societies; and some superannuation and pension
schemes. All are closely controlled by various Acts.

Industrial assurance business is the effecting of life insurance by means of premiums which are paid to collectors,
who make house-to-house calls for this purpose, at intervals
of less than two months. Only friendly societies registered
under the Friendly Societies Acts or authorized assurance
companies may engage in this business. Registered friendly
societies and insurance companies which effect industrial
assurance business are known as 'collecting societies' and
'industrial assurance companies' respectively.

Industrial and provident societies are incorporated with

limited liability. The shareholding of any member, except another registered society, is limited to £1,000. Important under this heading are the wholesale and retail co-operative societies.

As we have seen, investment in building societies is in the form of deposits or shares. By contrast trade unions receive contributions from members, and some provide sickness and accident, superannuation, funeral, and various other benefits.

Pension schemes

Pensions are often the only form of saving for retirement which a person will make. They are a part of the remuneration of the employee, deferred until he has finished active work, to which he has a right. This is only now understood. Formerly pensions were regarded rather as an act of grace on the part of the employer, in fact were often expressed to be payable 'at the discretion of the directors', or some such phrase.

The 1973 Social Security Act stated conditions for the recognition of a private pension scheme. Formerly these schemes were of two basic kinds, both shaped by the tax concessions which the authorities were willing to give. The first gave less tax allowance, but allowed part of the pension to be converted into a cash payment – commutation – on retirement. The second gave a greater tax allowance, but no right of commutation.

Some limit to pension benefits has to be set if these tax concessions are not to be abused, and therefore the maximum yearly pension amount under the rules is one-sixtieth of final year's salary multiplied by the years of service, being not less than ten nor more than forty. In other words, provided an employee has served at least forty years with the same company he can get two-thirds of his final salary by way of pension. Many schemes yield less than this and an employee changing his job may find his pension rights are less as a result.

The state pension

The basic principle of social security schemes adopted after 1945, following the Beveridge Report, was that pensions should become payable when people retired, rather than when they reached a certain age, as under the pre-war scheme. When the National Insurance Act came into force, a man aged 65 received £1·30 per week and a dependent wife 80p. These figures were raised from time to time as continuing inflation made a nonsense of them.

In addition to the basic pension it became possible for those who did not retire at the minimum pensionable age to earn 'increments', that is, when they did eventually retire, they would draw a rather higher pension.

Under legislation coming into force in 1961 a 'graduated' element was added to the basic flat rate pension. This was meant to provide a higher level of pension, which would be more in proportion to the income earned during working years, for those earning more than the national average. This system ended in April 1975. From 6 April the Social Security Act 1973 came into operation. From that date flat-rate and graduated contributions ceased to be payable for employees and were replaced by wholly earnings-related contributions. Stamp cards for employees were abolished at the same time, and the earnings-related national insurance contributions are now collected with income tax under the PAYE procedure.

The 1973 Social Security Act established a two-tier pensions scheme, a basic scheme plus a state reserve scheme. The basic scheme is available for everyone at 65 (60 for women) provided that they in fact retire at that age. This part of the pension is guaranteed by the state and is at present £19.50 per week for a single person and £31.20 per week for a married couple. The state reserve scheme paid benefits related to earnings. The payments were in two parts; the first a minimum sum, the second an additional sum which would depend on how well the invested funds of the state pension fund performed. Both employer and employee contribute to the scheme, the employers paying 2½ per cent of the employee's wages or salary, the employee 1½ per cent. These percentages are paid on all earnings up to one and a half times the national figure for average earnings.

An employee in a private pension scheme will be contracted out of the state reserve part of the state pension fund.

On 8 May 1974 the government announced modifications of the 1973 Social Security Act. The state reserve pensions scheme was scrapped, for the reason that it would leave thousands of people dependent for years to come on means-tested supplementary pensions. Also, it made particularly poor provision for widows and other women. At the same time, the government was in favour of good private pension schemes. Apart from the state reserve scheme, the basic provisions of the 1973 Social Security Act would remain.

This would include the change from the present graduated pension scheme, which would be wound up, to a system which would be fully related to earnings. Provisions to preserve existing occupational pension rights would also come into force as planned.

Those who since 1961 have been earning more than the national average will be entitled to graduated pensions if they did not contract out at the time. Those who did contract out have had to make contributions since 1966 and will receive some extra pension on this account when they retire. Although the graduated scheme was terminated in 1975, benefits that have accrued under it are preserved, although without interest. For most people these benefits are likely to be very small.

It is an unfortunate fact that the two main political parties hold differing views on pension principles. It is also true that the question is a highly involved one and that any scheme takes years to work out. Thus it may happen that when it is ready to be implemented there is a change of government and the scheme is lost.

A Social Security Pensions Act was passed in August 1975;

its provisions will come into effect after April 1978. This has the most important implications for those in occupational pension schemes, and for employers who must decide before December 1977 whether or not to contract out of the State scheme.

The new pensions system will be financed by increased National Insurance contributions and by a Treasury supplement coming from direct taxation. Benefits will be of two kinds: a basic pension, corresponding to the existing flat-rate pension, and an earnings-related pension, which will build up over twenty years and by 1998 will equal 25 per cent of each person's average yearly earnings between a lower and an upper limit. What these limits will be by the time we get to 1998 is anyone's guess, but the limits now are £17.50 per week and £120 per week respectively.

On today's figures a single person earning £70 weekly will have a total pension of £27·50 a week if retiring in April 1998, a married couple £35·40. (There is, of course, provision for earnings to be revalued. This means that they are increased in line with the way that average earnings have increased between the year the money was earned, and the year in which the person retires. Each year has to be revalued separately.) Those retiring before 1998 will have their earnings-related part of the pension scaled down. To get the maximum benefit a person has to work for 20 years after 1978.

Those employees who are members of an occupational pension scheme may like to know that if the scheme fulfils certain conditions it can be contracted out of the State earnings-related part of the pension (no one can opt out of the basic flat-rate pension). The conditions are that after April 1978 a scheme must provide pensions of at least one-eightieth of final average salary (or revalued average salary) for each year of service to retirement. It must also provide for a widow's benefit of half this amount. The general principle is that no employee can be worse off than he would be in the State scheme.

There are inducements to contract out. Both employees and

employers will pay reduced National Insurance contributions on earnings between the lower and upper earnings limits. Employers' contributions to occupational schemes attract tax relief.

It seems likely that small firms will find it impractical to contract out. If they already have a scheme going they have three choices; to keep it going to supplement the State scheme (particularly in the early years), to switch to a scheme which provides lump-sum cash benefits, or to discontinue the scheme (in which case, employees' pensions will be frozen until retirement).

Self-employed persons

The self-employed man or woman, or anyone else who wishes to provide for retirement, can take out an endowment assurance policy to provide a pension or a lump sum on retirement which can be invested; or can contract with an insurance company for an Individual Retirement Annuity.

Endowment assurance carries the same tax relief as for any other policy, but Individual Retirement Annuities get the same tax relief as is granted to an approved employer's scheme, a much better proposition. Any annuity is subject to the disadvantage that if you die soon after you have retired you have made a bad bargain. To cover this the annuitant should see that the annuity payments are guaranteed for five or ten years after retirement. If then the annuitant is dead there will be something to be passed to his dependants.

All pensions and annuities should have built-in provision of cost-of-living rises; otherwise continuing inflation will progressively eat away the real value of the payments at a time when the recipient is least likely to be able to do anything to supplement them.

Assurance companies

Insurance companies in this country began in the middle of the sixteenth century with marine risk insurance. We have seen how the association of underwriters known as Lloyd's developed. About the same time, round about the turn of the seventeenth century, the first fire and life offices were founded.

Insurance may now be said to fall into the main groups: life; property; marine, aviation and transport; motor vehicle; third-party liability; and personal accident and sickness.

The first and the last of these are means of saving, but life assurance is much the more important.

A certain amount of insurance is provided by friendly societies, but this is a small proportion of the total business, which is looked after by Lloyd's or by mutual or joint-stock companies.

All types of insurance companies are closely regulated by various Acts so as to protect the interests of those insured, and the Department of Trade is given power to supervise and to grant or withhold authority for new companies to act, or for an existing company to take on additional classes of business. Authority will be withheld if the Department is not satisfied as to the company's financial resources, its internal administration, and the fitness of the persons who control and manage the business. A minimum paid-up share capital is required, as is a certain solvency margin, that is, a certain excess of assets over liabilities.

The Department also has a number of powers relating to the annual returns of any company, and in certain circumstances may petition for the winding-up of a company, or may intervene at an earlier stage if it appears that a company's business is being so conducted that there is a risk of it becoming insolvent.

Companies carrying on life business are not required to have any specific solvency margin, but there must be an actuarial valuation of their assets and liabilities at least once in every three years, and this must make it clear that prudent margins have been allowed in the calculations.

All types of risk other than life are *insured* against, but a person's life is *assured*. An assurance company, therefore, is one dealing with life risks. Life assurance has three characteristics which are peculiar to it. It is essentially long term; it deals with something certain to happen (e.g. death or the attainment of a specified age); and an annual premium agreed at the beginning of the contract continues unchanged throughout the contractual duration.

Most of the companies are members of the Life Offices Association and Associated Scottish Life Offices, or the Industrial Life Offices' Association. There are about fifteen industrial life assurance companies and some seventy or eighty collecting societies.

Life assurance companies have very large sums for investment at their disposal and this form of insurance has become the largest single regular saving medium in the country. Over the last quarter of a century the growth of occupational pension schemes (not all administered by assurance companies) has greatly increased the rate of accumulation of funds for investment. These funds are invested roughly in government and industrial fixed stocks, as to one-half; and in shares and property, as to the other half.

Over the past fifteen years or so many life companies have introduced new forms of policies linked to groups of property and equity investments, in order to meet the demand for equity and property shares as a hedge against inflation. The variety of policies is now quite bewildering, but the basic forms are five in number: term policies, whole life policies, endowment policies, endowment or whole life with profit policies, and annuities.

Term policies insure your life over a certain period. If you wanted to insure yourself against the risk of an aircraft crash when you were flying on holiday you would take out a term policy for a few weeks. Term policies can, however, last for thirty years: it depends on the term.

If you die during the term your heirs get the benefit. If you survive the term there is no benefit. These are purely protective policies, with no investment element.

Whole life policies yield a lump sum on your death, consequently they are strictly for your heirs or dependants. As no one knows when you are going to die, no one can say what the exactly correct premium ought to be. But although the assurance company does not know when you are going to die it does know how many people die at what age all over the country, and from these statistics the actuaries of the company will fix the premium so as to show a profit for the company, while the same time offering a competitive proposition to the proposer.

Endowment policies offer a lump sum at a certain age, often 60 or 65, provided you live that long. Otherwise they will pay the lump sum on your death. These have the attraction that if you live to the age stipulated you will get the money yourself. It will then be up to you to provide for your heirs.

Either whole life or endowment policies may be obtained 'with profits' for an extra premium, and this means that the policies will share in the fortunes of the company by having bonuses declared every so often (usually every three years) added to the eventual sum to be paid. The bonuses are not the amounts you could get now if you drew them out, but the amounts you will get provided you leave the money in. If all bonuses are left in and the policy is allowed to lie undisturbed the with-profits policy will represent a very good investment, partly because the funds of a big assurance company are expertly managed, and partly because the tax relief, given by the authorities to encourage saving, will yield £15 in every £100 of premiums, as long as the insurance policy qualifies for such relief.

Index-linked policies began to appear in 1974. Under such a policy both the periodic premium payments and the benefits from the contract are adjusted in line with the movement of the General Index of Retail Prices. In this way compensation is made for the falling value of money in an inflationary era.

At first these concerned house buildings insurance and house contents insurance. Such policies contained an 'automatic escalation factor', which is a polite way of saying that the premium will go up by 4 or 5 per cent every year – but so does the cover. By the end of 1975 you could also get index-linked policies for family income benefit, flexible endowment assurance, and renewable term assurance. Insurance companies cannot offer inflation-proof savings-type contracts, because they cannot see any way to invest the moneys so as to keep up with inflation. Term assurance, on the other hand, can be index-linked. An example comes from the Legal and General, whose five-year convertible term assurance policy was said to be the first to link premiums and cover to the movement of the retail price index, adjusting both annually. The policy can be extended every five years, or it can be converted to a different type of life assurance – an endowment mortgage, or whole life cover, for example – to cater for changing insurance needs. To ram home the necessity of updating cover, the company made the point that during 1975 a £15,000 policy lost, through inflation, over £3,000 in real value.

With an annuity you pay a lump sum and the assurance company pay you an income for the rest of your life whether it be short or long. The later you leave the payment, the greater the income. If you come from a long-lived family you have the chance of making a good profit, but this will be balanced, as far as the company is concerned, by those who die earlier than the average.

Everyone who can should take out an endowment with profits policy. It represents a genuine saving, it gives cover for dependants against the premature death of the wage earner, it provides a lump sum on retirement, and it is a hedge against inflation. Furthermore, as its value increases over the years it becomes an acceptable security for a lender. A bank in particular will be reassured to find that the prospective borrower has demonstrated a saving disposition earlier in his or her life. This makes it more likely that repayment of any loan they grant will be duly made, and this in turn makes the bank more disposed to grant the loan.

Investment and unit trusts

The function of investment trusts and unit trusts is to raise
collective capital from the public and to direct it to where it
will do most good, that is, into profitable investment channels.
The two different types of organization enable the small
investor with limited capital to spread his risks over a wide
range of securities under full-time specialist management.

Investment trust companies

Founded soon after the introduction of the principle of
limited liability for joint-stock companies, investment trusts
are public corporate bodies registered under the Companies
Acts. Their capital is derived mainly from public issues of
debentures (see p. 322) and preference and ordinary stock
which are quoted and dealt with on the Stock Exchange.
They are companies formed for the purpose of holding
investments. The amount of the company's stock is fixed
until any further issue of capital, and new investors can
obtain holdings only by buying stock from existing holders.

The management of an investment trust is often carried
out by a professional management company, which will
take the policy decisions on what investments should be
held, look after the actual buying and selling of the securities,
and make the interest and dividend payments to the shareholders. Such management companies may come from firms
of solicitors or accountants, or from merchant banks, or
from specialized trust management organizations.

The debenture, preference, and ordinary stock commonly
associated with a corporate body serve to raise the capital
which the company needs in the first place, to buy the
investments which it is going to hold. If it needs any more
capital later on it can float a loan at a fixed rate of interest
or issue a further series of debentures. Investment trust
companies also like to build up a stock of US dollars so that
they can include American investments in their holdings of

securities (portfolios). This has led to the raising of loans in dollars, so that the assets of the company may consist of both sterling and dollar securities.

In the past, English and Scottish investment trusts have played an important part in overseas development by mobilizing private capital for employment in the Commonwealth countries, the British dependencies, and in several foreign countries. In the 1870s Scottish investors were able to invest quite heavily in American shares at a time when the United States dollar was weak following the Civil War. These movements of capital contributed much to the development of the United States in the period before the outbreak of the first world war, and the holdings now show an advantage when sterling is weak as against the dollar.

The Association of Investment Trust Companies was formed in 1932 for the 'protection, promotion and advancement of the common interests of members'.

Unit trusts

A unit trust is a method of investment whereby money subscribed by many people is pooled in a fund, the investment and management of which is subject to the legal provisions of a trust deed. The fund is invested in securities on behalf of the subscribers by a management company. The investments so acquired are held by a trustee, usually a well-known bank or insurance company. The management company and the trustee must be quite independent of each other. They are parties to the trust deed which defines their collective responsibilities towards the subscribers to the trust fund and sets out the rules for the operation of the trust.

The earliest unit trust in this country was formed in 1931, and the idea caught on rapidly, although control over new capital issues restricted the offering of new units for much of the post-war period.

A fixed trust spread the risk over a period of ten to twenty years with severe restrictions on the management's ability to vary the investments. Later it was appreciated that it was bad business to keep securities whose dividends were not maintained, or which had slumped or ceased to be quoted. In later companies the trust deed empowered managers to substitute securities at their discretion, although restricting their choice to a given list. Thus the unit trust idea moved nearer to the investment trust idea, where there is free discretion for the management company to buy and sell securities as it thinks best.

The advantages claimed for the unit trust idea of investment are a good yield, security, regular income distribution, and, above all, spread of risk. The units are not quoted on the Stock Exchange, but are bought and sold by the management company which works out purchase and sale prices ('bid' and 'offer') based on the market value of the underlying securities. The management company undertakes to purchase all sub-units offered to it, thus there is an assured market for those wishing to realise their investment.

The portfolio of securities is the unit. This is divided into some thousands of sub-units, which are sold to the public, the investor being given a sub-unit certificate. The value of this is based on the market price of the unit portfolio.

Before the units are offered for sale to the public a unit trust must be authorized by the Department of Trade. The Department will not issue a certificate of authorization unless it is satisfied that the trust deed is drawn up in a way to satisfy the Department's requirements.

The trust deed must provide for the provision of funds for future management expenses; for the audit and circulation to sub-unit holders of the accounts of the managers in relation to the trust; for the manner in which the sale and repurchase prices of sub-units and the advertised yield is calculated; for the examination by the trustee of all advertisements; and for changes in management if the trustee certifies that this is necessary in the interests of the sub-unit holders.

Through his subscription to the trust fund each subscriber acquires a fraction of interest in the block of securities in which the fund is invested, while the dividends received from the investments form the income of the trust. The net income is paid to all investors in the trust fund in proportion to the size of their holdings.

The primary functions of the trustee are to make sure that the terms of the trust deed are observed, to act as custodian of the capital and income of the trust, to hold in its name the securities in which money subscribed by the public to the trust fund has been invested by the managers, to take responsibility for the register of sub-unit holders and to ensure that advertising details are correct and not misleading.

The trustee company's remuneration comes from an agreed part of the loading charge, shared with the managers, and commission on stock orders. (The loading charge is the charge made for the administration of the trust, spread over the life of the trust.)

The managers are responsible for the administration of the unit trust, for the calculation of the unit offered and its price, for preparing income distributions, for managing the investment portfolio of the trust fund, and for maintaining a market in the units of the trust. The remuneration of the management company comes from a portion of the loading charge and from the 'turn' or difference between transactions at offer and bid prices.

The costs of running the trust are met partly by an initial charge which forms part of the price of the sub-unit and partly by a semi-annual service charge which is taken out of the income of the trust. The level of both charges is controlled by the Department of Trade.

Some unit trusts accept holdings as small as £10. The trusts differ considerably in character; some aim at securing a high income while others aim at capital appreciation. Some invest widely over all classes of ordinary shares, while some specialize in, for example, bank, insurance, or investment trust shares, or put a high proportion of their money in manufacturing or mining.

The Association of Unit Trust Managers was formed in 1959, in which nearly all the major unit trust management companies were represented. Its objects are to act as a consulting body, to standardize unit trust practice, to represent the management companies as a body, and to co-operate with other interested groups with regard to investment protection.

A number of banks and the Trustee Savings Banks Association have set up their own unit trusts. The insurance companies are also issuing policies linked with unit trusts. These represent a very long term investment, and holders can afford to treat the ups and downs of prices with a certain detachment. In fact, a slump in prices may even be to their advantage, because the lower the price of units during the currency of the policy, the more of them will be accumulated. A policy of this nature invests so much in sub-units every month. Over a period of years, monthly premiums will buy sub-units at a variety of different prices, but the lower the average price, the higher the ultimate profit will be when the policy is cashed in (always assuming that this takes place when unit values are high). This is called 'pound cost averaging'.

Some unit trusts are registered abroad in countries which offer tax advantages. They are sometimes called mutual investment funds. These funds can be used by United Kingdom investors, but they are not allowed to advertise in this country because they are not under the control of the Department of Trade. They frequently have much wider powers of investment than United Kingdom trusts, enabling them to invest in types of fixed-interest securities which would be taxed at a very high rate in a home-based fund.

Because they are not subjected to the same scrutiny as the United Kingdom trusts which are authorized by the Department of Trade, there must be an added element of risk, which suggests that intending investors in these 'offshore funds', as they are called, should stick to one run by one of the big unit trust groups.

One reason for the success of the unit trusts has been the

attraction of this type of investment to small savers who have been impressed by the performance of the unit trusts, and the administrative convenience of this form of investment. The larger investor has also found unit trusts a useful form of investment, and as a result a number of trusts have been set up which require relatively large sums of money from the prospective sub-unit holder, ranging from £1,000 upwards. These are called 'high-minimum' trusts.

Local authority loans

Local authorities are usually in need of money, being government on a smaller scale. They need to borrow money in advance of the yearly rates influx. To find large sums quickly they operate on the money markets, where they may obtain quite large amounts for anything from seven days to a year. For more permanent borrowing they may issue loan stock, which is quoted on the Stock Exchange. They also advertise for loans from the general public, the amounts which they are prepared to take being in this case as low as £100. These will be for fixed periods of between one and seven years, with no withdrawal facilities. The rate of interest will be competitive when the loan is made, but it will be fixed, so that the investor will do better if interest rates fall subsequently. Interest is paid with tax deducted, but investors paying a low rate of tax can reclaim the tax involved. Smaller councils may offer a slightly higher rate of interest, though all local authority loans are equally secure. Full details of the various offers available can be obtained from one of the information bureaux run by the Chartered Institute of Public Finance and Accountancy, and it usually pays to shop around a bit.

Local authorities, of course, borrow from a wide range of sources, one of them being the Public Works Loan Board, which is financed by the government. The Board, as well as lending in normal circumstances, will act as a lender of last resort.

Finance company deposits

The highest interest rates of all are offered by commercial companies describing themselves as 'banks', by finance houses, or by hire-purchase companies. Many of these should be treated with caution. The three points where difficulty may be expected are: Are there any facilities for withdrawal? Is the deposit for a long term of years? Is the sum to be invested fixed at a large minimum?

It may be considered as some protection if the finance company concerned is a member of the Finance Houses Association, or the bank concerned is a member of the Accepting Houses Committee or the Issuing House Association.

Revision Test 6

Put ticks in what you think are the right boxes.

(1) The first £40 of interest earned in any one year is free of tax on
    (a) a Trustee Savings Bank Account ☐
    (b) National Savings Certificates ☐
    (c) unit trust dividends ☐

(2) Interest on British Savings Bonds is paid
    (a) by accrual to capital ☐
    (b) twice yearly without tax deduction ☐
    (c) quarterly, tax paid ☐

(3) A person paying £5 a month in SAYE who makes no withdrawals can look forward to
    (a) £330 after five years ☐
    (b) £510 after seven years ☐
    (c) £720 after ten years ☐

(4) A person paying £30 a month under the Nest Egg Plan
    (a) gets life cover of £5,400 ☐

    (b) is entitled to a bonus of £360 after 10 years   ☐

    (c) has a right of conversion into British Savings
       Bonds after the first year   ☐

(5) Which of these can be bought and sold on the Stock
    Exchange?

    (a) investment trust stock   ☐
    (b) trust sub-units   ☐
    (c) building society shares   ☐

(6) Protection against inflation is incorporated in

    (a) National Savings Certificates   ☐
    (b) a with-profits endowment life policy   ☐
    (c) building society subscription shares   ☐

(7) A collecting society is

    (a) an industrial assurance company   ☐
    (b) a trade union   ☐
    (c) a registered friendly society   ☐

(8) An endowment assurance policy is a better proposi-
    tion from the tax allowance point of view for a self-
    employed man saving for retirement than an Individual
    Retirement Annuity

    (a) True   ☐
    (b) False   ☐

(9) Survival to a stated age will give a lump sum under a

    (a) whole life policy   ☐
    (b) term policy   ☐
    (c) endowment policy   ☐

(10) Purchases of Trustee Savings Bank trust sub-units may
    be made by means of

    (a) the Link-a-Loan scheme   ☐
    (b) National Savings Certificates gift tokens   ☐
    (c) investment in Harvest Bonds   ☐

Check your solutions with the answers on p. 395.
Take one mark for each correct answer.
Each Revision Test totals 10 marks.

Questions for discussion

1. Define (a) savings and (b) capital goods. What are the principal ways in which savings are channelled into capital goods?

2. In what broad respects does the role of a clearing bank in the economy differ from that of (a) a building society (b) a Trustee Savings Bank (c) the National Giro?

3. How does a unit trust work?

Part Two

The business of banking

7

Structure of a bank balance sheet

It is time now to look at the activities of a bank, and a good place to start will be with its balance sheet. The figures given here are of one of the large clearing banks and if we are able to read the figures, that is, know what they mean, we should be able to come to some conclusions as to how the bank is doing, how strong it is financially, how it is affected by any monetary restrictions in force at the time of the balance sheet, and what use it is making of the money it has.

Some people have a gift for figures and take naturally to the understanding of balance sheets. Others feel at a disadvantage when looking at an indigestible array of information which means nothing to them. In fact, of course, like everything else, it is quite easy when you know something about it. Let us start by answering the questions, what is a balance sheet, why is it produced, and by whom?

A balance sheet has been described as a photograph of a company's business at a moment in time. Every business needs money for something which it does and this at once raises two points, where is it going to get the money from, and what is it going to do with it when it has got it? Here is the introduction to the balance sheet. A public limited company gets its money by advertising itself to the public (by a prospectus, when it is just beginning) and selling shares in

National Westminster Bank Limited

Balance Sheet

at 31 December 1975

	1975 £000	1975 £000	1974 £000	1974 £000
ORDINARY SHAREHOLDERS' FUNDS				
Ordinary share capital	183,522		183,492	
Reserves	552,199		530,703	
		735,721		714,195
PREFERENCE SHARE CAPITAL		13,872		13,872
		749,593		728,067
LOAN CAPITAL		65,082		63,984
PROVISION FOR PENSIONS		—		9,090
DEFERRED TAXATION		58,739		65,826
AMOUNTS DUE TO SUBSIDIARY COMPANIES		55,675		56,604
CURRENT, DEPOSIT, AND OTHER ACCOUNTS		8,014,091		8,078,269
OTHER LIABILITIES				
Creditors and accrued expenses	10,334		11,747	
Taxation	3,130		5,564	
Dividends	8,200		7,704	
		21,664		25,015
		8,964,844		9,026,855

	1975 £000	1975 £000	1974 £000	1974 £000
LIQUID ASSETS				
Coin, banknotes, and balances with the Bank of England	336,650		308,987	
Cheques in course of collection on other banks*	324,225		332,753	
Money at call and short notice	1,045,160		1,208,444	
Bills discounted	246,540		307,574	
		1,952,575		2,157,758
SPECIAL DEPOSITS WITH THE BANK OF ENGLAND		160,695		169,915
CERTIFICATES OF DEPOSIT		134,620		37,450
INVESTMENTS – OTHER THAN TRADE INVESTMENTS		536,659		421,106
CUSTOMERS' AND OTHER ACCOUNTS				
Advances, less provision	5,189,411		5,429,568	
Other debtors and prepaid expenses	19,882		11,860	
		5,209,293		5,441,428
TRADE INVESTMENTS		97,969		95,394
SUBSIDIARY COMPANIES				
Investments – at cost less amounts written off	130,620		111,221	
Amounts owing	233,081		118,391	
		363,701		229,612
PREMISES AND EQUIPMENT		509,332		474,192
		8,964,844		9,026,855

*Although it is the practice in the National Westminster Bank to include this item under Liquid Assets, many other banks do not do so.

return for money subscribed. This money is a liability from the company to its shareholders, and by tradition appears on the left-hand side of the balance sheet.

It will spend the money on things it needs to do and have and so will acquire assets. These appear on the right-hand side of the balance sheet. (Some people remember which is right and left by thinking that liabilities begins with an L and goes on the Left.)

The bank balance sheet will show how much it has obtained from the public in this way and also what money it has obtained from other sources, such as customers opening accounts with it and depositing money in them. From the bank's point of view these are all debts, or liabilities, to go on the left-hand side of the balance sheet.

On the right-hand side we shall see what has been done with all this money. Some has been lent out, some may have been invested in subsidiary companies, some is with the Bank of England. Because we are dealing with one total sum of money, but looking at it from two points of view, we expect to find that the figures on each side of the balance sheet add up to the same total.

The figures present only a momentary glimpse of the business, for naturally most of the details specified in the balance sheet are continuously changing. Nor does it matter what point in time is chosen, as long as once fixed, the same date is kept year after year, so that when we compare this year's figures with last year's figures, we are comparing like with like, and can draw valid conclusions.

For many companies 31st December seems a logical time to present a balance sheet, others have theirs at the end of their financial year, whenever that may be.

It is stipulated by the Companies Act that alongside each year's figure must be stated the corresponding figure for the year before. In the example given these are shown in italics. Certain notes attached to the original have been omitted for the sake of simplicity.

We shall start with the Liabilities.

Shareholders funds

The first group of figures is sub-totalled. This is to give the exact amount of how much of this money belongs to the shareholders.

Preference share capital refers to those shares which carry a fixed rate of interest and which are entitled to receive this interest before any other payments out of profits to ordinary shareholders are made. If in any year the profits made by the company are only just sufficient to pay the preference shareholders, no other class of shareholders will get anything.

The ordinary share capital refers to the money put in by the ordinary shareholders, who have no preference at all. They are paid a dividend after the preferential shareholders have been looked after, and only if profits permit. In a bad year the ordinary shareholders may get nothing by way of dividend, whereas in a good year they will probably do very well. There is no fixed rate at which their dividend will be calculated, as there is with preference shares. The ordinary shares are sometimes called the 'equity' of the company. Their holders take the main risk (in banks of this standing this risk is so small one couldn't even guess what it might be).

The reserves are the total of those amounts which have over the years been prudently set aside for a rainy day, before the dividends were paid. They come, as do the dividends, out of past profits, which is why we say they belong to the shareholders, the risk takers who are entitled to any profit there may be. We can see these reserves have reached a pretty hefty total, more, in fact, than the ordinary share capital. This is an indication of the massive financial strength of this bank. This is reflected in the Stock Exchange quotations for the shares. Both preference and ordinary shares are of £1 each and the value of the ordinary shares can be seen any day from the financial page of any daily newspaper. Today they look like this:

				+	—
272	201	Nat. Westmstr.	210	8	

On this example we see that the highest these shares have been this year is 272p each, the lowest, 201p. Today's valuation is 210p and this is a fall of 8p on yesterday.

On the day you read this, look them up again and see how they compare. You will find them under the heading 'Banks, Discount, HP'. The example given above was at a time of depression on the Stock Exchange as a result of grave economic conditions coupled with internal industrial disputes. All shares of all classes had become very depressed compared with their standing earlier in the year.

Coming back to the Balance Sheet, we see that the shareholders own the enormous sum of £749,593,000. Last year it was £728,067,000. So this figure remains more or less steady, the rise we notice being due to inflation.

Loan capital

This item refers to the acquisition by the bank some years ago of a subsidiary company, engaged in hire purchase. The bank issued its loan stock in exchange for the ordinary share capital of the finance company. The shareholders who used to own ordinary shares in the finance company now own loan stock in the bank. They are not in the same position as the ordinary shareholders of the bank, but are treated as though they were people who had made a loan to the bank at a stated fixed rate of interest.

Provisions

Provisions are sums of money put on one side to meet known payments which have to be made. This sum was mostly for the payment of pensions to former staff of the bank who are now retired. The remainder was to meet certain exceptional expenses of reorganization which was taking place in the bank at this time.

Deferred taxation

The deferred taxation account is to cover corporation tax at the current rate on the difference between book and tax values of certain assets.

Amounts due to subsidiary companies

This item speaks for itself representing sums borrowed from other companies in the 'group' of companies.

Current, deposit, and other accounts

This is the total of the depositors' money. The different accounts on which customers can keep money are not specified here, but are all totalled together for the purposes of the balance sheet. Certificates of deposit issued by this bank come under this heading as deposits, although they are not separately specified (see also p. 190). By comparing this figure with that for last year we can get a good idea as to whether the bank is expanding its business. Even allowing for inflation, we see that this bank is expanding rapidly. Fresh customers are coming in, many more than old ones closing their accounts. This must mean that the banking habit is spreading, and also that the existing customers are either satisfied with the service they are getting from the bank or, at least, do not anticipate better service elsewhere.

The last heading is self-explanatory. Now let us turn to the assets.

Coin, banknotes, and balances with the Bank of England

We know that the banks have to keep a certain amount of banknotes and coin in their tills to meet the demand of their customers for repayment, and that they keep balances with the Bank of England so that the daily adjustments with other banks on the debit and credit clearings can be settled by a book transfer. We know that before Competition and Credit Control all the big banks by convention kept a cash ratio of 8 per cent. The cash ratio is the percentage which this item is of Current, Deposit, and other accounts.

As none of this money earns any interest, banks are naturally keen to keep the cash ratio as low as possible, consistent with prudence. When the inter-bank agreement came to an end, therefore, all the cash ratios fell. (Of course, this was partly due to the fact that the cash in their tills no longer counted as an eligible reserve asset.) If we compare the two figures:

Current, deposit, and other accounts	*Coin, banknotes, and balances with the Bank of England*
£8,014,091,000	£336,650,000

– we shall find that the cash ratio of the bank on the date of the balance sheet was 4·2 per cent.

Cheques in course of collection on other banks

We have seen how customers paying in cheques for the credit of their accounts get their accounts credited the same day, but that the clearing of those cheques takes three (or five) days to effect. During this time the total of money represented by all these cheques is said to be in the clearing pipeline. While it is in this pipeline it earns no money, so if it were possible to cut this time down the banks would be very pleased, even though some of it would reduce credit balances.

The Giro at Liverpool does not have this problem, because everything there is centralized at one place and their computer can make all the transfers between accounts on one day. But the banks are numerous and have the problems of sorting the millions of cheques before they can be presented. One day perhaps the banking computers will get to the point where one enormous computer with connections to all the banks in the country will be able to make transfers very much as Giro now does on a much smaller scale. The installation of the Bankers Automated Clearing Services Bureau in the Credit Clearing can be seen as a step towards this ideal.

So on any day a proportion of current, deposit, and other accounts is somewhere in the clearing pipeline. The figure varies with seasonal and other factors, but is normally about 4–7 per cent. If we compare the two figures in this balance sheet we shall see that on this date the proportion was 4·0 per cent.

If we add together these two items, Coin, banknotes, and balances with the Bank of England, and Cheques in course of collection on other banks, we can see that about one twelfth of the customers' money earns no interest.

The remainder is carefully invested in many ways. The balance sheet will tell us how this has been done. The general principles which the bank will keep in mind here are that investments must be spread so that not too much is lent in any one direction. Also, the bank must be able to get at the money, or some of it, quickly and without losses on realization, should the need arise. There must be liquidity. Some of the investments, therefore, will be in government stock (which can be quickly sold – but at market price) and in the money market (who will repay on demand or at a few days' notice). Other investments will be less liquid, such as money lent to other customers of the bank. Such loans will be technically repayable on demand, but will usually prove more difficult to recover than those already mentioned.

Liquidity usually goes along with risk. There must be some element of risk in every borrowing, but in some – say, loans to the government – there is virtually none.

The greater the element of risk, the higher is the interest rate which can be obtained. The bank has to remember not to lend too much at the higher rates of interest because if it did it would be taking unacceptable risks in the hope of greater profits.

Money at call and short notice

The bulk of these loans are to the discount houses and are mostly on a day-to-day basis, or at most seven days. This item represents the bank's most liquid item, after cash, and if the bank itself were short of cash this is where it would turn first to get some, by recalling its money at call.

Since Competition and Credit Control, overseas, merchant, and foreign banks had to start maintaining reserve assets as soon as they were brought into the system. A result of this was to give the discount houses more of a choice in where to go for their daily loans. The overseas, merchant, and foreign banks were quite willing to lend to them because money at call with the market qualified as reserve assets.

For a time less business came to the big clearing banks and the money at call and short notice for 1971 – £375,909,000 – showed a drop on the corresponding figure for 1970 – £529,562,000. It can be seen now that the figure for these loans had practically doubled in 1975, even though a sizeable part of it represents advances to institutions outside the money market.

The discount houses can as a last resort borrow from the Bank of England, but this must mean that none of the banks has any money to lend. There is a shortage of cash in the system as a whole. If this persists interest rates will rise. The Bank of England can engineer such a shortage (by open market operations) if it thinks short-term interest rates should go up, and can relieve it by feeding a fresh supply of money into the system by lending to the discount houses.

We have therefore a system through which the ebb and flow of cash in the banking system can be evened out. This entry is the evidence of this bank's participation in this system.

Bills discounted

The figure for bills discounted by the bank is shown in the notes to be made up of British government treasury bills

£107,625,000, and other bills £138,915,000. Banks keep a supply of treasury bills for their own account, as a safe way of investing money, which they increase or reduce quickly as their liquidity requirements vary. Other bills discounted reflect the bills which the bank has discounted for its own customers, and those which it has purchased from bill brokers. When anticipating requiring a certain sum at a certain date, the bank may buy first-class bills from brokers which will mature at the time it wants the funds. The bank obtains the endorsement of the brokers on the bills as an additional guarantee that the bills will be honoured when they fall due.

After this item the balance sheet is sub-totalled to show the sum of the bank's liquid assets.

Before Competition and Credit Control banks were required to keep a minimum ratio of all liquid assets to deposits of 28 per cent, and this figure could be checked from the balance sheet. Now the place of this liquidity ratio has been taken by a reserve asset ratio as a means of control. That ratio cannot be checked by reference to the balance sheet information, which does not tell us how to total up either the eligible reserve assets or the eligible liabilities.

The concept of liquidity, however, is still important. If the bank locks up in medium- or long-term loans which it has made more than is prudent it may find that it does not have enough ready cash to meet all its obligations. Although the bank can now borrow funds on the inter-bank market, and consequently the maxim that those who borrow short must never lend long has lost some of its force, it is still necessary to keep a reasonably liquid position.

If we compare the sub-total of liquid assets with the figure for current, deposit, and other accounts – i.e. £1,952,575,000 with £8,014,091,000 – we can work out that in this bank the liquidity ratio is 24·36 per cent.

So the bank's liquidity ratio is not very much lower than it used to be before Competition and Credit Control.

The liquidity ratio varies during the year. It is lowest in the spring when customers are borrowing heavily to pay their tax, and builds up for the Christmas demand for money at the end of the year.

Special deposits with the Bank of England

A special deposit is an instrument of monetary policy by which the Bank of England may restrict credit. It may call at any time for special deposits to be made with it by all the banks, and these deposits have to be taken from the liquid resources of the banks, thus cutting down their ability to lend.

Since they were introduced there have been various calls made by the Bank of England and later released, only to be imposed again in more difficult times. A call is for a certain percentage, usually 1 per cent, of eligible liabilities. If this does not have the required result another call may be made.

Certificates of deposit

Negotiable certificates of deposit describes a way in which banks take deposits for large sums. Unlike other forms of deposit, the depositor receives a certificate, which is a negotiable instrument, transferable by delivery. Certificates are issued for a minimum period of three months, up to a maximum of five years. The minimum denomination of a certificate is £50,000 and the maximum is £500,000. They are readily realizable at current market rates in London, where the discount houses provide a secondary market in them. This figure represents the total of the certificates of deposit, issued by other banks, which this bank is holding.

Investments – other than trade investments

The notes to the balance sheet show that practically the whole amount under this heading is invested in securities of, or guaranteed by, the government. These securities can be sold when the bank needs money, but the intention when the investment is made is that they shall be held until maturity, that is, until the government repays them. For this reason only dated stocks are taken, that is, stocks which quote the year in which they will be repaid. The value of these stocks may vary during their lifetime, but the value must come up in the final stages to what they are going to be worth when repayment is made. So as long as they can be held until maturity there must be a profit on them, but if they have to be sold before, there may be a loss.

Holdings are planned so that a proportion of them mature each year, thus lessening the risk of loss if the bank has to realize any of these investments. Most banks organize these investments into two groups, those maturing in five years' time and those maturing in five to ten years' time.

Customers' and other accounts

Now we come to the biggest item on the Assets side – the loans and overdrafts made by the bank to its customers. Here the risk is much higher than on money lent to the money market or to the government, and therefore the interest rate obtained will be much higher. In normal times this money will be lent to anyone who, being a customer, can satisfy the bank that the sum borrowed is within the borrower's capacity to repay, but in times of restriction the Bank of England directs the banks as to the classes of borrowers who may receive favourable consideration. This is usually for exporters (whose efforts tend to reduce the unfavourable trade balance with other countries), those producing equipment for National Defence (who add to the safety of the country), farmers (who produce some of the country's food), and those engaged in the building of factories and houses.

These are called qualitative restrictions. The Bank of England expressly reserved the right to make them when the conditions of Competition and Credit Control were published.

The bank traditionally lends for short periods and prefers normally to lend working capital for business and to provide bridging finance, that is, short-term loans pending the provision of longer-term finance from some other source. Of recent years, however, a willingness to lend for longer terms has been noticeable. Banks have become increasingly involved in house purchase and property improvement schemes, and some longer-period loans have been made to industry. For years the big banks have made quite long-term loans to encourage exports and home-based shipbuilding under government schemes.*

In this section of the balance sheet we find the source of the banks' greatest profit. At times when interest rates are raised to high levels the banks' profits go up automatically. In 1972 and 1973 the annual figures were larger than ever before. These record profits came at a time when prices and incomes were restricted, and other people were being stopped from charging too much. The banks would perhaps have liked to increase dividends, but they were pegged, or make better payments to their staffs, but here again they were forced to comply with the pay code then imposed by the government. The only thing left was to give way on the commission charged to customers – always a source of criticism – and late in 1973 all big banks announced new charging schemes (see p. 293).

In an attempt to maintain a fiction of liquidity all advances under this head are legally repayable on demand, but the ordinary borrower is not able to repay on demand. The farmer certainly is not. The best he can do is to take reducing amounts of accommodation so that the advance would – theoretically – eventually cease to exist.

It used to be accepted that as these loans were the riskiest form of lending the total of them should be limited to half of the deposits. This lending ratio was well observed even if it did occasionally creep up to 52 per cent or 53 per cent.

* See p. 399.

However, a fresh view of this has been taken since Competition and Credit Control and lending ratios have gone into the 70s. If we look at this one:

Current, deposit, and other accounts	*Advances to customers*
£3,239,542,000	£5,189,411,000

– we shall find that the lending ratio of this bank on the balance sheet date was 65 per cent.

When the bank suspects that a loan or overdraft is becoming bad it makes provision for writing it off. Thus advances are shown in the balance sheet, 'less provision', to indicate that the bad ones have been sorted out and already provided for; by implication what is left should all be good.

'Other debtors' needs no explanation. 'Prepaid expenses' are expenses paid earlier than they need have been. Anything paid in advance entitles the bank to show it as an asset until such time as the goods or services for which payment has been made are duly delivered or performed.

Trade investments

These include the bank's investments in affiliated banks and associated companies, for example the Agricultural Mortgage Corporation, in which the bank has a stake. For quoted investments a middle-market valuation is taken, half-way between the buying and selling price. Where the investment has no quotation the directors of the bank place a valuation on it according to what they think it is worth.

Subsidiary companies

Under this heading is shown the value of the bank's share holdings in its wholly-owned subsidiary banks and finance companies in this country and abroad. These include executor and trustee companies, a hire-purchase company, a merchant bank, a factoring company, and a company selling computer services.

Premises and equipment

Bank premises are traditionally shown at a very conservative valuation, thus building a hidden reserve into the assets. The National Westminster, whose figures we are looking at here, was formed by merger of Westminster, National Provincial, and District Banks in 1969. Of course it was found that in some places the new bank had too many branches and some must be closed down and sold. This process has been going steadily on, and indeed this rationalization is part of merger benefits, which ought to include a greater economy. Nevertheless, the total value of premises continues to rise steadily by about £30 million a year, a sign of the equally steady fall in the value of money. The bank is not buying more premises to account for this increase (although it is rebuilding its head office): on the contrary, it is reducing the number of its branches.

This heading also includes the value of the bank's computers.

So much for the balance sheet. Note the importance of the current, deposit, and other accounts figure. Everything flows from that. The percentage in the clearing pipeline, the proportion of funds re-invested at interest, the liquidity ratio, the cash ratio, the lending ratio; to work out any of them we have to go to the total of deposits. This total is the mainspring of any bank. The bank must advertise for these funds some of which it gets quite cheaply (in the case of a current account, for nothing) and must face fierce competition from other banks, finance houses, instalment trading companies; everybody wants money.

As well as getting new deposits, however, the bank must do its best to keep the deposits it already has. This is equally important. To do this it must see that its staff understands what good service is and then gives it to customers. It is ultimately in the opinion of its customers that a bank will succeed or fail.

A balance sheet is to give information. We have seen how much information we have got out of this one, and we have been dealing with it only on a very simple basis. It is the public who need the information, those who might be thinking of buying shares in the bank, and those who are already shareholders. They are entitled to know how the bank is doing.

Other critical eyes will be analysing the figures also. We can be sure that all banks watch each others' annual figures, and that the union representatives and bank staff associations are also keenly interested. The Companies Act says a balance sheet and other accounts must be presented to the shareholders within eighteen months of the company's incorporation and yearly thereafter. Copies must be registered at Companies House, where anyone may ask to see them on payment of a small fee. Various matters are required to be shown separately in the balance sheet, which must summarize the capital, liabilities, and assets of the company. The balance sheet is required to give a true and fair view of the company's affairs. A statement of the share capital, assets, and liabilities of the company must be exhibited twice yearly in each branch bank.

The bank's balance sheet is drawn up by the bank's chief accountant and his staff. When the figures are ready they are checked by an independent firm of chartered accountants who can ask any questions and make any investigations into the bank's affairs, as they wish. Big companies, like this bank, often put their annual accounts out to two such independent firms or companies.

When the accountants are satisfied that all is in order they add their Report. This will state that they have examined the balance sheet, together with the notes associated with it. They go on to certify that in their opinion, the balance sheet and associated accounts comply with the requirements of the Companies Acts and give a true and fair view of the state of the bank's affairs at the balance sheet date. (In this case, 31 December 1975.)

This report by qualified auditors is a guarantee to all reading the balance sheet that the figures are fair ones. If the auditors cannot get all the information which they want, or if they don't agree with the company's treatment of some of the figures, they must say so in their Report. No company would willingly see such a reservation attached to their balance sheet, so companies are likely to meet their auditors' requirements if they possibly can.

The Auditors' Report is a real protection for the shareholders. In the example given it was omitted, along with other accounts, for the sake of simplicity. It was there all right, though.

Revision Test 7

Put ticks in what you think are the right boxes.

(1) The item 'reserves' refers to
    (a) money kept at the Bank of England ☐
    (b) money belonging to the shareholders ☐
    (c) money put aside to meet bad debts ☐

(2) The cash ratio is found by comparing deposits with
    (a) liquid assets ☐
    (b) money in tills and at the Bank of England ☐
    (c) advances to customers ☐

(3) The equity of a company is
    (a) the sum set aside to pay pensions ☐
    (b) the preference share capital ☐
    (c) the ordinary share capital ☐

(4) Special deposits are
    (a) deposit accounts opened by customers at special rates ☐
    (b) moneys deposited at the Bank of England to restrict credit ☐
    (c) calculated by reference to eligible assets ☐

(5) Much the largest figure on the Assets side is
   (a) advances to customers ☐
   (b) money at call and short notice ☐
   (c) balances with the Bank of England ☐

(6) After Competition and Credit Control the lending ratio
   (a) went down ☐
   (b) stayed much the same ☐
   (c) went up ☐

(7) Certificates of deposit are
   (a) given by the bank to deposit account holders ☐
   (b) negotiable securities issued by banks ☐
   (c) issued for a minimum period of one month ☐

(8) Trade investments are
   (a) investments in associated companies ☐
   (b) investments in shipbuilding ☐
   (c) investments in government securities ☐

(9) A balance sheet may be produced
   (a) once in twelve months ☐
   (b) once in eighteen months ☐
   (c) once in twenty-four months ☐

Check your solutions with the answers on p. 395.
Take one mark for each correct answer.
Each Revision Test totals 10 marks.

Questions for discussion

1. Describe the main liabilities and assets of a commercial bank. To what extent do these reflect the banking services provided by a commercial bank?

2. What criteria govern the use that a bank makes of the deposits entrusted to it?

3. What are the ratios usually connected with the current, deposit, and other accounts figure and what is their purpose?

8

Business organizations

The business of banking has become so varied that it has become necessary to separate it into divisions, such as Personnel Division, Domestic Banking Division, International Banking Division, and so on. (A schematic representation of the organization of the United Kingdom Management Company of Barclays Bank Ltd. is shown overleaf. This comprises the domestic branches and the head office departments. The Financial Services Division has a separate structure of its own, although the various heads of sections report to the same General Managers.) The aim has been expressed as being able to meet all the varied financial requirements of large international companies, particularly those operating in Europe. Because of this country's entry into the European Economic Community our big customers have extended their business from these islands into the continent, established branches in foreign towns, learned to speak French and German, and are now trading on an international scale. The banks are in the process of doing everything that is necessary to continue to offer a competitive service to such customers.

However varied the banking business may be, it is carried on within the framework of the law of contract. When a banking account is opened there is an agreement between two parties – the banker, and the customer – which is intended to have legal consequences. This means that both parties have agreed to do certain things in the course of the relationship between them, and if one fails to do them, he may be sued for compensation by the other.

Of the two the banker is the more likely to know the ins and outs of the legal side. Many of his customers are private individuals not in trade. His customers who are limited companies will know the law which they need to know for carrying on their business, but perhaps little more. Only the banker has got to have a good working knowledge of the law as it affects all his customers, whoever they may be. He has to know this because he is in a contractual relationship with them. He has to know what they may legally do, and what they may not. When he is asked to lend money he has to know whether the customer has legal power to borrow money. Another way of putting this is, if the borrower does not repay, can he be made to do so by process of law? Can one person by his signature commit another to do some act, or undertake some liability? Can one person stop a cheque drawn by another? There is no end to the questions.

So although we may have big international companies demanding modern services we still have to be able to deal with smaller companies and with private individuals, all of whom are customers. Every banker starting out on his career, therefore, has to learn the basic elements of the business. Trading organizations range from the sole trader, through partnerships, to a variety of companies. The capacities in which one person may act are equally numerous – agent, trustee, liquidator, executor and many others.

When thinking about these customers we must always remember one thing, the bank is in business to make a profit. It needn't act like Scrooge, but it isn't a charitable organization either. The most profitable side of its many activities is the lending of money, which it eventually wants to get back again. Therefore the one question of particular importance to the bank manager in each and every case is, if he lends

BARCLAYS BANK U.K. MANAGEMENT LIMITED

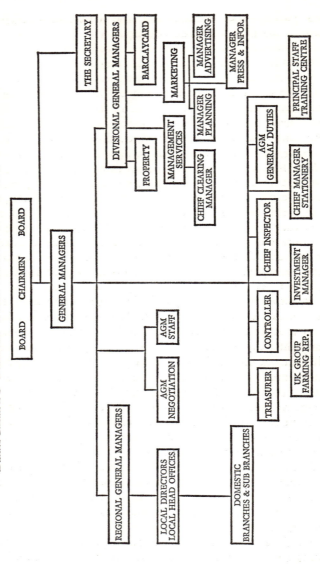

the bank's money, is there any reason why he shouldn't be able to get it back in due course?

Sole trader

A sole trader is in business by himself, for himself. He may be a shopkeeper, or he may be engaged in manufacture on a small scale, or he may be selling a service, such as repairing electrical equipment or building garages.

As long as he is of full age, he is responsible for his debts. If he cannot pay them out of his liquid assets then he may be made bankrupt by his creditors. His house and his car, and nearly everything that he has, can be taken and sold, all by due process of law. If he signs any document he is in general presumed to have read it and understood it, and to be bound by its terms. If he reads it and doesn't understand it he can go to a solicitor and have it explained to him. If it is a bank form then he can ask the bank officer dealing with the matter to explain it to him.

A bank officer of some seniority must therefore be able to understand and explain any of the bank forms in general use.

The account of a sole trader will not be very different in any way from an ordinary personal banking account, except that the rhythm of the account will be different. An ordinary individual getting his salary once a month, for example, will spend a lot of it as soon as he gets it, and then try to make the remainder last out the month. His banking account will reflect this procedure, and it will be more or less the same every month. A trader, however, is not paid monthly. He may send out his bills monthly, but they will be paid at any odd times. His account will not present such a regular appearance. Moreover, it will be affected by seasonal factors. To take an extreme case, a man producing Christmas cards will start in February, get orders in May, deliver to the shops in September, and get paid in January. A farmer has a similar annual cycle. On the other hand, hairdressers and undertakers have a steady demand all the year round.

The sole trader must keep accounts of his business – purchases of raw materials, sales of finished product, cost of transport, and so on. He may have a staff – wages and salaries. He must have an office – heating, stationery, telephone. At the end of the year he will have to pay tax on his profits and the tax authorities have to be satisfied that his return is made on correct figures.

So he needs an accountant, who will produce a balance sheet every year. If the sole trader is borrowing from the bank the manager will want to see this balance sheet. We shall see in a later chapter what lessons can be learned from this kind of balance sheet.

Partnership

When a sole trader gets tired of doing all the work himself he may take a partner. Or two or more individuals may start a firm. With a sole trader, the position is governed by common law. There is no Act of Parliament labelled 'Rules for sole traders'. But there is one labelled 'Rules for partners'. It is actually called the Partnership Act, and it was passed in 1890. Before we go on to say anything about that let us see what was meant by the phrase 'common law', for it can mean different things.

Before the reign of Henry II there was a variety of legal customs in different parts of the country, partly the residue of various tribal laws and partly the edicts of various lords of the manor. The country was unified in the sense that it had got past the stage of Mercia fighting Wessex, and now had one king over the whole country, but it did not have a single, common system of law.

Henry II, a great lawyer, sent his judges travelling all over the country, taking the law with them. In time they wove all the conflicting systems into one common system, which became known as 'common law'. (That part of the common law which deals with the customs and practices of business and commerce is called the law merchant.) The meaning of 'common law' can alter when it is compared with different things. Canon law is the law of the church. In this context, common law is all the law that is not canon law.

Statute law is law passed by parliament. Here common law is all the law that did not originate in an Act of Parliament.

Common law is compared with Equity. Equity was a second set of legal rules that grew up in protest at the way common law worked. Common law was rigid – you went strictly by the rules in the book. Equity tried to do what was fair.

Now back to partners. We have a legal definition of partnership: 'the relation which subsists between persons carrying on a business in common with a view of profit'. No written agreement or deed between the partners is legally necessary, though it often exists. All that is necessary is a written, verbal, or implied agreement between the partners.

Notice that the definition firmly points to a commercial relationship. Husband and wife are often described as partners, but they don't normally carry on a business in common with a view of profit. (Of course if they ran a hairdressing business together they would be partners in the legal sense.)

There can be anything from two to twenty people in a partnership. In a few cases, such as persons carrying on business as members of a recognized stock exchange, these may be more than twenty, but otherwise any group of people in excess of that number wishing to form a business to be carried on for gain must form themselves into a company. A partnership is a firm. A firm is the traditional form of business organization for professional men – doctors, dentists, solicitors, accountants, etc.

The firm has no separate existence. When people talk about the firm they mean all the partners who compose the firm. Anyone suing the firm is suing all the partners. Anyone making the firm bankrupt is making all the partners bankrupt.

A firm may borrow money. Does this mean that where a firm has eight partners, they all come in to see the bank manager about a loan? In other words, can one, or two, or less than all the partners make an arrangement which will bind the firm (all the partners)?

This is the first really important rule about firms: one partner may bind the firm by any act done in the ordinary course of the firm's business.

So if the firm is engaged in a financial business where it is borrowing and lending all the time, then yes, just one partner can come in to see the manager, arrange for an overdraft, deposit security in support, sign any papers the bank wants signed and the firm, not just that partner, will be legally liable to repay and can be sued if it doesn't.

But most firms are engaged in other types of business and they don't borrow money every day. In fact it is an event which happens occasionally for them. So all the partners will have to come in and sign the bank's forms. This is very inconvenient. Is there any way in which the bank can get round this?

Yes, there is. When the account is first opened the partners must all give the bank a specimen of their signature for the bank wants to know how cheques are going to be signed. For this purpose the bank has a form, called 'Application for a Partnership Account' which gives these details, and specimen signatures. What more simple then, than to slip into this form a clause like this:

'We agree that any act done by any partner in relation to the account shall be deemed to be done for carrying out the business of the firm in its ordinary course.'

Then any partner can arrange an overdraft and the firm will be liable to repay it. It is perhaps obvious to say that the bank is keen to have all the partners made liable for repayment, instead of just the one, because in that way the bank has a much better chance of recovering the money.

The second important rule concerning firms is, from the bank's point of view, that of the partners' liability for the firm's debts. The law says that all partners are fully liable (there is no principle of limited liability, as there is with companies), but that this liability is joint. If a firm owes a creditor £100, and there are four partners, all the partners together are responsible to pay £100. If they don't pay, and the creditor sues them, he only has one right of action. To have the best chance of recovering he ought to sue all the partners together. He ought to bring his action against the firm. If he sues only one partner, that partner is still liable to pay the £100 (there is no question of each partner being liable only for £25 – the liability is a joint one), but should he be unsuccessful he cannot after that sue the other partners. He has only one right of action, and he has used that up. (If he had been successful, and the partner had to pay up, that partner would have had the right to recover £25 from each of the others.)

If this were all it might not be too important. The bank wishing to sue would always be careful to bring its action against the firm. But there are important advantages, if the firm goes bankrupt, in making the partners individually as well as jointly liable for the money which the firm owes the bank. To be technical, the bank needs to establish joint and several liability. Then there would be as many rights of action as there were partners.

This is done by including another useful clause in the form of application for a partnership account (which has to be signed by all the partners):

'We agree that any liability incurred by us in connection with the account or in any other way shall be joint and several.'

This useful form will also say whether the partners are going to sign in the name of the firm, or on behalf of it. In the first case suppose the name of the firm is Brown, Robertson, Jenkins & Co. Suppose there are four partners. Then the form will show in the space for specimen signatures the name of the firm written four times, each time in a different handwriting.

In the second case each partner will sign his own name under the words 'on behalf of (or per pro.) Brown, Robertson, Jenkins & Co.'

The form will also say how many partners are to sign on these occasions. Partners are supposed to trust each other, so there may be only one partner signing on behalf of the firm. On the other hand, it is a useful check if two partners sign. Whatever the firm says, the bank will expect to see, not only on cheques which come in for payment, but also on any letters sent by the firm to the bank.

That example raises another point. The name of the firm mentioned three partners, but in fact there were four. How can this happen? Well, partners die or retire, and new ones join the firm. This firm did originally consist of the three men whose names still describe the firm, but Brown died, and Benson took his place. Later on the firm got a bit short of money and Hemmings invested a sum of money in it in return for a partnership. On both these occasions the name of the firm could have been changed to describe accurately the names of the partners after the change, but by then the name of the firm had begun to get known in the district as people who could be relied upon to do a good job, and it would have been a pity, by changing it, to lose the goodwill attached to the old name.

How then does the bank, or indeed anyone else having business relations with the firm, know who they are dealing with? One could not lend money to a firm, money for which the partners are jointly and severally liable, without even knowing who the partners are.

Provision has been made for this by parliament. Any firm where the firm name does not accurately describe the names of all the partners must register these details on the Business Names Register at Companies House, and anyone interested can look these up on payment of a small fee.

Partners can be general, dormant, quasi or limited. A general partner is one who takes an active part in the management of the firm's business.

A dormant or sleeping partner is one who has money invested in the firm, but takes no active part in it.

A quasi-partner is one who is not a partner, but has acted in such a way as to make other people think he is. Because of his misleading conduct the law may hold him to be liable for the firm's debts as if he really were a partner.

A limited partner is one whose liability for the firm's debts is limited to the capital he has invested in it. He has no power to take any active part in the firm's business. (A limited partnership must have at least one general partner who will be fully responsible for the firm's debts. It must be registered as a limited partnership, again at Companies House. Such partnerships are very rare).

Limited companies

By far the bulk of business is done by limited companies. Since the first Companies Act in 1862 there have been other Acts, the Companies Act of 1948 being a comprehensive summary of the law at that time.

Limited companies are built around the principle of limited liability. So far, with sole traders and partnerships we have been dealing with people who can lose everything if debts are not paid. Limited liability introduced a new system. The shareholder in a limited company can lose the value of his shares, but beyond that he has no responsibility for the debts of the company. In a partnership, the partners are 'the firm'. In a limited company, the shareholders are not 'the company'. There is one difference of great importance – 'the company' exists in law as a being in its own right. 'The company' cannot do anything for itself, so it has directors and a secretary to act for it – the arms and legs of the corporate body, as someone once said.

Types of company

We can divide up companies in at least two ways; the first division is into public and private companies. A public company is one which gets its capital from the public. When it is floated as a new company a prospectus is issued by way of advertisement for the company's future (this prospectus is closely regulated by law in case any over-optimistic or down-right inaccurate information should creep in) and an issue of shares is offered at a certain price, say, £1 each. The shares go out, the money comes in. The underwriters take up or pay for any shares not disposed of.

The company now has capital. Provided all the legal steps have been taken the company can now start to trade. We know it must produce a balance sheet within eighteen months and once every year thereafter. The balance sheet and accounts have to be sent to the shareholders before the annual general meeting. The company usually has a Stock Exchange quotation.

A public company must have at least seven members and at least two directors.

A private company does not appeal to the public for funds, but finds them from private sources. It limits the number of its members (shareholders) to fifty. Restrictions are placed on the transfer of its shares, which are not quoted. It may be a family business.

A private company must have at least two members and at least one director.

Often a man starts a business as a sole trader. After a time he takes in a partner. The business expands and prospers and eventually the partners decide to turn themselves into a private limited company for the sake of the advantage of limited liability and also perhaps because there may be advantages on the tax side (now they can both have a car and charge the petrol up as a business expense). If progress continues and the company does well, the time will surely come when more capital is essential. They might be able to get it in several directions, but the snag is always the same. The ones who invest invariably want to control the business and therefore ask for 51 per cent of the shares. The existing directors (the grandsons of the founder) have worked hard to build up this business and don't intend to let newcomers come in and take control.

The bank might lend, if the company has a good balance sheet, but will want the money back again. (Banks always do.) If, on the other hand, it were possible to go public, permanent capital will come flooding in.

This is a normal progression. Many of our present big public limited companies started when great-grandfather made the first clay pot on the kitchen table, or the first dining room suite on the second-floor landing, or conducted the first holiday group of ten people on a day trip to Dieppe.

Another way of dividing companies is into companies limited by shares, companies limited by guarantee, and unlimited companies.

Companies limited by shares are those where the liability of the shareholders for the debts of the company is limited to the amount of their shareholding. Thus if a shareholder buys 500 £1 shares at par (at the nominal value, 100p each) and the company does badly and finally has to be wound up, the shares will decline in value until they are worthless. The shareholder will lose £500 in this way, but that is the maximum he can lose. If he were a partner he could be made bankrupt, if necessary, to pay the firm's debts.

Companies limited by guarantee are those where the liability of the shareholders is limited to the amount they have each guaranteed to find if ever the company were wound up. Such companies are usually clubs, or societies which have been formed to promote the interests of their members, but are not intended to trade or make a profit.

Unlimited companies are those where there is no limitation to the liability of the shareholders for the debts of the company. As the whole idea of limited liability is to protect the shareholders from bankruptcy and ruin, there must be some compelling reason for any company to want to be unlimited. The reason is that an unlimited company is excused, if it can meet certain conditions, from the requirement, to which other types of company are subject, to file its accounts and directors' reports with its annual return, which the Companies Act says it has to make to the Registrar of Joint Stock Companies at Companies House. There the accounts will be made available for inspection by anybody, on payment of a small fee.

The point is that with these accounts is the figure for the profit or loss of the company for the year in question. In a competitive world it is a great advantage to be able to keep this particular detail secret. The law allows for this secrecy if the shareholders in return will give up their limited liability.

Of course, to be liable to an unlimited extent for the debts of the company is no worry while the company is doing well, making good profits, and paying its debts promptly. We may suppose that it is only this type of well-managed company which chooses to be unlimited.

Whatever the type of company, each is a separate entity at law, quite independent of the shareholders or members who compose it. How, then, can people doing business with such a company – a mere legal fiction created by parliament – be sure what the company can legally do and whether it can be made to pay? At once we come back to the banker who wishes to know whether the company can in fact legally borrow money, and, if it does, whether it can legally be made to pay it back again.

The Companies Act has provided that people who wish to inform themselves on these matters should consult the Memorandum and Articles of the company.

Powers of the company

The Memorandum of Association of a company is a document drawn by the founder members. It has six heads:

(1) the name of the company, with 'Limited' as the last word (if it is a limited company);

(2) whether the registered office of the company is to be situate in England or in Scotland;

(3) the objects of the company;

(4) whether the liability of the members is limited;

(5) details of the share capital, and how it is divided up;

(6) the Association clause. This is a declaration signed by each of the founder members, promising to buy at least one share in the company when it is incorporated.

Under the third heading is listed the objects for which the company was formed, the things it is going to do. Anything listed in those objects, the company can legally do, and be responsible for. Such acts are 'intra vires' (within its legal power). Anything else is 'ultra vires' the company, outside its powers.

The bank manager will look in the Memorandum under the objects clause to make sure that the power to borrow is mentioned there (it always is), but, equally importantly, to see that any proposed borrowing is for a purpose which is mentioned as one of the company's objects. Banks have lost money over this. Now we have joined Europe we have to study the European law on this subject, which seems to put an end to what has been called the 'ultra vires' rule. There the system is that a contract entered into in good faith by a person dealing with a company should not be set on one side on the ground that it is beyond the powers of the company.

Although this seems pretty clear, British bankers are a cautious lot and there are some questions which cannot be answered just yet. Until they can be we are likely to go on checking under the objects clause as we always have done.

The Memorandum of Association is a document which sets out the rules as between the company and the people and organizations with whom it deals. It governs the external relations of the company with the rest of the world.

The Articles of Association are contained in a document which is usually bound into a thin foolscap-sized book along with the Memorandum.

The Articles contain the rules for the internal conduct of the company, dealing with such things as the issue of shares, provisions about general meetings of the shareholders, appointment and duties of directors and secretaries, provisions as to the audit of the accounts, and so on.

The banker is interested in the powers of the directors, for it is they who usually authorize any borrowing by the company from the bank. We mustn't assume that they necessarily have the required authority to do this; occasionally, where the sum to be borrowed is a large one, the articles may say that the company must be called together to discuss the matter first. Then we might hear that 'the motion was put to the company and passed by a show of hands'. This motion is a resolution 'that the company be and hereby is empowered to borrow the sum of £x,000 from the Y bank against the security of (the company's freehold premises/stock exchange security owned by the company/ a guarantee by an outside company)'.

But this has not been authorized by the directors, but by the company. The Articles will say whether the bank needs to see a resolution of the directors, or a copy of the resolution passed by the company.

Shares in a company

The capital structure of the company is set out in the memorandum. It may be subsequently altered; if so, there will be a note of the alteration in the company's file at Companies House. Usually the shares will be ordinary shares (the equity of the company) with perhaps an issue of preference shares. However, there are other kinds of shares.

Preference shares

Preference shares carry a fixed rate of interest, which is usually specified in the Articles. Such shares receive their regular interest out of the company's annual profits (always assuming the profits will run to it) before any other classes of shareholders receive anything. The preference may also extend to repayment of capital if the company fails.

A non-cumulative preference share has the disadvantage that in a year where profits were not sufficient to pay the whole, or any interest on this type of share, the unpaid interest would be lost for ever to the shareholder.

In a cumulative preference share, however, such lost interest would be made up, profits permitting, at a later date. Preference shares are of the cumulative kind unless otherwise stated. Participating preference shares participate in the retained profits of the company when share capital is repaid on a winding-up.

Ordinary shares have no preference. They are paid after the preference shares and then only if profits permit. In a good year, however, ordinary shares come into their own. Preference shares will still get their $5\frac{1}{2}$ per cent (or whatever the rate is), but ordinary shares may pay a dividend of 20 per cent or more.

Deferred shares are rare. They are sometimes issued to the promoters of the company. They get a dividend after the ordinary shares and then only if the latter have been paid up to an agreed maximum (say 15 per cent).

Directors' qualification shares are found where the Articles stipulate that directors must have a personal stake in the company by investing in a certain minimum number of the company's shares.

Shares are for a round value, possibly 10p, 50p, or £1. Stock is capital in a mass and can be split up into pounds and pence to arrive at a more exact holding.

Shares in a public company can be easily valued by reference to their Stock Exchange quotation. Moreover they are readily saleable. These are two qualities which commend them to the lending banker as security. Neither of these virtues applies to shares in private companies. As they have no quotation, the only way to find out what they are worth is to do a calculation from the balance sheet. If some have changed hands recently it might be possible to ask the secretary of the company at what figure they changed hands. They are not saleable. In such companies it is always import-

ant for the existing directors to retain control of the business.
Therefore the Articles are sure to put restrictions on the
transfer of the shares. Often they have to be offered to the
other directors, or to nobody.

Such shares are not, therefore, good banking security.

Banking account for a new company

When the promoters of the company have completed all the
preliminary details and submitted all the necessary documents
to the Registrar of Joint Stock Companies at Companies
House, and have paid the necessary fee, the Registrar will
register the company and issue it with a certificate of incorporation. This is the company's legal birth certificate.

In the case of a public company, further formalities are
required and when those have been complied with, the
Registrar will issue a trading certificate – the official permission to commence business. The new company will want to
open a banking account. The bank manager must see the
Certificate of Incorporation, and, if necessary, the Trading
Certificate. He is usually given a copy of the Memorandum
and Articles to keep in the bank. He will need signing
instructions – perhaps all cheques will have to be signed by
a director and counter-signed by the secretary – names and
specimen signatures of all the directors and the secretary
and a copy of the resolution authorizing the opening of the
banking account.

Until he sees the Certificate of Incorporation he must not
allow the company officials to draw any money out or even
to have a cheque book, for the company has no power to do
anything. Any money lent would be 'ultra vires' and might
not come back. The most the bank can do is to let the company pay in, if it wants.

Unincorporated bodies

There are many associations of persons grouped together
for the pursuit of a common interest and with no thought

of commercial gain, such as sports clubs, social clubs and horticultural societies. Such groups are managed by officers and committees elected from their own number, and they will need a banking account for the receipt of the subscriptions of the members, for any grants which they may receive, and for the payments out which they will have to make.

The bank account is usually opened in the name of the society and operated by the treasurer together with one or more members of the committee. Details of the persons authorized to sign, together with specimens of their signatures, must be supplied in the usual way and a copy of the resolution of the society which appointed the treasurer and any other signing officers must be kept in the bank's records.

Those signing officers will change from time to time, and each change must be notified to the bank with a new specimen signature. The notification must be signed wherever possible by the old officers whose signatures the bank already has, and in this way a thread of authority is kept running which will enable the bank to check that all payments out are being properly signed by the right persons.

Such associations have no legal entity that can be sued for repayment of any borrowing. If the society wants to borrow, therefore, someone connected with the society must undertake personal responsibility. Usually a guarantee is taken from such a person in terms which make him directly responsible for the debt. Sometimes a joint and several guarantee will be signed by the members of the committee and this will be acceptable provided that they are persons of some standing.

Agents

Turning from groups to individuals, we see that some persons acquire special legal powers and shoulder special legal responsibilities, which they would not have as ordinary individuals. This is because they have been appointed to some office, or have concluded some agreement or made some contract, which gives them special duties and rights.

The relationship called agency involves a principal, and an agent. An agent is employed to do work for his principal and to make contracts on his behalf. The agent may be a firm or a company. The bank is continually acting in the capacity of an agent for its customers, as we shall see. We are familiar with travel agents, estate agents and insurance agents.

Agency involves a triangle of three parties, the principal who must tell his agent exactly what he wants him to do; the agent who does it; and the third parties who contract with the agent. A person wishing to take out life assurance will obtain a suitable policy through an agent who will make the arrangements with the life assurance company. A person wishing to fly abroad will make the arrangements through a travel agent who will book the flight for him. In the first case the principal is the life assurance company and in the second, the airline company. Export and import agents arrange the movement of goods between this country and abroad for a variety of principals. An agent may receive a regular salary or he may work on commission.

As a general rule the agent should incur no personal liability, for he stands in the place of his principal. Although the agent makes the contract with the third party, it is the principal and the third party who are the contractual parties. For the agent to incur no liability (which should be the usual rule) he must keep strictly within the powers which his principal has given him. If his principal has told him to bid at an auction for a picture 'up to £100', and the agent buys the picture, but pays £105 for it, then he has exceeded his powers. The result will be that the principal is not liable on the contract at all. The agent is.

The other time an agent might be liable is when he has made a contract without letting the third party know that he is only an agent. The third party may conclude that he is dealing with a principal. If later the third party wants to bring an action on the contract, and he has discovered the true state of affairs, then he may take proceedings against either the principal, or the agent, as he may choose. One or the other, but not both.

The rules of agency run from the top to the bottom of the business structure, and the essence of the relationship is summed up in the question, when can one person bind another by his actions? The agent binds his principal when he has completed some task within the powers conferred on him. Each general partner is an implied agent for the firm and makes his co-partners liable on debts incurred by him on behalf of the firm in the ordinary course of the firm's business. Each stockbroker is an agent employed to transact dealings in stocks and shares and his principal is bound by the rules of the Stock Exchange. The banker is an agent for his customer in some cases and not in others. When a customer is cashing a cheque, or paying in cash himself there is no agency, but as soon as a third party enters, agency is found. Thus where the customer draws a cheque payable to a third party, or pays in a cheque for collection which is drawn by someone else, the banker becomes an agent. He is an agent when he is buying stocks or shares for his customer, arranging insurance for him, remitting money abroad for him, and in many other cases.

Agency is an old institution and the common law long ago worked out the rules to which an agent must work. There are six of these:

(1) He must do the work he has agreed to do with care and diligence.
(2) He must keep his principal well-informed and up-to-date with what is happening.
(3) He must not pass on confidential information entrusted to him by his principal.
(4) He must not delegate his duties to anyone else.
(5) He must see to it that his private interests never conflict with those of his principal.
(6) He must not make any secret profit. That means that if he receives something extra, over and above his

commission, in the course of his duties, then it belongs by rights to his principal.

In return he is entitled to be paid his commission or remuneration when he has earned it, and he is entitled to be reimbursed for any payments out which he personally has had to make while carrying out the business of his principal.

The bank is sometimes an agent for another bank. We saw how banks with no seats in the Clearing House have to have their cheques cleared by banks which have. Another case is when a customer wants to cash cheques at a town in which his bank does not have a branch. Arrangements are therefore made for the customer to use the branch of another bank. Or sometimes one bank will ask another one to get a form signed by someone who lives nearby. These are all agency arrangements.

Customers, too, can appoint agents to deal with the bank on their behalf. The most usual case is where a customer gives some one else power to sign on his account. The bank likes to have its own form completed in such a case, because the principal's authority to his agent has got to be precisely worded. In this case, for example, the bank will want to know if the authority given is restricted to signing cheques or whether the agent can also negotiate overdrafts and deposit the principal's security in support.

Bailment

Where one person (a bailor) entrusts goods to another (a bailee) for a specific purpose, there is a contract of bailment. Customers entrust their boxes, parcels containing valuable documents, and jewellery to the bank for safe keeping. The banker does not usually make any specific charge for this service and is called in law a gratuitous or unpaid bailee. As such he has to show a good standard of care in keeping his customers' articles safe, but not as much as if he were a paid bailee. In practice this is an artificial distinction because the banker sets a high standard of care in any case.

Bailment has been suggested as a basis for the legal relationship between banker and customer, but the courts have held that the proper relationship is that of debtor and creditor, the banker being the debtor. The argument was that bailment refers to certain specified property. When the customer pays in to his account in cash, and later draws a cheque and cashes it at the bank counter, he gets paid in notes which are different from the notes he paid in. If he had put those in a bag, and got the bag back later, that would be bailment, for the notes would be the same.

The debtor-creditor relationship is reversed when the customer overdraws his account.

Trustee

A trustee is a person to whom property is entrusted so that he may deal with it in accordance with the directions given by the creator of the trust. A common example is where a man sets up a trust for the benefit of his children. To do this he has to choose a trustee and give over to him the securities which form the trust property. As the securities produce interest at regular intervals, the trustee pays the money out to the children in accordance with the terms of the trust instrument.

A trustee must take as much care of the trust property as a reasonable man would do of his own property. He is not allowed to make a profit out of the trust. He may or may not be free to vary the investments in the trust as he thinks fit. If he is to have this power, there must be an express authority for it in the instrument setting up the trust.

The person setting up the trust is called the donor. Those who are to benefit under it are called beneficiaries. Trustees are found in many different capacities; perhaps the most familiar is a trustee in bankruptcy, whose task is to take charge of the assets of a bankrupt, turn them into money, and then apply that money as far as it will go in settling the debts of the bankrupt. Another is a trustee under a deed of arrangement, which is a kind of alternative to bankruptcy, if the creditors will agree to it. The trustee administers the property of the debtor for the benefit of the creditors.

Banks and other financial institutions have set up trust corporations which administer trusts and wills of customers. The big clearing banks have a range of trustee branches which co-operate with the banking branches who find them their business. As trustees cannot make a profit at common law, a special 'charging clause' has to be included in the will or in the instrument setting up the trust. Trusts can arise under a will when all the debts of the deceased have been paid, and all the legacies and bequests discharged. What is left of the deceased's property – the residue – is then paid to the residuary legatee; but if the will has left money to children who are not to have it until they come of age, then a trust will be set up until that time.

Personal representatives

A man dies and may or may not leave a will. He dies 'testate' or 'intestate'. If he leaves a will, he may or may not name in it a person to be his executor. An executor is the person appointed in the will of a testator to administer his estate, to pay his debts, and to distribute his assets as instructed in the will. The law presumes that there is a bond of trust between the testator and the executor, that the testator has asked the executor to act for him because the testator knows him and trusts him to do the work well.

The executor nominated in the will may not actually do the work. He may refuse it when the will is read, saying that this is the first he has heard of it. He may be unable to act (too old or infirm) or unfit to act (he may be a criminal in prison). He may die before the testator does.

Where a will has nominated an executor but he does not act, or where a will has nominated no executor, or where no will has been left, then an administrator will be appointed according to a set of rules which the law provides. Very often the administrator is a relative of the deceased, but in the case of any administrator there is no presumption of any bond of trust between the testator or the intestate, and the administrator.

An executor (or an administrator) is called a personal representative. He represents the dead man. All the latter's property passes to him on death, not for himself, but so that he can deal with it as the deceased wished; or if the deceased left no wishes, as the law lays down.

The executor and trustee banking corporation will act as a personal representative. This has at least two advantages for those who benefit under the will or intestacy. The first is that the estate will be competently administered by experts who will know how to keep the capital transfer tax down to the lowest possible figure. The other is that there will be the benefit of continuity. The trust corporation will not die as mortal executors or administrators do.

So a banker may appear in a number of capacities. Suppose a customer keeps a current account in credit, has a parcel in safe custody, draws cheques payable to third parties, and has asked the bank to administer his will. The banker is a debtor, a bailee, an agent and a trustee. All these are accommodated within the contractual framework of the banker-customer relationship.

Receiver

When a customer dies his personal representative carries on for him. A customer may lose his legal powers to look after his own affairs in two other ways, by his bankruptcy, when a trustee is appointed to take over, and by becoming mentally ill, when the Court will appoint a Receiver. A Receiver is a person authorized to receive and administer the assets of a person certified to be mentally incapable, under the direction of the Court. The term is found with other meanings.

Where a creditor has petitioned the Court that his debtor should be made bankrupt, as it seems as if this is the only way in which he is likely to get any money at all, the Court will make a receiving order. This means that the Court has appointed one of its own officers, the Official Receiver, to take charge of the debtor's estate as an interim measure. If the debtor is eventually made bankrupt, the estate will be passed on to a trustee.

Where members of a firm are in disagreement, a partner may perhaps apply to the Court for dissolution of the firm. For this purpose the Court will appoint a Receiver for Partnership. When a person has deposited the deeds of his house as a security for a loan, he has mortgaged them. He is the mortgagor, and the lender is the mortgagee. If the mortgagor fails to repay, the mortgagee can exercise a power of sale over the property. He may choose instead to appoint a Receiver of Rents to collect the rents from the property (say a row of houses) and manage the estate.

Liquidator

An individual is made bankrupt and has a trustee appointed. A limited company goes into liquidation and has a liquidator appointed. A liquidator is a person appointed by the Court (in a compulsory liquidation) or by the creditors of a company (in a creditors' voluntary winding up), or by the members of a company (in a members' voluntary winding up) to get in what is owed to the company, to take charge of the assets and turn them into money, to pay the company's debts, and then if there is anything left, to distribute it amongst the members in proportion to their shareholding.

A compulsory winding-up is administered through the Court. It is usually the result of a petition from creditors.

A creditors' voluntary winding up does not go through the Court, but is supervised by the creditors.

When the reason for winding-up is nothing to do with shortage of money, but is for some amalgamation or merger with another company, or because the purpose for which the company was formed has now been achieved, no supervision by creditors is required, and the winding up is called a members' voluntary winding up.

Revision Test 8

Put ticks in what you think are the right boxes.

(1) Statute law is
    (a) the law of the church ☐
    (b) common law ☐
    (c) law made by parliament ☐

(2) The firm
    (a) has a separate legal existence ☐
    (b) cannot be made bankrupt while any partner remains solvent ☐
    (c) is administered in bankruptcy by a liquidator ☐

(3) Where joint and several liability has been established
    (a) each partner is liable to the firm's creditors for his share of the firm's debts ☐
    (b) the creditor has as many rights of action as there are partners ☐
    (c) the creditor has only one right of action ☐

(4) A 'quasi-partner' is one who
    (a) is not a partner, but has said or implied that he is ☐
    (b) has limited his liability for the firm's debts to the amount of the capital he has invested in the firm ☐
    (c) takes an active part in the management of the firm's business ☐

(5) A private limited company
    (a) issues a prospectus ☐
    (b) does not have to register its annual accounts at Companies House ☐
    (c) limits the number of its members to fifty ☐

(6) A Memorandum of Association
    (a) shows the objects of the company ☐

    (b) sets out the rules for the internal administration
       of the company ☐
    (c) advises the shareholders of the date of an Annual
       General Meeting ☐

(7) Preference shares
    (a) must be held by every company director ☐
    (b) are sometimes called the 'equity' of the company ☐
    (c) carry a fixed rate of interest ☐

(8) Shares in private companies
    (a) can be easily sold ☐
    (b) are not good banking security ☐
    (c) are quoted on the Stock Exchange ☐

(9) A company
    (a) can be made bankrupt on a creditor's petition ☐
    (b) is wound up by a liquidator ☐
    (c) has no separate legal entity from its members ☐

(10) A man dies without leaving a will. His affairs are
    settled by
    (a) his executor ☐
    (b) his receiver ☐
    (c) his administrator ☐

Check your solutions with the answers on p. 395.
Take one mark for each correct answer.
Each Revision Test totals 10 marks.

Questions for discussion

1. How does an executor differ from an administrator and
   in which cases is the latter appointed?
2. What are the duties of an agent and when is a banker so
   acting?
3. Compare and contrast limited companies and partnerships from the point of view of their business advantages and disadvantages.

9

Bills of exchange, cheques and promissory notes

As we have seen, the common acceptance of the Gold Standard between the trading countries of the world made international trade simpler and easier in that gold was acceptable by all merchants in these countries in payment for their goods which they had sold. However, it was not very convenient to send bars or coins of gold from one country to another, because of the risk that it might be stolen on its journey.

The bill of exchange was invented to overcome this difficulty and seems to have been used in Italy as long ago as the twelfth century. It was first used in this country in the fourteenth century and the first recorded mention of its use was in a statute of 1379.

The basis of the system which the merchants worked out was to 'marry up' as far as possible, two separate transactions, that is, the payment to be received for goods going out of a country, with the payment to be made for goods coming into the country. Suppose A in London exported some cotton to B in Paris, and about the same time C in Paris exported some wine to D in London. The cotton was worth £5,000 – B has to pay that to A – and the wine was worth £4,000 – D has to pay that to C. In each case the contract between the two sets of merchants stipulated that payment was to be made three months after the dispatch of the goods.

In due course A would draw a bill on B, and would send it (nowadays with the bill of lading and the insurance policy covering the consignment of cotton) to his agent in Paris. That gentleman would then present the bill to B and B would accept it by signing his name vertically across the bill. In present times the agent will then hand B the bill of lading and the insurance policy. The bill of lading is a document of title to the goods. Before B can claim the consignment of cotton from the ship's master at the French port where it has been sent, he must hand over the bill of lading. This proves to the ship's master that B has a rightful claim to the cotton, in fact, that he is the owner of it, and therefore he hands it over.

The insurance policy is to cover the risk of loss or damage to the cotton while it is on its journey. It might be damaged by storms or, worse still, the ship and its cargo might be sunk. In that case B doesn't get the cotton for which he has paid, but he does get instead the proceeds of the insurance policy, which will compensate him.

A's bill might have looked something like this:

£5,000

68, Tooley Street, London.
4th January 1858.

Three months after date pay to me or to my order the sum of Five Thousand Pounds, value received.

(signed) Alan Andrews

To Bernard Berthold,
14, Place de la Concorde
Paris

The date mentioned is the date of the bill, so payment is due to be made to A on 4th April. There used to be what was called three days of grace allowed to the acceptor (the debtor), giving him another three days on top of the period mentioned in the bill to find the money with which to pay it; this is no longer the case. The original stamp duty has been ignored as there is now no stamp duty on bills in this country.

C's bill drawn in Paris on D in London would be similarly expressed.

Each bill is accepted by the debtor and returned to the creditor. We now have an accepted bill (now called an acceptance) for £5,000 in the possession of A in London, and an acceptance for £4,000 in the possession of C in Paris. (We have supposed for simplicity's sake that C drew up his bill in sterling – more likely, of course, it would be in French francs, £4,000 being the sterling equivalent.)

Now if B, in Paris, could somehow be put in touch with C, in Paris, B could buy from C the bill for £4,000, accepted by D in London, and payable in London. If then B can find another, similar, bill for £1,000, and buy this also, he can then pay his debt when the three months are up, simply by sending the accepted bills to A. Once the bills are in A's hands he will have no trouble getting the money, because in each case the bill is payable in sterling in London. If the bills were originally drawn in francs, they would be converted at the time of payment into sterling at the current rate of exchange.

B and C have dealt with each other, in francs, in Paris, and A and D similarly, in London, in pounds sterling. No gold, or silver, has had to be sent either from Paris to London, or from London to Paris, but the shipments of cotton to Paris, and wine to London, have been satisfactorily financed.

Of course, the banks now actually do the work of exchange, which has been simplified considerably since the date mentioned on the bill. Today B would not have to worry about finding a French exporter to help him pay his debt for British cotton. He would simply ask his bank to arrange for the bill he had accepted to be met on the due date (the day of payment at the end of the three months) in London. His bank would contact a bank in London and between them they would see that the acceptance was paid in sterling to A (or to A's bank for credit of his account) in London, the equivalent in francs being debited to B's account with his bank in Paris. Both banks would charge a commission for their services.

The parties to the bill

The bill may be between two parties only, as in the example we have seen, or it may name three parties where the drawer uses the bill to pay off a debt he himself owes to a third party. That is, B owes A money as before, but this time A, when drawing the bill, directs B to pay the money, not to him or his order, but to P or his order.

£5,000

68, Tooley Street, London.
7th January 1979.

Three months after date pay to Peter Pitt or his order, the sum of Five Thousand Pounds, value received.

(signed) Alan Andrews

To Bernard Berthold,
17, Place de la Concorde,
Paris.

As before, the bill once drawn is sent to B, who accepts it and then returns it to A. A sends the accepted bill to P in settlement of his debt to him. When the bill is due P sends it to his agent in Paris who presents it to B for payment. Or P gives it to his bank in London and it is sent by them to another bank in Paris, who present it for payment. The proceeds are passed back to P.

Let's be sure we understand who all the parties to the bill are, and then we can go on to some other types of bill.

In this example we have supposed that A and B are merchants who have agreed to supply goods and to pay for them, respectively. A is the seller, B the buyer. A is the creditor, B the debtor. B could have paid in a number of ways. He could have sent gold or silver, or he could have sent a cheque. Instead, the parties to the contract have agreed that payment will be by way of a bill payable at three months. The bill is dated 4th January, and is payable on 4th April. The goods are sent when the bill is drawn, so let's say they arrive in Paris after a fortnight and the bill and documents of title are presented to B on the 18th January and after he has accepted the bill he is given the bill of lading and claims the goods from the ship which has taken them from England to France. He then has two months and two weeks in which to re-sell the cotton. Perhaps he makes the cotton up into shirts and sells them to the big stores in France. Whatever he does, he hopes to dispose profitably of all of the cotton, and have the money for all of his sales in, before he has to meet the bill which he has accepted. This is what the three months are for. It is a period of credit. The period may be more or less – this depends on what the merchants agreed upon originally.

When B has got all his money in, he has made a profit. But if the ship has been sunk, the bill of lading is obviously worthless and in that case the document of title is the insurance policy. This policy must be made out for the value of the goods plus a certain percentage, say 10 per cent or 20 per cent, which will represent the profit which B would have made.

A is the drawer of the bill. He is also the seller and, until he is paid, the creditor.

B is the drawee of the bill, the person on whom the bill is drawn. He is the buyer, and, until he pays, the debtor. When he accepts the bill he is called the acceptor, and the bill is called an acceptance. P is the payee of the bill. He is the person who will eventually get the money unless he passes the title on to someone else, i.e. negotiates the bill. He can do this if he wants to, because a bill of exchange is a fully negotiable instrument. Suppose P owes R £6,000. He decides to pass on this bill to R, thus bringing his debt to him down to £1,000. If you like, it is a payment on account. The original wording said the money was to be paid to P or his order, that means, as P orders.

P will pass on the proceeds of this bill by endorsing it, that is, by writing his name on the back of the bill. If he simply does that, the bill will become payable to anyone who is in possession of it (the bearer). P is the endorser and he is said to have endorsed the bill in blank. Then he can send the bill to R. But there is a risk here. If the bill goes astray between P and R anyone can get the money. It would be better for P to endorse the bill specially.

A special endorsement specifies the person to whom, or to whose order, a bill or cheque is to be payable.

The special endorsement here would read:

Pay Richard Rowley or order, (signed) Peter Pitt.

Then the bill will be payable only to R or to whomever else R chooses to endorse it. Suppose he keeps it and tells his bank to collect the money for it. Before he gives it to his bank he will have to endorse it himself, as a receipt for the money he is getting. Just his signature will do, under the special endorsement made by P.

Then we shall have P called the first endorser, and R the second endorser. The chain of title to the money will have passed like this:

A ————————→ P ————————→ R
(drawer)   (first endorser)   (second endorser)

If for any reason P did not want R to pass the bill on to anyone else, he could write on the back:

Pay Richard Rowley only, (signed) Peter Pitt.

This is called a restrictive endorsement. It destroys the transferability of the bill. A could similarly have drawn the bill restrictively, by substituting for the words 'or his order' on the face of the bill, the word 'only'.

The various parties to the bill, drawer, acceptor and endorser, all have their duties defined in the Bills of Exchange Act, 1882. These duties may be summarized by saying that each person who signs his name on a bill in effect guarantees that it will be paid. This means that if on presentation for payment the bill is unpaid or dishonoured, the holder may sue any previous party for the sum – anyone whose signature appears on the bill, in whatever capacity, when he receives it.

The holder of a bill is the person who is in possession of it. He may be either the payee, or an endorsee, or the bearer.

The bearer of a bill is the person who is in possession of a bill or note which is payable to bearer. A bearer bill is one which is expressed to be payable to bearer, or one which is endorsed in blank. An endorsee is the person to whom the bill is endorsed over.

Types of bill

You can see that there are plenty of definitions to learn for anyone who needs to find his way around the Bills of Exchange Act. We have made a start with:

drawer	endorser
drawee	endorsee
acceptor	blank endorsement
payee	special endorsement
holder	restricted endorsement
bearer	

These terms, new and strange at first, rapidly become familiar as study progresses.

Now let us take another look at the bill. The one we have been using as an example is called a term bill, because it incorporates a term of credit. You will remember that we allowed a fortnight for the cotton to get from London to Paris, so that B did not actually get three month's credit, only two months and two weeks. He didn't mind this, because it still left him with enough time to resell the goods and get the money in.

But suppose the goods had had to travel, not from London

to Paris, but half-way around the world, to a place where steamers did not run very often, so that no one could say for certain how long they would be. Then serious inroads would be made into the period of credit. One way round this would be to increase the term of credit to, say, six months, in the original negotiations between the merchants.

However, there is a better and more precise way out of this difficulty. The drawer simply substitutes in his bill for the words 'after date' the words 'after sight'. Then the three months will run not from the date of the bill, but from the date when the importer (drawee, acceptor) first sees the bill. If the bill travels on the same ship as the goods, that must mean that the importer gets to see the bill when the goods have become available to him.

In this case, he will have to add to his signature of acceptance the date when he sighted the bill, so that the term of the bill may be calculated and the due date ascertained. His acceptance will then look like this:

(signed) Stephen Soames
Sighted 6th June 1978

So if this were a case where three months' credit had been agreed, and the bill was dated 31st March 1978, the due date would be 6th September and not 30th June.

A bill of this nature is described as one payable after sight. The word 'after' is important because a bill payable at sight (a sight bill) is one payable immediately, as soon as the drawee sees it.

A term bill, or a bill payable after sight, has to be presented twice, once for acceptance, and once for payment. The bill can be dishonoured at either of these stages: if the bill is dishonoured by non-acceptance there is no point in presenting it for payment. Of course the bill is the visible evidence of the agreement entered into by the parties. A contract (unless under seal) must be accompanied and supported by consideration. (Consideration has been defined as 'some right, interest, profit or benefit, accruing to one party, or some forbearance, detriment, loss or responsibility given, suffered or undertaken by the other'.) That is the point of the words 'value received' which the drawer includes in his form of words. Then when the acceptor signs he is agreeing that he has had the goods and this is proof that the contract was supported by consideration. These words do not have to be included in the wording of the bill, but it is usual to see them.

The acceptance is the signification by the drawee of his assent to the order of the drawer. It confirms the original contract. It implies that the goods which have just reached him are satisfactory in every way.

The acceptor may accept indicating that when the bill is presented for payment it should go to his bank. In this case he would write across the bill the words 'Accepted payable at the London & Provincial Bank, 12, Throgmorton Street, London', followed by his signature.

Such an acceptance is said to be domiciled at a bank.

Of course any fraudulent person could pick a name and address out of the telephone directory, draw a bill on that person, and send it to him. Such a bill would be neither accepted nor paid. There is no transaction to which the bill refers. There is no consideration for the bill.

Bills which are to go abroad may possibly get lost and so a bill may be written out in a set of three, and sent by different posts. Such a bill might be worded:

Thirty days after sight pay this First of Exchange (Second and Third of the same date and tenor being unpaid) to Thomas Trotter or order the sum of Two Thousand Pounds.

This 'first part' will be matched by a second and third part similarly worded. The second part will impose the condition that the first and third parts should be unpaid, and so on.

The debt is only to be paid once, of course, and the drawee must be careful to accept only one of the three parts. If the first part is delayed or lost he may get the second part first, and then he accepts that. Once one part is accepted, the other two are valueless.

All bills drawn abroad, and payable in this country, and all bills drawn in this country, and payable abroad, are foreign bills. Bills both drawn and payable in this country are inland bills.

Bills as instruments of credit stand or fall by the reputation of the acceptor and the drawer. The acceptor has promised to pay, by his acceptance; and the drawer, by drawing the bill, has guaranteed that the acceptor will be willing and able to pay on the date, and if he does not, he, the drawer, will.

Very often, therefore, an importer in London would get his bank to accept bills on his behalf. The bank's name would be very much better known than the merchant's, therefore the bill would command more confidence and subsequent negotiation would be more easily effected.

Term bills can be negotiated either before or after they are accepted. Those who take them for value before acceptance by the drawee are relying on the name and reputation of the drawer. Those who take them after acceptance (but, of course, before payment) have two names on which to rely.

As banks continued to accept bills on behalf of their customers, there grew up in London firms and merchant banks which specialized in accepting bills on behalf of their merchant customers. These were the accepting houses, you will remember. A bill bearing the name of a member of the accepting houses was looked upon all over the world as absolutely good. Such a bill gave rise to the phrase, the Bill on London, than which there was nothing more reliable. So trade all over the world was financed by the undertakings of London bankers. Goods sent from Rio de Janeiro to Freemantle, from Hong Kong to San Francisco, never went anywhere near London, but the trade was financed from there. Bills bearing the name of a London accepting house fulfilled the function of an international medium of exchange. Some writers have described them as international money.

Now let us look at an inland bill payable on demand.

£500·60   4, Tarrant Street, London.
                                              1st January 1979.

Pay to my order on demand the sum of Five Hundred
Pounds and Sixty Pence, value received.

                                    (signed) Robert Cully

To Charles Freeman,
4, Argyll Street, Durham.

Here there is no element of credit in terms of time. The bill
is to be paid as soon as it is presented. The bill may perhaps
start 'Pay bearer on demand . . .' or, where the proceeds are
to go to X.Y., 'Pay X.Y. on demand . . .'. The words 'at
sight' may be used instead of 'on demand'.

As there is no term there is no need for an acceptance, so
this bill is presented once only, for payment. It is presented
at the usual place of business of the drawee, in this case 4,
Argyll Street, Durham. The drawer would not himself make
a special trip from London to Durham to get the money,
but would give the bill to his London bank, which would send
it to their Durham branch (or to another bank in Durham
if it did not itself have a branch in Durham) to be presented
locally.

The bill of exchange is defined in the Bills of Exchange
Act as 'An unconditional order in writing, addressed by one
person to another, signed by the person giving it, requiring
the person to whom it is addressed to pay on demand, or at
a fixed or determinable future time, a sum certain in money
to or to the order of a specified person, or to bearer'.

This definition nowhere requires the bill to be written on
paper. The humorist and jurist A. P. Herbert once wrote out
a bill on an egg, and had it cleared by the bank. Since then
in the silly season one regularly reads in the papers of bills or
cheques written on pieces of tentcloth, handkerchieves, or
slabs of paving stone.

This defect of the statutory definition shows how hard it is for the draftsmen of acts of parliament to anticipate every single thing which may happen. In every other respect the definition is an example of precision and lucidity.

Cheques

A cheque is a special form of a bill of exchange, namely, one payable on demand and drawn on a banker. It differs from the bill of exchange proper. It does not require acceptance, the drawer is the person who has to pay it, although he may stop payment of the cheque, and it is always drawn on a banker and not on a private person, firm, or company.

Cheques first came into use about 1680. An order cheque was one payable to a named person or his order, a bearer cheque was payable to the bearer, who, as we have seen, was the person in possession of it. The period of bank expansion was at its height in the middle of the nineteenth century when most cheques were bearer cheques. This was due to the fact that at that time bearer cheques were subject to a stamp duty of 1d per cheque, while order cheques were subject to ad valorem stamp duty just like bills. They were charged according to the value of the cheque. The greater the amount the order cheque was made out for, the more the stamp duty.

Bearer cheques, although cheap, were subject to the drawback that if they were stolen, they could be cashed by the thief. So when in 1853 the Stamp Act provided for the issue of a 'draft or order for the payment of any sum of money to the bearer or to order subject to stamp duty of one penny' there was a great increase in the use of order cheques.

(Stamp duty, later increased to twopence, was abolished altogether in 1971.)

Now the order cheque can be said to be the main method of settling debts. The amounts represented annually by the cheques passing through the Clearing House are greatly in excess of the total of all banknotes and coin in circulation. But like the bill of exchange, a cheque is not money. It is a claim to money. When a payee receives a cheque from the drawer, he is no better off in terms of cash until he has paid the cheque in to his bank, and his bank has obtained the money from the drawer's bank and credited his account with it. Sometimes, of course, a cheque can be passed from hand to hand for value (in exchange for cash or for goods) and in that case it does act as a medium of exchange. But although a cheque is a negotiable instrument, less than 5 per cent of all cheques are in fact negotiated (passed from hand to hand for value). The great bulk of them are paid straight into their bank accounts by the payees. The negotiated cheque does not fulfil the function of money long enough to affect the money situation in any way.

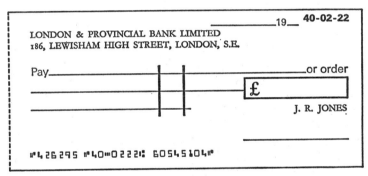

Example of an order cheque.

If we look at this form of cheque we shall see that it is an instruction from a depositor (customer) of a bank to that bank, instructing it to pay some of his money away. The drawer's name appears in the bottom right-hand corner. It is printed by the bank before the cheque book is issued to the customer for his use. Its purpose is to assist in the sorting of cheques into alphabetical order. Below the printed name is a space for the drawer's signature. The bank is the drawee and, whatever name the drawer writes in after the word 'Pay' will be the payee.

In the top right-hand corner is the space for the date, followed by the national number of this particular branch bank. This number is repeated at the bottom of the cheque in magnetic ink characters which the computer can recognize, and there also are to be found the number of the cheque (on the left) and the number of the customer's account. As soon as this cheque is paid back into the banking system the collecting bank will add a further set of magnetic characters indicating the amount of the cheque. The computer can then debit the right amount to the account of the right customer at the right branch. The confusion which was sometimes caused because of the existence of customers with similar or the same names and initials has been much reduced, if not altogether eliminated, by the introduction of an account number which is different from all other account numbers at that branch.

The two vertical lines constitute a crossing, which will be explained shortly. Cheques can be obtained with or without pre-printed crossings.

Bearer cheques are the same as in the example given with the difference that the words 'or bearer' take the place of the words 'or order'. Bearer cheques are uncrossed.

It is for the customer to tell the bank what sort of cheque book he wants. If he is likely to send most of his cheques through the post he will ask for a crossed order book. If he is likely to be cashing most of his cheques at the bank, across the counter, he will ask for an open order book. Bearer cheques are much rarer but are still in use, particularly in the City where there is a tradition that members of the Stock Exchange settle with each other by means of bearer cheques. This was originally to avoid the bother of having to endorse them, but although endorsement has been practically abolished (by the Cheques Act, 1957) the custom persists.

If the customer has the wrong cheque book for any particular transaction he wants to enter upon, he can amend the face of the cheque in ink. If he has a bearer cheque book and he wants an order cheque he can run his pen through the word bearer and the cheque will automatically revert to being an order cheque. Or, to make matters quite clear, he may write in the word 'order' over the deleted 'bearer', possibly adding his signature or his initials.

If he has an order book and he wants a bearer cheque he can delete the word 'order', write in 'bearer' and authenticate the change to his bank by adding his signature. In this case the customer is introducing an element of risk in making a bearer cheque and this is why the banks insist on the authentication.

If he has an open book and he wants a crossed cheque, the customer can add the crossing in ink. If he has a crossed book and he wants an open cheque he can write between the vertical lines of the crossing 'Pay Cash' and authenticate the alteration with his full signature. The one thing he cannot do is to make any alteration to the line of magnetic ink characters at the bottom of the cheque, or make an alteration to the branch of the bank where he wants the cheque presented. This might perhaps happen where a customer has two accounts at two branches of the same bank, and has a cheque book on each. If he wants to debit his account at branch A he may go to his cheque book and find that he has used the last one. He must not then take a cheque from the B branch book and alter it in ink, because the computer does not recognize the strokes of a pen, only the magnetic ink characters.

Crossings

Crossings were invented in the Bankers' Clearing House, where it became a practice among the banks exchanging cheques with each other, to indicate which bank a cheque was to go to. It became generally adopted as soon as the public recognized what a good safeguard against fraud or theft it was.

Crossings may be general or special.

A general crossing consists of two parallel transverse lines with or without the addition of the words 'and Company'

and with or without the addition of the words 'not negotiable'.

A special crossing consists of the name of a bank, with or
without the addition of two parallel transverse lines and with
or without the addition of the words 'not negotiable'.

The words 'and Company' or 'and Co.' originated when
the drawer of a cheque wished to cross it to the payee's
bank, but not knowing which it was he wrote the words
across the cheque leaving a space for the payee to complete
it himself, as it might be, 'Coutts and Company'.

The words 'not negotiable' turn the cheque into a non-
negotiable instrument and we shall see presently what
negotiability is. The words have no effect on the transferability of the cheque. The words are not used on a bill of
exchange other than a cheque, for a bill of exchange is the
supreme example of a negotiable instrument. Where a person
takes a crossed cheque which bears on it the words 'not negotiable' he shall not have, and shall not be capable of giving a
better title to the cheque than that which the person from
whom he took it had. (A person has a good title to a bill or
cheque when he has received it honestly and is entitled to the
money which it represents. If he has received it by mistake, or
gained it by fraud, he is said to have a defect in his title.)

The effect of crossing a cheque is to oblige the paying
banker, when the cheque reaches him, to pay the proceeds
only to another banker. If the crossing is a general one, he
may pay to any banker; if a special one, only to the banker
named on the cheque. (A bill of exchange other than a cheque
cannot be crossed.)

So if a cheque is stolen, and the thief forges the endorsement and tries to cash it across a bank counter, he will not
be able to do so if the cheque is crossed, for every banker
knows that he cashes a crossed cheque over his counter at
his own risk.

Now to illustrate the action of a crossed order cheque.

D the drawer owes P the payee £100 and decides to post
him a cheque for the sum. P banks at the Northern Bank,

Carlisle, and D banks at the Southern Bank, Brighton. D makes out the cheque and posts it. P pays it into his banking account in Carlisle and the Carlisle branch send it to their London office, in with all the other cheques to be cleared, the same evening. The Carlisle bank, London, transfer it through the Clearing House to the London office of the Southern Bank, who send it to their Brighton office by post, and they check the signature and then debit it to P's account. We could show this as follows:

D → P → Northern Bank, Carlisle → Northern Bank, London → Southern Bank, London → Southern Bank Brighton

The check of the signature at the Brighton bank is an essential part of the operation, for the cheque is D's instruction and authority to his bank to pay away some of his money deposited with them. If the signature of D is forged the bank has no authority to pay. If they do they will have to refund D's account when he finds out about it. It follows that all the staff in all the banks must be able to identify correctly the signatures of all their customers. If they are in doubt, they must compare any particular signature with the specimen signature which each customer has to give to the bank at the time when he first opens the account.

If the order cheque is not crossed, and if D and P live in the same town, P may choose to go into D's bank and present the cheque himself across the counter for payment in cash. Then the cheque will not go through the clearing house.

D → P → D's bank

In this case P will have to endorse the cheque before presenting it across the counter, partly as a receipt for the money, and partly to identify himself. The cashier at D's bank will not know P's signature, only that of D, but he will check that the endorsement appears to be correct. The idea of this is that if the presenter is not in fact P, but a thief who has stolen the cheque from P, or someone who has found it in the street because P has lost his wallet, then he may be disconcerted at suddenly having to forge P's endorsement, and perhaps leave the bank without the money because he is afraid of being caught.

A bearer cheque may likewise be directly presented for payment, but in this case the holder will not have to endorse, because bearer cheques are payable to whoever is in possession of them, and possession is the only criterion: there is no question of identification.

Of course, both open order cheques and bearer cheques may be paid into the holder's banking accounts and go through the Clearing House as the crossed cheques do. They do not have to be presented directly.

Negotiability

Negotiability is that quality which enables the holder of a bill or note to maintain a good title to it even though a previous holder had a bad one. The characteristics of a negotiable instrument are:

(1) Mere delivery of the instrument by one person to another passes the full legal title. In some cases endorsement is necessary before delivery.

(2) No notice of the transfer need be given to the person liable on the instrument.

(3) The title to the instrument passes free from all counter-claims between previous parties and from defects in the title of previous parties. The transferee (the person who has received the bill or note) must give value for the instrument and must act in good faith and without any knowledge of any doubt affecting the title of the transferor.

(4) The transferee may sue in his own name if this becomes necessary.

As to (1) we should note that while a bearer cheque passes by simple delivery, an order cheque passes by endorsement and delivery.

With a bearer cheque the legal right to the proceeds of the cheque passes from the drawer to whoever presents it for payment.

With an order cheque the legal right to the proceeds of the cheque passes from the drawer to the payee. If the payee wishes to pass it on to another person he must endorse the cheque, to pass the title on. The endorsement may be in blank, in which case the title passes to the bearer, or special, in which case the title passes to whoever it was specially endorsed to.

As to (2) there is no need, when a cheque is endorsed over, for either the endorser or the endorsee to inform the drawer. This may seem obvious, but such a characteristic is not true of non-negotiable instruments: for example, when an assurance policy is assigned, say as security to a banker, notice of the assignment must be given to the assurance company, who is in this case the debtor.

As to (4) an action at law may become necessary if the cheque or bill is dishonoured when presented for payment. If that happens the holder of the bill can sue as a person in his own right: he does not have to claim through the person who transferred the cheque to him.

Instruments which are fully negotiable are banknotes (and other promissory notes) bills of exchange (including cheques – unless crossed 'not negotiable'), bearer bonds, dividend warrants (unless crossed 'not negotiable'), bearer scrip, debentures payable to bearer, share warrants to bearer, treasury bills and certificates of deposit.

Promissory Notes

Many of us will perhaps be familiar with the gambler who writes an IOU for his debts. This piece of paper contains an acknowledgement of debt and implies that one day – some time – repayment will be made. It is on this point of the date of repayment that it differs from a promissory note.

A promissory note is an unconditional promise in writing

made by one person to another, signed by the maker, engaging to pay, on demand or at a fixed or determinable future time, a sum certain in money to, or to the order of, a specified person, or to bearer.

This definition has many of the words and phrases to be found in the definition of the bill of exchange. Both definitions come from the same Act, the Bills of Exchange Act, 1882. But this is a 'promise', not an 'order'. It is 'made' to another, not 'addressed'.

The writer of a promissory note is a 'maker'. To complete

£500   Liverpool, 30th June 1978.

I promise to pay bearer on demand the sum of
Five Hundred Pounds.

                                        (signed) George Jessel

---

Example of a promissory note payable on demand.

£400   Liverpool, 30th June 1978.

Three months after date I promise to pay William
Smith or order the sum of Four Hundred Pounds.
                                        (signed) George Jessel

---

Example of a promissory note drawn for a term.

the note, if it is to maker's order, he must endorse it. The note is incomplete until it has been delivered to the payee or bearer.

Promissory notes issued by private persons are hardly ever seen in banks nowadays. But this is made up for in the banknotes which banks continually handle. The banknote is the most celebrated promissory note of all. It starts 'I promise to pay'. It is payable on demand, and signed by the Chief Cashier of the Bank of England. Banknotes, like other promissory notes, cheques, and bills of exchange other than cheques, are all governed by the Bills of Exchange Act, 1882.

Bills of exchange, cheques, and promissory notes other than

banknotes, are not money, although they perform very similar functions. They are sometimes called 'near money'. The bill of exchange finances international trade, the cheque finances nearly all domestic transfers. These two instruments supply nearly all the power to keep the wheels of commerce turning. It is essential, therefore, to understand their functions.

Revision Test 9

Put ticks in what you think are the right boxes.

(1) Here is a specimen endorsement: 'Pay Sam Small or order. (Signed) P. Pitt'. Is this
  (a) an endorsement in blank ☐
  (b) a restrictive endorsement ☐
  (c) a special endorsement ☐

(2) A restrictive endorsement destroys the
  (a) negotiability ☐
  (b) transferability ☐
  (c) acceptability ☐
  of the bill

(3) The acceptor of a bill of exchange, before he had accepted it, was called
  (a) the drawer ☐
  (b) the drawee ☐
  (c) the endorser ☐

(4) A bill of exchange begins 'Three months after date . . .' Is this
  (a) a demand bill? ☐
  (b) a sight bill? ☐
  (c) a term bill? ☐

(5) A demand bill
  (a) is one domiciled at a bank ☐
  (b) does not require presentation for acceptance ☐
  (c) is payable immediately after acceptance ☐

(6) Documents of title to goods include
    (a) a bill of sale ☐
    (b) a bill of lading ☐
    (c) a bill of sight ☐

(7) The drawee of a cheque is
    (a) the person who gets the value ☐
    (b) a banker ☐
    (c) the person whose bank account will be debited ☐

(8) A special crossing consists of
    (a) the name of a bank ☐
    (b) two parallel transverse lines ☐
    (c) the words 'not negotiable' ☐

(9) The title to a bearer cheque passes by
    (a) endorsement ☐
    (b) endorsement and delivery ☐
    (c) mere delivery ☐

(10) Which is the negotiable instrument?
    (a) a share certificate ☐
    (b) a bearer bond ☐
    (c) a postal order ☐

Check your solutions with the answers on p. 395.
Take one mark for each correct answer.
Each Revision Test totals 10 marks.

Questions for discussion

1. What are the main forms of money in modern society? What factors distinguish money from 'near money'?

2. In what circumstances might payment of a debt be made by way of bill of exchange rather than a cheque?

3. What is the purpose of an endorsement on a cheque and when will one be found?

10

Banking services

The term 'wholesale banking' has been used to describe the banks' operations in the money market dealing with other financial institutions, and the term 'retail banking' has been used to describe the dealings with bank customers. In this country merchant, overseas and foreign banks are wholesale banks. They do not provide retail services because they have no branch network in the country. Some merchant banks, how ever, are beginning to open branches in provincial centres.

Building societies, some finance houses, and savings banks fulfil some banking-type functions although their deposits are not officially counted in the money supply and they are not part of the banking sector.

Only the large clearing banks, with their thousands of branches, can offer every type of service to their customers. It is only in the last decade that they have realized this, but now they are moving aggressively forward into spheres of banking business formerly dominated by the merchant and foreign banks. They have begun to think in terms of banking supermarkets, where the customer shops for the services he wants.

The list of available services is now so long that it is asking a lot to expect one man to comprehend it all. Yet the modern view is that the cashier on the bank counter is the selling outlet to the customer. His job is not only to take in credits, and pay out cheques, but to talk to the customer, finding out in the course of the conversation what opportunities there may be to suggest other banking services to him.

One solution suggested is for branches to be organized round a regional centre. Branches would provide the bread and butter services, the centre would be staffed by those who could explain the details of the more specialized services and arrange for them to be made available.

Banking covers so many services that it is difficult to define it. However, three basic services have always been recognized as the hallmarks of the genuine banker. These are, the receipt of the customer's deposits, the collection of his cheques drawn on other banks, and the payment of the customer's cheques drawn on himself.

From this historic foundation has been built a wide variety of services. These have been arranged under eight heads, as described below.

A further useful division of services which can be made is into services for personal customers and services for business customers. Many services fall into both these categories, so that three lists are required:

Advances

A bank lends money to a pre-arranged limit principally by overdraft, loan or personal loan.

Overdraft

With the overdraft, interest is calculated on a daily basis. Consequently the customer pays only for what he uses. The overdraft is by far the cheapest form of borrowing, but it can only be obtained if the bank manager is satisfied on a number of points. His first four questions will be, to all propositions, how much? what for? how long for? what is the source of repayment? If these are all answered to his satisfaction he may ask a fifth question, is there any security?

But not necessarily so. He may be content to rely upon the customer's integrity. In the case of a limited company he may very well be content to lend because the customer's balance sheet shows a healthy position.

Loan

A loan is more expensive. The amount agreed is made available by transfer from a loan account in the customer's name, to his current account. The loan is supposed to be reduced at agreed intervals, often once a month, by an instalment from the current account. If the money is not forthcoming the bank cannot make the transfer, and will probably write to the customer pointing this out. The customer then knows that he may find any cheques he has drawn dishonoured if the account would be overdrawn should they be paid. With the loan method the current account should be kept in credit. There is no point in transferring an instalment of loan reduction when the only result is to increase an overdraft.

The loan is easier to supervise from the bank's point of view. It is much harder to see if an overdraft is being reduced methodically.

Loan interest will be charged quarterly or half yearly on

the amount of the loan outstanding and debited to the current account. That account may well still have on it some, most or all of the original amount of the loan, but there is no allowance for interest earned set off against loan interest. There may be what is called 'interest at a notional rate' (fixed by the bank) earned by this money, which goes to reduce a commission charge, or to extinguish it altogether.*

Personal credit plan

Midland Bank is alone among the four major clearing banks in offering this type of scheme. Prospective borrowers agree to pay a fixed sum (minimum £10) each month and are then entitled to credit of up to 30 times this amount. The ceiling is £1,000. To encourage borrowers to build up their PCP accounts, the bank pays a 6 per cent annual interest on the money deposited. It charges a true 18 per cent interest for credit.

The scheme is aimed at borrowers who may not want an immediate loan but are anxious to prepare for future emergencies. The chief advantage is that customers do not have to visit their bank managers repeatedly: the credit can be used how and when it suits them.

Personal loan

The personal loan was intended as a cheaper form of hire purchase. The interest is added to the amount borrowed and the total is then repaid by regular monthly repayments over an agreed period, usually six months to three years or, in some cases, longer. The applicant makes out and signs a bank form giving certain details of his income and regular outgoings. The bank manager usually has no way of checking the accuracy of some of the details given, but where one of his customers is concerned he has the history of the account to help him. Personal loans are not limited to existing customers, however, and when strangers to the bank go in off

* See p. 401.

the street to ask for a personal loan – as they are entitled to do – the manager must use his judgement, which is what he is paid for.

As interest is added to the capital borrowed at the outset of the advance, each repayment will consist partly of capital and partly of interest. The effect of this will be to make the true cost to the borrower – the effective rate of interest – much more than the flat rate, which is the rate at which the interest is calculated for addition to the capital. The exact figures will vary according to the length of the personal loan, but will be somewhere between one and a half and two times the flat rate. This is true of all hire purchase, of course, but can mislead the unwary borrower. The Consumer Credit Act, 1974, requires both flat and effective rates to be quoted in all cases.

The personal loan, unlike commercial hire-purchase contracts, gives the bank no rights over the object purchased with the money lent. The personal loan agreement states that if any instalment is not paid on time the whole of the debt will fall due for repayment immediately. This gives the bank a right to bring an action for the money, which it hardly ever feels is worth doing. This particular service is obviously open to abuse, but so is any bank service. It is often said that anyone can defraud a bank once, but in these times few customers can afford to be anything but honest with their banks. They will need their help too much, and too often, to take risks with their credit rating in the bank's eyes.

Personal loans are granted from £50 to £2,000.

All advances must be subject to a plan for regular repayment, so that the return of the bank's money can be clearly visualized from the start. If the customer cannot adhere to the agreement he has made, he should give the bank manager a good explanation. Otherwise he will lose his reputation in the bank's eyes, and will find, next time he wants to borrow, that things are very much more difficult to arrange.

Specific mention should be made of three common types of advances.

Bridging loan

A bridging loan is usually in connection with the sale of one house and the purchase of another. A customer in this position may find that the money for the house being bought is required before the money comes in for the house being sold. The banker is asked to 'bridge' the gap. This should be a short-term loan and the banker will usually lend after he has seen an undertaking by a building society to lend any balance required on the new house; has been advised by the solicitor acting that contracts for the house being sold have been exchanged; and has received the undertaking of the solicitor to pay the sale moneys into the customer's account. The solicitor must be known to be reliable.

Farming advance

Banks traditionally help the farmer, who usually takes the advance year after year. These are long-term advances really, often only cleared off on the death of the farmer and the sale of the farm (see p. 324).

Probate advance

This is an advance to a personal representative so that he can obtain probate of a will, or letters of administration where there is no executor who can act. The advance is made to the personal representative personally and is to be repaid out of the first sale proceeds from the estate. These advances are short term and usually quite safe. The money is wanted for the payment of estate duty, without which no probate or letters can be granted.

Deposits

Current account

The normal banking account is the current account, running from day to day, a balance being shown at the end of any day on which there has been a debit or credit entry. No interest is normally allowed on a current account.

The bank is always seeking to attract new customers as it works to extend its business. Nevertheless, the holder of a current account must be carefully checked before he is issued with a cheque book. Two references are normally required, and the referees must themselves be considered of satisfactory status. Statements of the account are sent to the customer quarterly or half-yearly, or more often if he wishes. The account may remunerate the banker because a good average credit balance is kept, but if it does not a commission charge may be debited to the account quarterly or half-yearly (but see page 291).

Deposit account

It is perhaps a little confusing that the term 'deposits' is often used to describe the money which customers of all kinds leave with the banks on both current, deposit, and other accounts, but if a current account is defined as an account which is opened so that cheques may be drawn on it, then a deposit account can be defined as an account which is opened to earn interest. Deposit interest is paid at a rate determined by the bank's base rate, at present $1\frac{1}{2}$ per cent below it. As between the banks there may be temporary small differences between deposit rates offered, but these never last for very long.

No cheques are supposed to be collected for deposit account holders and no cheque book is issued. Consequently it is unnecessary to take up references.

Withdrawals are nominally at seven days' notice, but can be obtained on demand, although in such a case seven days' interest on the sum withdrawn will be foregone. Deposit books which had to be produced for every transaction are giving way to statements. Interest is credited to the current account, if there is one, half-yearly, otherwise it is added to the balance of the deposit account.

Fixed deposits are sometimes arranged for a fixed sum at a fixed rate. Normally deposit interest rates are not very exciting, but in the exceptional conditions of the last half of 1973 the banks' base rates went to up 13 per cent, which would have made the deposit rate an unheard-of 11 per cent. Because the building societies complained that the banks were gaining all the deposits the Chancellor stepped in to limit deposit rate on sums up to £10,000 to 9½ per cent. Depositors of sums over this amount, however, were free to negotiate with the banks for a fixed rate for a fixed period.

Banks are required to make a return of deposit interest paid to customers to the Inland Revenue authorities, where the amount is £25 or over.

Safe custody

Articles of value, locked boxes, wills, and many other things are left by customers in bank strongrooms for safety. Boxes should be locked and parcels sealed by the customer before handing them in to the bank. The banker will issue a receipt if so required. He must be careful to hand them back only against a signature by his customer or a properly-appointed agent who is known to the bank. Such a safe-keeping is a contract of bailment. If the banker makes a specific charge for the service he is a paid bailee. If he does not he is a gratuitous bailee. The paid bailee has to show a higher standard of care in dealing with the safe custody articles than does a gratuitous bailee.

Safe deposit

Some banks maintain a safe deposit service where the customer is taken into a strong room and himself puts his documents or articles of value into his box, or compartment, to which he alone has the key, or takes them out. The bank keeps duplicate keys in case of emergency, but does not use them except in the presence of the customer or by his express authority.

Statements

An account of cheques paid, credits received, and resulting balances is prepared by the computer and sent to the customer at varying intervals. Big companies will require their statement daily, small private customers usually get theirs three- or six-monthly.

The statement stems from the old passbook which was written up by hand and showed debits and credits sub-totalled in pencil. Very often a balance was put in, also in pencil, just before the customer had the book out to look at it, or he could work it out for himself. When machined statements came in many systems were tried. The passbook had sometimes suffered from illegible handwriting, now the statement sometimes suffered from poor typing by machine clerks who were not typists. The detailed statement, which gave payee's names, was largely replaced by the statement which gave symbols for recurring items and numbers of cheques for others. With all their faults, these statements were up-to-date when the customer got them.

The computer did away with bad typing, but it did not give names, only numbers and symbols. Moreover, it was usually several days behind.

Finally, escalating postal charges persuaded the banks to give up returning paid cheques with the statements. In future customers must check their debits against the information on the counterfoils of their cheque books. This is not impossible, but it takes much longer. The cheques are kept for six years in the bank's storage depots, and then destroyed.

This slowly deteriorating service is due to the vast increase in the number of customers and the increasing need to standardize procedures in order to cope. In one respect, however, a truly personal service is given. Two of the big clearing banks provide statements in braille for blind customers. A braille transcription service has also been introduced. This enables a customer to write to his bank manager in braille and receive a braille letter in reply.

Stops

If for any reason a bank customer who has issued a cheque wishes to stop payment of it, he may telephone his bank, which will accept a countermand of payment in this way provided that written confirmation follows without delay. The customer must quote the number, amount, date, and payee's name of the cheque concerned, taking these details from his cheque counterfoil. Sometimes the customer has not filled this in, and dictates the details from memory, so that some of the information supplied may be incorrect. The bank will do its best to apply the details given, but the customer must get one detail right – he must be certain of the number of the cheque.

On receiving such a countermand the bank will first check that the cheque has not already been paid; if not a stop order will be placed on the cheque, which will be returned by the bank when it is presented for payment with the answer 'Orders not to pay', or 'Payment countermanded'. If the customer's written confirmation has not yet arrived the answer will be 'Awaiting confirmation of orders not to pay'. Any of these answers will indicate to the payee that he must now take the matter up with the drawer.

Financial services

Acceptance credit facility

An acceptance credit facility is an agreement whereby a bank or accepting house agrees to accept bills for a customer on a regular basis, up to a certain limit. Such bills, once accepted, become prime bank bills and are readily discountable. The customer pays a commission for the acceptance service.

Bills discounted – see p. 96.

Business advisory service

By arrangement the bank sends an executive trained in the running of small businesses, particularly from a financial viewpoint, to spend up to a week with the customer at his place of business. In that time the banker will study the accounting procedures in use, methods of invoicing, debt collecting, and forecasting the cash flow; will analyse the budgeting, costing, stock control, and assessment of overhead costs. His recommendations, which are confidential, will suggest how the customer can save money, improve the efficiency of his business, or use additional capital.

Business development loan

This type of loan is designed to meet the needs of smaller businesses for extended credit with planned and agreed repayments, which include interest charges. It is available in the range £2,000–£100,000 for expenditure on property purchase or extension, the purchase of plant, machinery, or vehicles, the purchase of a business or professional practice, or by way of additional working capital for a new or existing business, or any other approved project.

A term of 1–5 years is usual, or, in exceptional cases, up to 15 years. The term is phased on an appraisal of the profit flow and expected life of any assets purchased with the proceeds of the loan.

Interest is added to the initial amount of the loan and the total amount repaid in ecual monthly instalments over the agreed period of the loan. Interest is at 7·5 per cent per annum on secured loans and 9 per cent on unsecured loans, the effective rates being 14·6 per cent and 17·5 per cent respectively. In addition, an arrangement fee, not exceeding 1 per cent of the amount of the loan, is payable at the outset to cover the cost of setting up the borrowing agreement.

The borrower is normally required to have a life policy covering the amount of the loan.

Computer services

The bank may sell time on one of its computers to a customer who has no computer of his own, but really has a need for the use of one at certain times. An example might be where the customer is a big employer of a labour force which has to be paid once a week. The computer, given the necessary details, will quickly produce a list showing what each man or woman should get after allowing the deductions for tax, holiday pay, insurance, short-time working, and so on (a service known as the pay-roll service). At every payrun the employer is supplied with a detailed summary of tax, National Health Insurance, stamps, graduated pension, and all allowances and deductions applied in that payrun.

Other possible uses might be to analyse the results of an advertising campaign, or to arrive at the best use of farmland. Stockbrokers and building societies find a use for computer services.

Such services may be made available through a subsidiary company of the bank.

Dollar certificate of deposit

Negotiable certificates of deposit were issued by American banks some years ago. The certificate is evidence of the deposit with the bank of a sum of dollars for a specified time at a fixed rate of interest. It differs from the deposit book or statement in that it is a negotiable instrument which can be sold by the depositor at any time he wishes. At the same time the bank is assured of the deposit for the whole of the specified time.

Executor and Trustee business

The clearing banks maintain special trustee branches to handle executor and trustee business. The work consists of handling the estates of deceased persons, agreeing and paying the capital transfer tax, and supervising and carrying through the administration of trusts and settlements for the benefit of beneficiaries.

The bank may be appointed executor in a will, or it may be approached to act on a death. If a will is in question it should contain a charging clause empowering the bank to pass its fees to the debit of the estate. Without such an express clause the bank could not pass any charge unless it could obtain the permission of all the beneficiaries, for the bank in this business is a trustee, and trustees are not allowed to make a profit from their trust unless so expressly authorized.

The bank charges an acceptance fee on a percentage basis on the value of the estate as ascertained for transfer tax purposes, an annual fee for administration, which may well include the judicious investment of trust funds, and a vacating fee on termination. It will act alone or jointly with a named executor.

Factoring

Factoring has its seeds in the Industrial Revolution, when the textile mills in the north of England, exporting to North America, appointed agents, or 'factors', to sell their product and to get the money for them and send it back. In time these factors became more involved with their clients in America than with their principals in Britain. Commission on sales made became less than profits to be made in providing collection, credit insurance, and other services for American businessmen.

As their profits increased they were able to finance the long collection of money due period involved in the American trade by offering British suppliers payment on export.

During the development of the United States industries the factors specialized more and more in 'home' trade rather than import trade and the business grew, although, in view of its origins, it was still mostly concentrated in the textile trade.

During the last two decades, however, there has been a mounting diversification and a growing volume of industries using the factoring services.

The first factor in Britain started business in 1960. After an uncertain start the major clearing banks became interested and are now all involved either through their own subsidiaries or through associated companies. 'Factoring' is a term sometimes used rather loosely. There are in reality three kinds of factoring services.

Non-recourse factoring

The factor operates by buying from his client, a trading company, their invoiced debts. The client has fulfilled an order, dispatched the goods, and now awaits payment. Some debtors are slow to pay up, some may never pay at all. The credit control in the trading company may be lax. The factor becomes responsible for all credit control, sales accounting, and debt collection. If a debtor fails to pay the factor accepts the loss (he has no recourse against his client). Thus companies are able to sell their outstanding book debts for cash. The selling company receives payment for the debts purchased on a calculated 'average settlement day' instead of haphazard. The company passes its invoices to the factor as soon as it has made them out.

The full factoring service has four elements – the maintenance of the company's sales ledger (including the dispatch of statements to debtors and any follow-up procedures as may prove necessary); credit control over the customers of the company exercised by the factor, who carries out his own credit checks; 100 per cent protection for the client company against bad debts due to insolvency; and collection from the customers of the money they owe, paid across by the factor to the client on the average settlement day (the 'maturity date').

Two further optional services are: (1) payments on account (i.e. ahead of the maturity date) up to a maximum of 80 per cent of factored sales, which enables a client effectively to turn a major proportion of credit sales into cash for more profitable use in the business. For example, extra stocks may be carried, or advantage may be taken of any cash or bulk discounts offered, or seasonal working capital problems can be eased. (2) Sales analysis giving a wide range of information. This assists in market and sales planning.

Factors are usually interested only in a company which has a large turnover, say £100,000 or more. The factor makes a service charge of $\frac{3}{4}$–$2\frac{1}{2}$ per cent of the factored company's turnover, depending on the complexity of the sales ledger to be administered and the likely incidence of bad debts. The optional sales analysis service is evaluated separately depending upon the particular requirements of each client. Clients who choose to take payments on account before the maturity date pay a discount charge on the funds which they actually use. This discount rate is usually a little over current bank lending rates.

The benefits to clients of the full factoring service are considerable. The expense of and management time involved in running a sales ledger is saved; no provision need be made for bad debts; detailed information in relation to a company's progress is made available; cash flow (the money coming in and available for the company's use and to provide profits) in respect of factored sales is accurately established and is often improved; and heavy involvement with slow payers and doubtful customers is avoided. It all adds up to a very much easier life for the company's managers.

Recourse factoring

Recourse factoring is similar to non-recourse factoring with the important exception that the factor does not extend to the supplier any credit protection. All indebtedness is handled by the factor with full recourse to the supplier in the event of the insolvency of the customer.

Both recourse and non-recourse factoring can be either disclosed or undisclosed. The former, which is by far the most common arrangement, involves notification by the supplier to his customers that payment must be made to the factor; the latter involves some form of arrangement that disguises the factor in order that customers believe they are still paying direct to their suppliers. This stemmed from the belief that factoring was not quite reputable, a belief which died when the major clearing banks took an interest, bringing with them backing and respectability. A better understanding now prevails of its value in strengthening the businesses using factoring services. These companies are in a firmer position in respect of both their suppliers and their customers.

Invoice discounting

Invoice discounting is the provision of loans against money yet to come in ('receivables') without any of the service elements of factoring. The purpose of invoice discounting is to enable a supplier to get his money earlier, so as to improve his cash flow, or to use the money for obtaining discounts, or for any other reason useful in his business. He pays an interest rate rather in excess of a bank overdraft rate – indeed, this was precisely the type of business which banks in the old days did not care to support. Now it is seen that the advance is made against the security of certain debtors – those approved by the factor – the criteria being good status rating and regular orders. There is, however, no credit control and none of the other factoring services. In fact, invoice discounting is really lending pure and simple, and strictly should not be described as factoring at all.

Invoice discounting is undisclosed, the supplier's customers knowing nothing of the arrangement.

Export factoring

Export factoring provides for British short-term exporters all those services which are available in the domestic market, plus the ability to invoice their customers in their own currencies. The factor looks after the exchange risks and the collection from the customers overseas. The factor's client enjoys an immediate sterling equivalent, has no problems dealing with difficult payers in a foreign language, and is not concerned with fluctuating exchange values between date of invoice and date of payment. Customer collections are made by local staff in the factor's own office, or through correspondence factors. Where the factor has his own overseas offices it is possible for the client company to arrange for factoring services to be provided for its overseas sales subsidiaries by the overseas offices of the factor.

A few of these factors are members of the British Export Houses Association (BEHA), which includes also confirming houses and finance houses interested in export finance. A recent development has been the establishment of the Association of British Factors, the members of which consist of those companies providing full factoring services as their main business, as opposed to those interested only in invoice discounting.

There is little doubt that factoring is here to stay, as a solid administrative and financial support for growing companies. The company using the full range of services regularizes and usually speeds up its cash flow and in place of a wide range of assorted customers has only one undoubted debtor – the factor. Services based on advanced and sophisticated computer systems developed for sales accounting and credit control have now been in use for many years with the result that many well-known companies are making use of factoring, both for their home and export sales.*

Farm development loan

This type of loan is available to sound, practical farmers for such purposes as purchase of stock, machinery and plant, and farm improvements.

*This section is largely based on a paper by Mr R. A. Pilcher, Managing Director of Credit Factoring International, Ltd.

The loans are available for amounts up to £50,000. Interest is charged on the full amount of the loan for its full term, loan and interest being repayable in equal monthly instalments up to a period of five years, or, exceptionally, seven years. The borrowing term will be fixed to take account of the expected life of any machinery and plant purchased with the proceeds of the loan. The lending bank will require a clear farm business plan and certain related information. Typical interest rates would be 7·5 per cent per annum for a secured loan and 8·5 per cent for an unsecured loan, giving effective rates of 14·2 per cent and 16 per cent respectively.

Hire purchase

All clearing banks now have subsidiaries or linked companies which deal in hire purchase and the banking branches will put business their way when they can.

The investment by the clearing banks in hire-purchase finance companies has led to new forms of lending. Normal instalment finance was largely provided for the private consumer and covered such goods as cars and commercial vehicles, household and other goods. Relatively little effort was made to develop the industrial and commercial business. The banks, through their subsidiary and associated companies, have met the diverse needs of modern business enterprises by introducing factoring, contract hire, and leasing. These facilities are available not only for the banks' own customers but through their hire-purchase connections for many who have no other link with the bank.

Leasing contracts have proved acceptable to industrial and commercial customers. A company may need expensive capital equipment which it cannot really afford to buy without causing an excessive drain in its working capital. This difficulty can be overcome if a finance company buys the equipment and then leases it to the company. Leasing contracts may also carry taxation advantages for the company (see p. 130).

Income tax management

The bank's income tax department will handle the tax affairs of any private customer, and for this purpose may be supplied with duplicate copies of the customer's account by the banking branch. The work consists of preparing the customer's annual statement of income and outgoings, claiming allowances, and generally seeing that the customer pays no more tax than necessary, and claiming any rebate to which he may be entitled. The income tax department will also advise on how the customer's affairs should be arranged in order to minimize tax, possibly through setting up trusts for the benefit of children, or in other ways.

Insurance

The bank's insurance department will arrange cover for almost any contingency. The most usual requests are for marine insurance, fire insurance, comprehensive house insurance, car insurance, goods in transit, and holidays abroad. The latter would cover insurance against the risk of air travel, loss of baggage or personal effects, illness while abroad, personal injury, and extension of car insurance to named countries. The department will advise on any travel restrictions or health requirements in the countries to be visited. It also handles life assurance and annuities.

The bank does not act as a principal in this business, but deals with Lloyd's and other brokers, obtaining the best rate possible. A big advantage for customers of insurance cover effected through a bank is the complete reliability of that cover. There have been many examples of the failure of cut-rate insurance concerns, underlining the desirability of placing one's premium only with a reputable company.

The Midland Bank not only has an insurance department but also owns, through an intermediary, a firm of Lloyd's brokers. Barclays Bank successfully applied in March 1976 to transact business at Lloyd's, and since then Barclays Brokers International have placed business, originating from many countries, direct with Lloyd's underwriters. They also, of course, place Barclay's own in-house insurance business similarly.

Investment management

The bank's investment department will manage the portfolios of customers, attending to registrations, rights issues, or bonus issues. The investments are transferred into the bank's name and thereafter the bank will collect dividends and interest, crediting them to the customer's account, review the securities from time to time, make any sales or purchases as seem desirable and maintain a valuation of the portfolio. Any changes made may be with prior consultation with, and approval of the customer, or entirely at the bank's discretion. If the customer is working or spending much time abroad, or if he is unskilled in investment, or uninterested he will probably find it convenient to leave matters entirely in the hands of the bank.

The bank charges an annual fee, based upon the market value of the portfolio, for this service.

Leasing – see p. 130.

Merchant bank services

Of recent years the clearing banks have no longer been content to leave to the merchant banks that business in which they had always traditionally excelled. Instead, the clearing banks formed alliances with an existing merchant bank, or used one of their subsidiaries for merchant bank activities, and now are able to offer many new services. A complete registration service is provided for companies, local authorities, and public boards. Modern computer techniques are employed. A Registrar's and New Issues Department acts as receiving banker for public issues, offers for sale, rights issues, and local authority bonds. It will deal with capitalization issues, and advise and represent companies in mergers, amalgamations, and takeovers. It will manage investment of pension and similar funds, whatever their size or diversity.

Purchase or sale of stocks and shares

The banker may be given a specific order by his customer, or he may be asked for advice as to the investment of a sum of money. In the first case he will transmit his customer's instructions by telephone to his broker, confirming the order in writing on the same day. Particular care is required in transmitting the order to the broker correctly. Any limits set down by the customer must be obeyed, any conditions linking one purchase with another sale scrupulously noted. The banker takes one-quarter of the broker's commission for this service.

Where he is asked for advice as to investment, he will not himself give advice, but will pass the request on to his broker for his recommendations. At the same time he must give the broker some idea of the circumstances of his customer, whether he is looking principally for security, or is willing to take some degree of risk in the hope of capital appreciation. He will inform the broker of any existing investments which his customer has already made, and whether the sum in question is to be invested in one amount, or spread over a number of stocks and shares.

When the recommendations are to hand the banker will pass the information to the customer, so that the latter may make the actual choice.

Sterling certificates of deposit

Certificates of deposit were first issued in dollars by American banks, but sterling certificates of deposit were issued by British banks from the end of 1968. Certificates are fully negotiable bearer documents transferable by delivery and therefore have to be lodged with an authorized depositary after issue. (Authorized depositaries are banks, members of the London Stock Exchange, certain specialist financial institutions, and solicitors practising in the United Kingdom.)

Certificates are issued by British banks for a minimum period of three months, up to a maximum period of five years, in denominations of £50,000 to £500,000. A market in them is provided by the discount houses.

Foreign services

Bills for collection

Where the bank's customer is an exporter, he is dispatching goods to a buyer abroad. Usually the exporter will draw a bill of exchange at a term on the importer, and ask his bank to collect the proceeds. The bank sends the bill to its agent in the foreign town where the importer lives, and has the bill presented for acceptance, and at the end of the term, for payment. It then brings back the proceeds, converts them into sterling, and credits the customer's account.

There are many variations on this. The customer may himself get the bill accepted by the importer through the post, and then later bring it to the bank, with the documents of title to the goods attached, for presentation for payment. If a bill has such documents attached it is called a documentary bill, if not, a clean bill. The customer must instruct the bank whether documents are to be released against acceptance by the importer (D/A) or only against payment (D/P).

The bank's remuneration for this service is a small percentage charge on the total sum involved, plus costs of mail or other transmission charges.

Bills for negotiation

The customer may not wish to wait for the proceeds of a collection to reach his account. As an alternative he may ask his bank to negotiate the bill, i.e. he sells the bill to the bank.

If the bank agrees to buy the bill it will pay the customer the face value of the bill, less discount. This part of the procedure is exactly the same as if the bank were discounting a bill, but as far as foreign bills are concerned the practice is termed 'negotiation'. In many cases, of course, the bill will be drawn in a foreign currency.

The banker is naturally concerned to safeguard his position if the bill should be dishonoured on presentation, and therefore he negotiates 'with recourse'. This means that the customer agrees to pay the banker if the acceptor does not. The banker may ask for security to be deposited to back up the customer's promise, and if the bill is a documentary bill the banker will certainly regard the documents as part of his security. Once he has bought the bill he is collecting the proceeds on his own behalf.

Documentary credit

An exporter of goods abroad will send his goods by sea, receiving in exchange a bill of lading from the ship's master. He will make out an invoice showing the cost, and describing and specifying the goods. He will insure them against the perils of the journey. The bill of lading, the insurance policy, and the invoice are the relevant documents. These have to be conveyed to the importer, who must have the bill of lading before he can claim the goods at the port of entry. (Other documents may be called for by the importer, but the three mentioned are the essential ones.)

Both parties have their problems. The exporter does not want to part with the documents of title (i.e. lose control of the goods) until he has been paid for them. The importer does not want to pay until he has had a chance to look at the documents to make sure that the description, cost, and quantity of the goods are in agreement with the contract between the parties.

The banker solves the difficulty by offering a documentary credit.

The exporter must stipulate in the contract how payment is to be made. If he makes it a condition that payment be by documentary credit, the importer, assuming he agrees, will instruct his bank to open a documentary credit in favour of the exporter. In his instructions to his bank he must list all the details which must be shown on the documents which he requires the exporter to present before he is given payment.

The importer's bank will choose a correspondent bank – a bank to act as its agent – in the exporter's country and will send to it a notification of the opening of a documentary credit in favour of the exporter. The agent bank will forward this to him, keeping a copy. When doing this it may add its confirmation, i.e. its own undertaking, that the provisions for payment against the documents will be duly fulfilled (a confirmed credit).

The credit may also be revocable or irrevocable. Once the latter has been opened, it cannot have any of its terms altered without the agreement of all parties.

Once the exporter has received this notification, he can feel easy in his mind that he is going to be paid, and will prepare his goods for dispatch. The credit should be opened for a period of time which will give the exporter adequate opportunity to ship the goods, plus a margin for unforeseen delays. It will, however, name a certain date as the last day on which payment can be made.

Before this day the exporter ships the goods and presents the documents of title to the agent bank for payment. That bank checks the documents carefully against the conditions of the credit and if all is in order, pays the exporter.

The agent bank forwards the documents, which are all in duplicate, by two separate air mails (a precaution against the accidental loss of one set), and debits the importer's bank with the cost plus its charges. There will be an extra charge if it has itself confirmed the credit.

The importer's bank checks the documents again, refunds the agent bank, sends the documents to the importer, and debits the importer's account, adding its own charges.

Both parties are satisfied. The exporter receives prompt payment and the importer knows that the documents of title have been subjected to two expert scrutinies.

There are many variations of the documentary credit. The main one used in international trade is, however, the confirmed irrevocable documentary credit.

Eurocheque scheme

Under this scheme holders of cheque cards or Barclaycards can cash their personal cheques abroad for travel expenditure only. A limit of £500 per journey is imposed. The extension of the use of the cheque card abroad relates only to the encashment of individual cheques, normally up to £50 at any one time, at banks participating in the scheme (nearly all European banks) and does not cover payments to hotels, restaurants, or shops. Payment will be made in the currency of the country. Any surplus foreign currency still in the hands of the traveller on his return home must be exchanged for sterling at his own bank.

Although these Eurocheque cards cannot be used at present to guarantee the payment of cheques in continental stores or hotels as in this country, British banks are currently considering whether they wish to become more fully involved (see p. 287).

Foreign currency

Any branch bank will obtain foreign notes and coin needed for a holiday, or buy foreign notes and coin left over after a holiday. These are comparatively small amounts. Foreign currency required to settle trading transactions will usually involve larger sums. At any time the Bank of England may have imposed controls on the amount of foreign currency which may be bought, and permission may have to be sought for larger amounts. The bank will make the application on behalf of its customer.

Not all branches keep stocks of foreign currencies, although they can get them very quickly, but certain of the larger ones maintain foreign tills in the better-known currencies. Branches at airports and main railway stations are also prepared to deal in currency.

The bank remunerates itself by a commission which is built in to the rate of exchange quoted. Such rates will probably be the best obtainable and will certainly be very much better than one could obtain, say, on a cross-channel ferry.

Forward exchange

A forward exchange contract is a way to guard against fluctuations in the exchange rate between two given dates.

An importer who has to pay in currency for the goods he is getting may buy the currency in advance through his bank. An exporter, who has to quote the price of his goods in a foreign currency, needs to be sure that when the time comes for him to receive payment, the sterling proceeds will cover his cost of production and his profit figure. He can guard against a possible fall in the value of sterling, as measured in terms of the foreign currency, by selling the foreign currency in advance to his bank.

In either case the bank commits itself to a deal at an agreed rate of exchange when the time comes, irrespective of how the actual rates may have moved in the interval. The bank will cover itself by 'matching' the contract to sell with another one to buy, and vice versa.

Forward exchange rates are quoted in terms of premiums and discounts on the spot rates (the rates now). For currency rates (i.e. so many units of foreign currency to the pound sterling) a premium is under spot (the rate is lower than the spot rate. The currency at a premium is dearer and so fewer units of it will be received for £1.) Conversely, a discount is over spot. Forward rates may be a little dearer or a little cheaper than spot rates, depending on supply and demand. Forward rates are quoted for 1, 2, and 3 months forward.

An outright forward contract specifies a date for completion, but if a person knows approximately but not exactly when he will want to sell foreign currency or buy it he can ask the bank for an option forward contract. This will give a certain choice to the customer. He still has to complete the contract, but he can do it any time he likes between two fixed dates.

In the major trading currencies such as US dollars, Deutschemarks, and French francs forward exchange cover may be obtained for periods of up to five years and even beyond. In other, less important, currencies cover may be restricted to a maximum of one year, or not obtainable at all. At any time facilities for cover in any currency may be suspended or curtailed by exchange control regulations, but this will not affect existing contracts.

International money order

In February 1974 Barclays Bank announced an improvement in its overseas services available to British customers – the international money order. The advantage of this over bank drafts and mail transfer, which it will supplement or replace, is that customers will be able to send sums to the recipient direct rather than to a specific branch of a specific bank. The international money orders can be purchased for cash from any Barclays branch and cashed at most banks throughout the world.

The amount that can be sent is limited to £500 or $1,000 and there is a 40p charge on purchase. Encashing banks may also make a charge.

Letter of Credit

A customer proposing to stay abroad for a period may ask his bank to arrange for a letter of credit so that he may always be sure of obtaining money abroad, without having to carry it about with him. The bank will inquire the name of the foreign town where drawing facilities are required, and the total amount required over the period in question. It will then debit the customer's account in advance and write to a correspondent bank or agent authorizing him to cash on demand any cheques or drafts drawn by the beneficiary, charging the sums to the debit of the issuing bank. A specimen of the customer's signature is sent to the agent bank. The letter of credit is given to the customer who must present it to the agent bank each time he wants any money, so that a note of the amount he has had may be written on the back.

Where only one agent is used the letter of credit is sometimes called a direct letter of credit. If the customer is travelling about it will not be possible to send individual letters to all the agents he may wish to use. A circular or world-wide letter of credit is then issued to the customer which will be available at the offices of any agent of the issuing bank in any country in the world, and the customer is supplied also with a letter of indication having a specimen of his signature. He must use this letter, which can be printed in several languages, to identify himself when he wishes to draw money.

If the total sum involved is over a certain amount, at present £500, it will be necessary for the Bank of England's prior approval to be obtained before the letter of credit is issued.

Letters of credit are still found, but they have been superseded by travel cheques for the ordinary holiday traveller. Another alternative is to use the Eurocheque scheme.

Letter of introduction

A customer travelling abroad or emigrating may be recommended by letter of introduction from the customer's bank to agent banks abroad. The issuing bank will explain the purpose and nature of the customer's visit and request the agent bank to assist him wherever possible. This assistance may take the form of temporary finance; sometimes the agent bank can assist the customer to find employment. Where the customer is an important person the agent bank may appoint an officer to meet him and to introduce him to leading figures in the neighbourhood.

Mail and cable transfers

A customer wishing to make a payment to a person abroad may instruct his bank to transmit equivalent sterling from his account to a foreign bank which will notify the beneficiary, who can then go in and get the sum authorized, in the currency of the country. Normally this advice will be sent by mail, but in cases of urgency a cable will be sent. The customer pays a commission plus mail or cable costs in addition to the sum sent out. He can stipulate that all charges are for the account of the payee, in which case they will be deducted from the money paid out.

The foreign bank will be remunerated by a credit to the sterling account which it keeps with the head office in London of the customer's bank.

Passport service

The bank will obtain or renew a passport for a customer wishing to travel abroad. This entails getting the customer to complete and sign an application form, witnessing the customer's signature, and certifying on one of the two passport photographs supplied that it is a true likeness of the customer. In verifying the application and vouching for the applicant as a fit and proper person to receive a passport, the bank must speak from personal knowledge of the customer.

The complete application form, the photographs, and the old passport, and, if the application is the first one, the birth certificate of the customer, are sent to the Passport Office, with the appropriate fee. The passport is obtained in due course and sent to the customer.

Travel cheques

Travel cheques are issued in sterling or in certain currencies by banks to their customers wishing to travel abroad. In sterling they can be obtained in denominations of £2, £5, £10,

£20, and £50. Each cheque has a space for the customer to sign immediately he gets the cheques, and another space for him to sign in the presence of the paying agent at the time he is cashing the cheque. In this way he identifies himself as the correct and proper person to receive the money. The cheques take the form of drafts drawn on the head office of the issuing bank. The customer pays for them, in full, plus the bank's commission, when he is issued with them, and must then keep them in a safe place. If he loses them or has them stolen through no fault of his own the bank when notified will replace them free or send a mail or cable remittance for an equivalent amount to the foreign town where the customer happens to be.

Travel cheques can be used in shops and hotels at home and abroad. If sterling travel cheques are cashed in a foreign bank payment will be made in the currency of the country. It is very much better for the traveller to take currency travel cheques, for the rate of exchange will be calculated by his British bank and is likely to be more favourable to him than a series of rates calculated by various foreign banks one at a time as the travel cheques are cashed.

Most banks can arrange for the supply of travel cheques in most currencies. The American Express, for example, offer travel cheques expressed in United States or Canadian dollars, French or Swiss francs, Deutschemarks, and Japanese yen. Cooks have travel cheques in United States dollars, the French Swiss and German currencies, and in pesetas.

These foreign currency travel cheques do have one drawback, however. The issuing banks may not offer automatic reimbursement for lost cheques.

Money transmission

Collection of cheques

This is one of the three basic services and needs little description. The customer receives cheques from his debtors on which his name appears as payee. He pays these into his bank either over the counter or through the post, making out a credit slip. A duplicate credit slip is returned to him as a receipt. The cheques are then presented through the Clearing House to the payee banker in the manner already described. The amounts of the cheques are credited to the customer's account on the same day that he pays them in, but he should not draw against them before they are cleared unless he has an arrangement with the bank, whether express or implied, that he may do so.

Direct debiting

A customer making periodical payments to a building society may send a cheque through the post each time, make a personal payment at the local office each time, or give his bank a standing order. A logical development has been to allow the creditor to make a direct claim on the customer's account, to be paid by the bank on each occasion. This saves time and money, and is very suitable for large creditors such as finance houses, insurance companies, and building societies. The customer will have to approve this arrangement before any transfers are made, and he must authorize his banker to meet the claims, for the banker cannot pay away his customer's money without his authority. Normally this authority takes the form of a properly completed cheque, but in this case a single signed form (provided by the creditor) will suffice to authorize the regular payments until further notice.

Emergency payments

Circumstances may arise whereby a customer urgently wishes a sum of money to be paid out in a distant town as soon as possible. An example might be where a weekly salaries and wages cheque sent out from a head office in London by post has failed to reach a factory in the provinces, so that they cannot take it to their local branch.

In such a case the payment would be authorized by telephone from the company's London bank. Banks have a code system whereby they can identify calls between branches as genuine.

Where a payment is required at another bank, the request will have to go through both head offices, because each bank has its own code. The customer's bank will therefore telephone a coded message to its head office, where a typed request will be prepared, signed by authorized officers. The letter is taken to the head office of the paying bank, who have copies of all signatures of all signing officials of all head office banks, the signatures are checked, and a coded telephone call is then made to the paying branch.

Standing orders

Customers having regular payments to make, such as mortgage instalments, club subscriptions, or monthly rate instalments, may give details to the bank and authorize it to make the payments on their behalf, as and when they fall due. The customer must see that on the due date there is enough money on the account to meet the transfer, and if the customer is persistently careless in this respect the bank will be justified in notifying him that it has cancelled his standing order and that in future he should make his own arrangements to deal with the matter.

Savings

Budget scheme

This scheme allows a customer to even out the regular payments which he has to make. He gives the details of his usual outgoings to the bank, who total the annual cost, open a budget account for the customer, and issue him with a special budget account cheque book. The customer should remember in his list to cover everything and a suggested series of headings might be rates; electricity; gas; telephone; fuel; life, house, and car insurance; car and television licences;

season ticket; school fees; clothing; holidays; subscriptions; car maintenance and depreciation; and Christmas expenses.

Thereafter the bank will debit the customer's ordinary current account and credit the budget account with a monthly sum which will be one-twelfth of the annual total. Sometimes the budget account will be in credit, sometimes in debt.

The service costs a few pounds each year. It is essential that the customer, paying his bills from his budget account cheque book, is not tempted to draw on it for things not included in the original list.

Savings Accounts

Most banks used to supply small metal safes with an inbuilt lock and a slot for coins and notes. These were originally designed to encourage thrift and to nurture a link with the bank which would, hopefully, end in the opening of a current account. When the safe was full it was taken to the bank and opened by a cashier. The contents were credited to the individual's savings account.

These 'home safes' have proved rather wasteful of a cashier's time, and not all that productive in new current accounts. They are not now, therefore, pressed quite so strongly, although lately some new and attractive variants of the old home safe have been produced.

Savings Accounts carry interest. Withdrawals may be made at any time.

Unit trusts

Unit trusts on sale through the banks may be those where the trustees are the bank concerned and the managers who administer the trust and invest the money are a subsidiary company of the bank. Some clearing banks have partnered a merchant bank who runs the trust, the clearing bank having the advantage that its branch network provides a country-wide series of selling points for the sub-units of the trust.

Unit trusts vary widely in the type of shares included in the

share portfolio and in the proportion of money invested in
fixed-interest stocks or gilt-edged, as opposed to shares. Unit
trusts designed to sell to the customers of large clearing
banks must have safety of capital as their prime objective, and
this must mean that such unit trusts will never be in the top
scorers of the unit trust league table. Nevertheless, they can
be a very suitable investment for people of limited means
who cannot afford to accept even a small degree of risk.
Such people can be absolutely sure that the strict control
exercised over all unit trusts by the Department of Trade,
coupled with the name and reputation of the bank, mean
that their unit trust investment will be handled with scrupu-
lous care and absolute honesty.

Services of place or time

Cash dispenser

A bank opening an account for a customer undertakes to
repay on demand. Certain legal limitations have been placed
on the repayment. It must be sought at the branch where the
account is, and during business hours.

The banks are closed at what the business community
regards as an early hour. Sometimes they have fixed their
closing time at 3 p.m. and sometimes at 3.30 p.m. This is
because there is a lot of work to do after the bank is shut to
the public. Unlike other business organizations, the banks
have to complete one day's work the same day. If they kept
open until 6 p.m. they would please their customers, but
rapidly lose their staff, who would be going home between
8 p.m. and 9 p.m. They have experimented with one late
night a week in certain areas.*

One help in this situation has been the most useful cash
dispenser. There are different designs of this machine, but
basically it consists of a safe let into the outer wall of the
bank, containing packets of £10 in £1 notes. The customer is
issued with a cash card having punched holes which is fed
into the machine for electronic checking. If this is satis-

* See p. 401.

factory the customer is then given access to a keyboard of ten numbered buttons on which he taps out his personal code number. The machine will then deliver the £10 packet. It retains the cash card, which initiates a debit to the customer's account and is then returned to him for further use.

More recent developments are the cash dispenser inside the branch, to supplement the cashiers' work, a computerized cash dispenser called 'Cashpoint', which is capable of dispensing variable amounts of cash, and 'Servicetill'. Servicetill dispenses cash and can tell customers what their balances are. Customers can also order cheque books and statements through this machine, which takes a Servicecard bearing a magnetized strip. This is returned to the customer at the time of operation. The service is controlled by a personal credit limit contained in the strip, arranged with the customer at the time of issue. Up to £100 can be issued at any one time in varying denominations of £1 and £5 notes.

The banks are installing these handy gadgets as fast as the makers can produce them.

Credit established

A customer who may wish to draw money at a branch other than the one where he keeps his account may, of course, use his cheque card, which is limited to £50 a time. If, however, he anticipates requiring more than this, perhaps while he is on a fortnight's holiday, he may arrange with his branch to have money made available for him at the bank's branch in the town where he is going to be, or, if the bank does not have a branch there, at the branch of another bank.

His own branch will need to know the dates between which he will be drawing, the amount which he expects to want, and the town where he wants it. The account-holding branch will then send these details, together with a specimen signature of the customer, to the branch bank which is going to pay the cheques, and the customer can then draw his money there.

Drive-in bank

A branch office having a cashier so posted that he/she may pay money to, or receive money from, a customer through the window of the customer's car. Like so many other ideas, this was American in origin, and it has never really caught on in the UK.

A similar system may be found where the bank is on the first floor of a building (having perhaps rented out the ground floor). A customer wishing only to cash a cheque or pay in does not need to climb the stairs (or go up the escalator) if a booth is provided having a means of conveying a credit and money or cheques up to the counter and down again. Vision and sound between customer and cashier are provided by a closed-circuit television link.

Mobile bank

A mobile bank is a motorized caravan fitted out as a small bank, which can tour outlying districts on one or more days a week, or go to fairs or agricultural shows. There is usually a staff of two to four who provide a counter service.

In a similar category are the fixed but temporary bank stands erected during exhibitions such as the Ideal Homes, Camping, or Do-it-Yourself exhibitions at Earls Court and Olympia.

Night safes

A customer wishing to pay in regularly at a time when the bank is shut may be offered a night safe wallet. The service is particularly suitable for a shop-keeper wishing to bank his day's takings rather than leave them in the shop overnight or take them home. He puts his credit and the cash in the leather wallet supplied, locks it, and then 'posts' it down a chute through the bank's exterior wall into the bank's night safe. The entrance to the chute has a locked cover to prevent undesirable items being inserted, but the customer has a key to this.

In the morning the bank staff clear all the wallets out of the night safe and list them in the night safe record book. Wallets are of two kinds, one to be opened by the bank staff and the proceeds credited to the customer's account; the other to be handed back to the customer, or his agent, during banking hours, because he prefers to open his wallet and then pay in himself.

The customer who can combine this service with the use of a cash dispenser can make an entirely automatic use of his bank.

Special clearance

A customer who pays in a cheque for collection will normally get it cleared in 3–5 days. However, if he is in a hurry to know whether a particular cheque is paid he can find out by paying it in separately, marking the credit boldly at the top 'Special Clearance'. The bank will then present the cheque directly by first-class post to the paying banker, telephoning next morning to enquire as to the fate. The result is then telephoned to the customer, who is this way learns the fate of the cheque the next day. If the paying bank is within messenger range the cheque can be presented the same day.

A charge of 50p–£1 is made for special clearance by post, or more if a bank or district messenger is used.

Credits may also be dealt with in a similar way. In the absence of postal delays or other exceptional circumstances, credits should reach their destination on the second business day after receipt. In case of need, however, a credit can be sent direct to the recipient's bank, so that it arrives earlier than it would through the clearing. A special fee of 50p is payable for this service.

Status services

Banker's draft

A banker's draft is an instrument rather similar to a cheque, but instead of being drawn by a customer on his banker, a banker's draft is drawn by a branch of the bank on its head office. As it is certain to be paid on presentation, it commands much greater acceptability than an ordinary cheque. A person completing the purchase of land, or wishing to pay for a car, or engaged in any transaction where the other party refuses to accept his cheque, may ask his banker for a draft, authorizing him at the same time to debit his current account accordingly. Banker's drafts are usually issued for approved customers without charge.

For sums up to £50 a customer's cheque backed by a cheque card is acceptable: bankers' drafts are usually seen for larger figures.

Cheque card

A cheque card is a piece of plastic about 85 mm by 54 mm bearing an amount of £50, the name of the bank, the name and signature of the customer, his code number, the card number and the expiry date. It is renewed yearly.

The issuing bank undertakes that any cheque not exceeding £50 will be honoured as long as the cheque has been signed in the presence of the payee, is drawn on a bank cheque form whose code number agrees with the code number on the card, and is authenticated by a signature which agrees with the specimen signature on the card. The cheque must be drawn before the expiry date of the card, and the card number must be written on the reverse of the cheque.

In this way the customer may pay hotel bills (or the first £50 of them) or purchase goods in shops, without using cash. The card will also allow a customer to withdraw up to £50 in any major British or Irish bank.

Cheque cards should be kept separate from the cheque

book. Where both are lost or stolen together fraud is almost inevitable. There is always a steady loss to the banks through cheque frauds. Organized criminals include middlemen acting as distributors of stolen cheque books and bank cards to gangs which tour the country passing £50 cheques at bank counters, shops, and hotels.

Customers using cheque cards are not supposed to use them for more than one amount of up to £50 in any one transaction. This condition is stated on the back of the card. If they do, the bank must pay the cheques if they comply with all the conditions, but it can withdraw its customer's cheque card, or, if he will not part with it, refuse to issue any further cheque books to that customer.*

Credit cards

Credit cards are similar in size and general appearance to cash cards, and contain similar details. The best known cards in this country are Barclaycard, Access, Diners Club, and American Express. Barclaycard doubles up also as a cheque card. With the credit card, goods can be bought in a shop, petrol at a service station, hotel bills paid, air fares met, in many parts of the world. The retailer sends in his account to the card company, which sends monthly statements out to each cardholder. Interest at $1\frac{3}{4}$ per cent per month starts to run between 25 and 60 days after the statement is sent out. Diners and American Express charge an entrance fee, but allow unlimited purchases, to be paid for on receipt of the account (unless a loan is agreed). Access and Barclaycard have no entrance fee, but impose a credit limit of £100 to £1,000.

Credit cards have been criticized for making borrowing too easy. When they are used to create or stimulate a burst of consumer spending there can be no doubt that they are inflationary. Some of the advertising has seemed to suggest that luxury goods can be bought right away, while not emphasizing that in the end they have got to be paid for – credit cards make most profit for their sponsors when the card

See p. 401. *

carrier is permanently in debt. On the other hand, there can be no element of inflation when the cards are used instead of cheques for a necessary purchase which is going to be made in any case. Used thus they are a convenience. However, credit cards cannot make more than a very small difference to prices as a whole, because in spite of the fact that there are nearly 7 million cardholders in the UK they account for a very small percentage of what people spend (one estimate puts it at less than 2 per cent).*

In December 1973 the Chancellor limited the cash withdrawal facilities to £30 at one time, until further notice. Repayments of amounts outstanding were to be at a minimum of 15 per cent of the balance, or £6, whichever was the greater, each month.

Guarantees and indemnities

A customer who has lost a share certificate may obtain a duplicate certificate from the company concerned, but it will want a banker to add his guarantee to the application, as a check on the genuineness of the request.

Similarly, a customer wishing to make application for the payment of money to him from a deceased person's estate may request the banker's assistance. This would arise where the estate is too small to attract estate duty and therefore no probate or letters of administration have been applied for. Without such authority, however, no money can be paid over, however small the sum, unless a banker certifies that the facts are as stated and that the application is a genuine one.

In these cases a banker covers himself against the (very unlikely) risk of loss by taking a counter-indemnity from his customer.

Performance bond

A customer engaged in the building or construction industry may tender for a contract and be asked to supply a perform-

* See p. 402.

ance bond. Such a requirement is often found in contracts for work overseas. The authority inviting tenders is really asking to be reassured that the builder or contractor who gets the job will be able to finish it, and won't go bankrupt or into liquidation half way through.

The bank, if satisfied that its customer is technically capable of handling the job, and financially strong enough to see it through, will issue a bond for due performance. This will enable the customer's tender to get to the stage where it will be considered.

The bank takes a counter-indemnity from the customer to cover its own position.

Status inquiries

The bank will answer status inquiries on its customer and will make similar inquiries about other people's financial position on his behalf. For exporters it will obtain reports on traders abroad (and on markets in particular goods).

To preserve the secrecy about the customer's affairs which banks must maintain, certain rules have to be made. The bank will only answer inquiries which are put to it by other banks or reputable trade organizations and it will only answer to such groups. It will not answer private inquiries, nor disclose addresses. Recent legislation has imposed a duty on a creditor or hirer to disclose on request the name and address of the credit reference agency consulted, and a subsequent duty on the credit reference agency to furnish the consumer with a copy of the file relating to him kept by the agency. It does not appear, however, that a bank comes within the definition of a 'credit reference agency', and therefore it seems that the present system whereby one bank answers in confidence to another will continue. The practice of giving a confidential report on a customer to one of the organizations established for the protection of trade, however, will have to stop.

The replies to all inquiries must be carefully considered

and tactfully phrased. If a favourable reply cannot be given a form of words must be used which conveys the right impression, but does not harm the customer's credit.

When the customer has requested that an inquiry shall be made he must give the name, address, and bank account of the person or company to be inquired about, and the amount and purpose of the inquiry, e.g. 'whether good for £500 in the normal course of business over twenty-four months'; 'whether good for £250 in one sum'; 'whether suitable as a tenant paying £14 per week'.

Recently some attention has been focused on the banks' procedures. In the course of business certain inquiries may be received, and answered, for customers who do not know that an inquiry has been made. The banks have always considered that it is to the benefit of the customer to have a reference given when properly requested on a business matter, and that the customer gives his implied authority to what is a normal banking custom by the act of opening his account. To request his permission before answering each inquiry, as was thought desirable in the Report of the Committee on Privacy (July 1972), would add anything up to a week or even more to the time required before the inquirer got an answer, besides adding to the work and expense involved.

Other cases concerned private inquiry agents, one of whom said in court that he could build up a complete financial dossier of any person by consulting existing records and telephoning his bank, pretending to be another branch making the inquiry. It may be that inexperienced clerks have been tricked in this way, and the remedy is to ask the inquiring 'branch' for the code number.

Another person said he could get anyone's balance for £10. There is no evidence that any bank clerk has been bribed to disclose information. Every clerk on joining the bank signs an oath of secrecy, and if it were found that any clerk had broken this oath he would be dismissed.

Charges for services

All services have to be paid for, and many have been the devices and names under which a charge has been made. In many of the services described above the bank will make a charge for the particular service at the time the service is given. Examples are mail or cable transfer, obtaining a passport, giving a performance bond. Other services such as a night safe wallet attract a specific quarterly, half-yearly, or annual charge. Other services are not directly charged for at all. Examples are use of the cash dispenser, use of a cheque card, status inquiry, safe custody. These are the privileges of the current account holder (who gets paid no interest) and are not available to a deposit or savings deposit account holder (who gets paid interest). For these and other benefits the current account holder pays, or may pay, a commission charge.

Looking back now, it can be seen that banking before the war offered a comparatively simple life. In those days branch managers scanned the accounts of their customers four times a year and 'estimated' a charge. Sums of 2s. 6d, 5s, 7s 6d per quarter were common.

After the war all prices jumped, but the banks made no increase in their commission charges for ten years. In that time their customers had got thoroughly spoilt. When the banks realized that the world was changing into a harder, less friendly place, that staff costs were going rapidly up and would continue to go up, that, in fact, everything was more difficult and more expensive, they addressed themselves to the problem of the commission charges. They realized that until then the good accounts had paid for the unremunerative accounts. Any customer who complained loudly enough had his charge reduced, and if he threatened to take his account away altogether he had the whole of it remitted.

Now a new approach was in the air. Each account must pay for itself, either by keeping a good average credit balance or by paying a proper commission. Each bank now tried to find out first what a current account did cost. No one knew. Various exercises were done, at the end of which most banks thought that 1*s* per entry, whether debit or credit, on the current account should cover them. It became possible to cost an account, allowing at first 1 per cent, later 2 per cent, as a notional credit interest. Managers counted up the number of debit and credit items in an account, kept figures to give an average credit balance, and arrived at a commission charge.

e.g. 128 entries at 1*s*. each   £6. 8. 0
Av. cleared credit balance £420
Interest thereon at 2 per cent for three months   2. 2. 0

Commission charge   £4. 6. 0

At least this had the merit of being related to the work given. A prolific cheque-issuer clearly gave the bank more work than a more modest user.

But the new charges made no allowance for various associated services. Standing orders began to be charged over and above the 1*s* for the account entry. Interview time was talked about. Safe custody charges were in some cases imposed, 1*s* per item per quarter. A bridging loan was a very useful service, but because the period involved was so short the interest gained was small. The arrangement fee made its appearance. The cost of counter service, of providing change, of handling monthly salary lists, was discussed with the larger customers.

The branch manager began to dread the quarterly arithmetic. Then the whole lot went on to the computer, and the process became automatic.

By now the public was thoroughly aroused. The Press, which never took much interest in the rising prices of whisky or cigarettes, united in criticism of banking charges.

At the present time this interest remains unabated. Bank charges are always news. In the meantime we have had decimalization.

We have had (in 1972 and 1973) unusually high interest rates which inflated bank profits to record figures, forcing the banks to rethink their commission charges. One after another they announced terms which effectively allowed nearly all their credit customers to escape all commission charges if they maintained £50 minimum, or £100 average, balance on current account, or some similar formula. At the same time they published tariffs of costs for those who overdrew, specifying the charge per debit item, the notional rate allowed on credit balances, and the maximum charge which the bank would waive each quarter or half year.

This happy stage of affairs continued until 1976 when continuing inflation and increasing costs forced the banks to apply, one after another, to the Incomes and Prices Board for permission to increase their commission charges. When all the dust had settled down a national newspaper was able to publish, in July 1976 the following details:

Co-operative bank

The Co-operative Bank, remains the cheapest and intends keeping its present tariff structure for some time yet. All the customers receive free banking if their accounts remain in credit.

For accounts which become overdrawn the bank charges 4p for each debit entry and 7p for standing orders and direct debits, although the amounts of 25p or less are waived.

Trustee Savings Banks

The Trustee Savings Banks are also cheap. A customer pays nothing on his current account if he keeps a minimum balance of £50 during the six monthly charging period. Should the balance fall below that figure, each debit item attracts a charge of $2\frac{1}{2}$p.

The TSBs do not operate their charging system on the average credit balance principle nor do they allow customers a notional interest offset against the money held in the account.

Williams & Glyn's

Williams & Glyn's is not making any change to its tariff. With a quarterly rather than a six-month charging period, customers receive free banking if they simply stay in credit. Should the account become overdrawn, a charge of 6p is made for each standing order or direct debit, 8p for each other entry (including credits), less notional interest of 5 per cent a year on the average daily credit balance offset against any charges incurred.

Midland

Midland will now allow free banking if customers maintain a minimum credit balance of £50 where previously the criteria for the absence of charges were either if the account always remained in credit or if the average credit balance was £50 or more over the six months. For those accounts not meeting the new minimum £50 balance charges for debit items go up from 7p each to 9p.

The rebate of 5 per cent a year on any money kept in the account and the absence of the charge for credit items remains unchanged. Charges of 25p or less will be waived.

Lloyds

Personal customers of Lloyds will have free banking if their cleared credit balances in the current accounts average £150 or more over the half year.

Those that do not reach the minimum requirement will be charged 9p per debit item, and the total charge will be reduced by an allowance of 4 per cent on the value of any money kept in the account. Credit entries will continue to be free of charge and service charges under 25p will be waived.

National Westminster

National Westminster is the only London clearing bank not to raise its minimum ledger balance qualification for free banking from £50 nor is the off-set allowance of 5 per cent a year on the total charge being altered. Credit entries also remain free of charge.

But if the balance falls below £50 debit items will be charged at 10p each, not 7p as under the previous tariff.

Barclays

Barclays is lifting the criteria for free banking from an average credit balance of £100 or a minimum of £50 to an average of £200 and a minimum of £100. For those accounts with balances below the minimum the cost to the customer of each cheque entry or standing order goes up from 7p to 10p. The notional interest allowance of 5 per cent on the value of the money in the account remains unchanged.

This mass of detail shows how keen the competition is, and how difficult it can be for any customer to work out where to keep his account at least cost. Here we must remember that the two 'cheap' banks, the Co-operative Bank and the Trustee Savings Bank, do not provide the same range of services as the clearing banks, although, as we have seen, they are working their way towards doing so.*

The banks are right to base their charges on the use made of the account, as measured by the number of entries on it, and they are right to expect professional men earning good salaries, private individuals in comfortable circumstances, and anyone in business, especially limited companies, to pay a fair price for the services they receive. In other walks of business life this happens without comment.

Of course, many customers paid less than the full rate anyway. Students' accounts are well publicized as being kept free, by all banks. This reflects a hope that the student will later become a man with a good income, and that he

See p. 403. *

will always keep his account with the bank which looked after him when he was young and broke, except for his grant.

In fact, there is a lot of truth in this. People do tend to stay with one bank, although to read the press report quoted above one would think that customers were constantly hunting around, moving their accounts here and there in response to every slight financial inducement.

Banks seldom charge other than nominal rates for such customers as nurses, policemen, servicemen, and those engaged in public service of any kind, as long as they stay in credit. If they choose to borrow money that is another matter, especially if they take it without asking.

Big employers have often used their influence to negotiate privileged rates for their staffs with the banks. In many individual cases the banks would hardly charge a widow whose husband, when alive, had been a good customer of the bank, but whose death had left her in reduced circumstances.

Service

'Services' have been discussed. 'Service' is the basis on which all banks stay in business. Good service as a general commodity is becoming rarer and rarer. In the banking world 'service' means answering letters by return, being cheerful and polite on the counter, trying to help in the manager's room, giving respect and fair play because these are the usual standards in banking. 'Service' is not given out of servility, but out of self-respect. 'Service' is answering the branch telephone promptly and pleasantly, 'service' is addressing the customer by name; in a word, 'service' is the relationship between the branch staff and the customer, where the customer is made to feel that the bank manager and his staff are genuinely interested and concerned to be helpful. It is this personal relationship which is at the core of real banking. It is the reason why the National Savings Bank, the Giro, and the money shops can never make anything other than a slight impression on the clearing banks. This atmosphere in a branch bank can be detected instantly. It also embraces the relationship between the senior officers and the junior staff. The tone is set from the top, and goes down to the bottom. The customer responds.

Many years ago a young man went into the suburban branch of a clearing bank with a request for a loan of £100 unsecured to start a holiday camp. After an interview the manager granted the loan. Twenty years later that holiday camp business had grown into a nationally known multi-million pound concern. The valuable account was still kept, at considerable inconvenience, at the suburban branch which originally had the vision and the trust to lend unsecured, to that particular customer.

Another man, a customer of a clearing bank which had some branches in Belgium, was an engineer working in Belgium on the outbreak of war. When the Germans invaded Belgium he was arrested and kept for some time in a foreign nationals camp. Back in this country after the war he was talking to a clerk in the bank.

'Your manager in Antwerp somehow got into the camp and came round asking if there were any Westminster Bank customers there. When I said I was he cashed me a cheque for £20 in Belgian francs which I used to supplement the meagre diet we were on. In 1946 I got a letter from the head office of the bank asking whether it would be convenient if they debited my cheque.' He paused for a moment. 'That's what I call service,' he said.*

Revision Test 10

Put ticks in what you think are the right boxes.

(1) A man on holiday in the north of England was able to draw £30 at a local bank by showing a card. Was it his
  (a) cheque card ☐
  (b) credit card ☐
  (c) cash card ☐

See p. 401. *

298 The Elements of Banking

(2) A bank customer repays his borrowing in equal instalments covering both capital and interest. Has he got
(a) a loan ☐
(b) an overdraft ☐
(c) a personal loan ☐

(3) A bank customer is granted a probate advance. Is he
(a) an administrator ☐
(b) an executor ☐
(c) a trustee ☐

(4) A man opening an account with a bank is asked to supply the names of two referees. Is he opening
(a) a current account ☐
(b) a deposit account ☐
(c) a savings account ☐

(5) A bank customer asks the bank to buy a documentary bill. Is this
(a) a collection ☐
(b) a documentary credit ☐
(c) a negotiation ☐

(6) A direct debit is
(a) a commission charged by a banker ☐
(b) a claim on a current account by a creditor ☐
(c) a withdrawal by a savings account holder ☐

(7) An exporter receives a document from the master of a ship on which he has loaded his goods for carriage abroad. Is this a
(a) bill of exchange ☐
(b) clean bill ☐
(c) bill of lading ☐

(8) A customer giving a bank a stop order must get one detail right. Is it
(a) the payee's name ☐
(b) the number of the cheque ☐
(c) the amount of the cheque ☐

(9) A customer whose account is in credit leaves a parcel with his bank for safe custody. Is the customer
(a) a debtor ☐
(b) a bailor ☐
(c) a factor ☐

Check your solutions with the answers on p. 395.
Take one mark for each correct answer.
All Revision Tests total 10 marks.

Questions for discussion

1. What are the main methods of making payment within the UK through the banking system? Trace the payment of an insurance premium through any one of these methods.

2. What methods of payment are available to a UK importer for settling transactions with a foreign supplier through his UK bank? Discuss their relative merits with regard to speed, safety, and convenience.

3. List and briefly describe the main services offered by the major banking groups, distinguishing between those likely to be of greatest use to (a) personal customers, (b) business customers.

11

Lending against security

Don't forget the four questions which the borrower must be asked.

(1) How much does he want?
(2) What is it for?
(3) How long does he want to borrow for?
(4) What is the source of repayment?

When all these have been answered it is time to think about security. No advance is to be made just because it is secured. The banker's decision will be influenced by many factors, of which the most important are the character of the borrower, the risk involved, the profitability of the transaction to the bank, the lending policy of the government (and therefore that of the bank), the best interests of the borrower and of the community generally, and, of course, the answers to the four questions.

The perfect advance will be safe, liquid and profitable. It will be for a suitable purpose. Needless to say, these requirements will not always all be present at the same time and the banker will therefore search for an acceptable compromise.

Security is taken as a kind of insurance. The real security is the character of the borrower. Unsecured borrowing, in the shape of balance sheet advances to big established limited companies, may account for nearly half of the bank's lending in any particular year. These advances made to trusted borrowers are usually far less trouble than the secured advances, which require a certain amount of work before the advance is taken to see that the security is perfected, that the bank has control over it.

We can work out some simple rules by asking ourselves some simple questions:

(1) Why does the bank take security (in those cases where it does)?
   Obviously, to sell it if the borrower defaults.
(2) How does the bank know it could sell, if it wanted?
   There are two answers to this one:
   (a) Only an owner can sell. Therefore the bank must either be the owner of the security, or be in a position to get the ownership if it wants.
   (b) There must be a market in the security taken, from which it follows that a bank must only take marketable securities.
(3) How does the bank know how much the security is worth?
   It must not only be possible, but easy, to value the security. The bank should try to take only those securities for which there are current valuations.

Applying these rules, we can write out a list of suitable types of securities, which are both easy to value and easy to sell.

Bearer bonds	Life policies
Stock exchange securities	Land

Over the centuries various types of security have been known by various names. Thus land is mortgaged, assurance monies are assigned, bearer bonds are pledged. A pawnbroker takes the actual article by way of security – this is a pledge, too – and keeps it until his loan has been repaid. The banker does not take the actual article, but he takes some kind of paper which shows the customer's title to the security – a share certificate, a life policy, deeds. These are 'valuable paper'.

Lien

A lien is the right to retain property belonging to another person, until a debt due from the owner of the property to the possessor of the property is paid. The lien has nuisance value, in that the owner of it cannot get it back until he has paid up. The possessor of the property cannot sell it, and so get the money owing to him, because he is not the owner, although sometimes a right of sale is given by some statute.

There are different sorts of liens but basically they all have one thing in common. A is doing some service for B. B owes for the service. During the course of the service property of B comes into the possession of A as a result of the service. A has a lien over the property.

A carrier has a carrier's lien over the goods transported.

An innkeeper or hotel owner has an innkeeper's lien over the luggage of the traveller or guest.

A warehouse keeper has a warehouse keeper's lien over the goods he stores in his warehouse.

A banker has a lien (if the customer is overdrawn) on any property of the customer coming into his hands in the ordinary course of his business as a banker. Cheques for collection would fall into this category, but articles deposited for safe custody would not. There is a certain lack of logic here. Taking articles on safe custody is really just as much in the ordinary course of the banker's business now as is collecting the proceeds of cheques, but the argument is that the article has been deposited by the customer for a specific purpose and that this is enough to destroy any claim to a lien.

Any person having any sort of lien over any kind of property should never part with it (unless he is paid). He cannot claim a lien until he is in possession of the property and he will lose it if he parts with the property, even temporarily.

Pledge

A pledge is a delivery of goods or documents of title to goods by a debtor to his creditor as security for a debt, or for any other obligation. The subject of the pledge will be returned to the debtor when he has paid his debt.

The pledgee (the creditor) can sell the goods if the debt is not repaid.

The lender should not part with his pledge before he is paid, or he will lose his remedy.

The banker takes bearer bonds by way of pledge, and also documents of title to goods.

Mortgage

A mortgage is the conveyance of a legal or equitable interest in real or personal property as security for a debt. Deeds are mortgaged (real property) and so are share certificates (personal property).

The distinction between legal and equitable rights or interests stems from the historical development of our law in the common law courts and in the courts of equity. A legal right is where a person has the ownership of property. He can do what he likes with it, sell it, destroy it if he wants – he is the owner. A person having an equitable interest does not have anything more than a claim on the property. He cannot sell it, for he is not the owner. Moreover, other people may have similar claims on the same property.

Real property is freehold land. Everything else (including leasehold land) is personal property. The distinction is again a historical one. An action 'in rem' was an action for the land itself, nothing else would do. An action 'in personam' was an action against an individual, a person, who might have to pay damages or make restitution in some way.

Assignment

An assignment is a transfer by a creditor to an assignee of the right to receive a sum of money, or some other benefit, from a debtor.

A contract between two people raises rights and duties for each of them. These rights and duties can be enforced at law. A right is often, to receive money. One party to the contract renders a service, the other pays for it. In our earlier history the law courts refused to recognize that the right to receive a payment under a contract could be passed by the contracting party to someone else – the assignee. They would only hear an action by one of the contracting parties, not by an assignee.

Thus if A and B make a contract, under which A owes money when B has rendered a service, then the sequence of events might be:

B renders the service.
B assigns the benefit of the payment to C.
A does not pay.
C wants to bring an action against A.

No, said the law courts, we can only hear B in this court. B must obtain a judgement, get the money, and then give it to C. There is no legal assignment.

To fill this gap equity gave an equitable remedy to C. So there was an equitable assignment.

The common law was modified in 1873 and confirmed in 1925. A legal assignment could after 1873 be obtained, on conditions: notice of the assignment has to be given to the debtor in writing; the assignment itself must be in writing, and it must be unconditional.

The banker is interested in the assignment of book debts (so are factors) and of life policies.

Bearer bonds

Now we look briefly at the charging of security against an advance. The customer has requested accommodation and answered the four questions to the satisfaction of the banker, who has then stipulated for security to be deposited. It is for the customer to say what security he has got, if any. Sometimes the security may be whatever it is he is going to buy with the money the bank is going to lend him.

The customer may be an individual, which includes sole traders, partnerships, married women, minors, unincorporated associations, executors, trustees, solicitors and many more; or a limited company which exists independently of the members who compose it. The banker has to know in each of these cases whether the borrower has legal power to borrow, and whether there are any obstacles in the way of getting his money back.

Bearer bonds are negotiable instruments. Ownership is passed from hand to hand and that act, as long as it is coupled with intention, will be enough to give the transferee a right to sell.

Contrast:

(1) A customer hands his bank bearer bonds with the intention that they are to be security for a loan which the bank is granting the customer.

The bank has a right to sell the bearer bonds if the customer does not repay.

(2) A customer hands his bank bearer bonds with the intention that the bank shall keep them in safe custody for him. The banker has no right of sale. The bearer bonds do not belong to him.

The bearer bond meets all three attributes of negotiability.

These are:

(a) Mere delivery transfers a legal title to the transferee.

(b) No notice of the transfer need be given to the debtor.

(c) The title passes free from equities (the transferee must give value and act in good faith).

Equities are counterclaims. Suppose company A issued a series of bearer bonds, and B possessed some of them. A is the debtor, B the creditor. But B also owes company A some money for work which the company has done for him.

B transfers the bonds for value to C, who receives them free of equities. He is not concerned with company A's claim against B, that is between the two of them. The existence of the counterclaim does not reduce the value of the bonds which he now holds.

Bearer bonds pay interest quarterly, half-yearly, or from time to time. In the latter case the company will advertise when the next date of payment is to be.

The company which issues the bonds has no idea who is holding them all. There is no register or list of the names of bond-holders. As they are negotiable, and keep passing from hand to hand, it would be impossible to keep such a list. Therefore there has to be a system whereby the company knows who to send the interest to each time it falls due. So each bearer bond has attached to it a number of tear-off coupons, rather like a sheet of stamps. The coupons are numbered. The holder of the bonds sends to the company the correct coupon, just before interest is to be paid, and this is proof that he is entitled to receive the interest.

Bearer bonds cannot now be held in the physical possession of individuals. They have to be lodged with 'an authorized depositary', such as a bank, stockbroker or solicitor. This system started at the outbreak of the last war, when the government was concerned for the safety of bonds. They might be taken abroad or fall into enemy hands. After the war the problem had changed into how to safeguard scarce foreign currencies, so authorized depositaries were forbidden to recognize any transfers of bearer bonds unless such transfer was accompanied by evidence that they were not going abroad.

Authorized depositaries can transfer the bonds on behalf of the owners amongst themselves. So when a customer offers bearer bonds as security it may be that his bank already has them, as his 'authorized depositary'. If some other authorized depositary has them arrangements must be made to have them transferred into the bank's keeping.

(The first rule of lending against security – take and keep the security, whatever it is.)

The customer is asked to sign a Memorandum of Deposit, which in this case is mainly important because it is evidence of the intention of the customer. Then the customer can take his loan. The security has been perfected. It can be valued, from the Stock Exchange List, and it can be sold by the bank if necessary. The bank has the power of sale, and there is a ready market on the Stock Exchange.

While the bank holds the bearer bonds as authorized depositary for the customer, the bank will tear off the coupons when they become due, submitting the coupons on the right date to the paying authority, collecting the proceeds, and crediting them to the customer's account.

Registered stocks and shares

Where the security offered is a registered stock or share certificate, the banker must think how he is going to put himself in a position to sell, if need be.

Stocks and shares are transferred from one person to another by completion of a stock transfer form, signed by the transferor, which is sent, together with the registered certificate which has on it the name of the transferor as owner of the shares, to the registrar of the company which has issued the shares. The transfer is registered in the books of the company and a new certificate is issued to the new owner, the old one being cancelled.

In effect then, the registered share certificate not being a negotiable instrument (the certificate does not pass from hand to hand on a change of ownership), the company concerned does know where all the owners of all the shares are, and it keeps a list of the names. On receipt of the stock transfer form (a request to transfer, a proof of intention, and an authority to the company) the company registrar simply crosses out one name against the numbers of the shares being sold or transferred, and writes in another.

The banker could get his customer to complete a stock transfer form in favour of the bank, take from him his registered share certificate, send both to the company registrar, and get himself registered as owner. Then he could sell, if necessary. He would have taken a legal mortgage over the shares. The customer would have lost his ownership and have left as his only interest in the shares a right to have them re-transferred to him when he has repaid the loan.

The banker may be content to take an equitable mortgage. This would leave the customer as owner. Something, therefore, will have to be done about acquiring the right to sell, if necessary.

In each case, legal or equitable, the banker will take the customer's share certificate and will get the customer to sign a memorandum of deposit. In the case of a legal mortgage the banker will, as we have seen, send the certificate to the registrar of the company. In the case of an equitable mortgage he will just keep it. Having possession of it the banker effectively stops the customer from charging it elsewhere: not that he would, of course, but it's part of banking to take no avoidable risks.

The memorandum of deposit has several clauses and does several things. We have seen that it establishes the intention of the customer to charge the named security – otherwise, of course, he wouldn't have signed the form. Another clause opens the door for the banker to acquire ownership later on, if need be, as a preliminary to selling the security. This clause extracts a promise from the customer that he will later sign anything which the bank wants in order to perfect its security. This would be a Stock Transfer form. A disadvantage is that the customer might refuse when the time comes, in which case the bank would have the trouble and expense of taking him to court.

Another solution is to get the customer to sign a blank undated Stock transfer form at the same time that he signs the memorandum of deposit, i.e. before he takes the borrowing. This blank stock transfer form can be held by the banker together with the share certificate against the possible day of need.

(This leads us to the second rule of lending against security – always get the customer to sign anything, do anything, which is necessary *before* any borrowing is taken. He may not be so willing afterwards.)

In the preliminary negotiations the customer should be given to understand that the bank will let him know when the security has been perfected, and therefore when he is free to start taking the accommodation.

One danger with an equitable mortgage is that, unknown to the bank, a prior equitable interest may already exist. An example would be where the customer is in fact holding the shares as a trustee. If he does not disclose this, and if the share certificate does not describe him thereon as a trustee, the bank has no way of knowing. In such a case the earlier equitable interest (which would here belong to the beneficiaries under the trust) would take priority, to the detriment of the bank.

The only way to guard against this risk – which is negligible in the case of an honest customer – is to take a legal mortgage. If the customer is not honest he should not be an account-holder.

Life policies

The bank must take from the customer his life policy, and get him to sign a form of assignment over the policy monies. A life policy is not a negotiable instrument; it does not pass free from prior equities, and it is necessary to give notice to the debtor (the assurance company) in order to get a legal assignment. Only the latter will give the banker the right to sue the assurance company in the (highly unlikely) event of its refusing to pay, in his own name.

Valuation is obtained by asking the company to state the surrender value of the life policy, saleability is assured by surrendering the policy to the company in return for payment to the bank of its value.

Prior equities in the case of a life policy are likely to be a previous loan from the company to the policy-holder, which is still outstanding. So the bank will enquire of the company if there are any prior assignments still outstanding, and at the same time ask the company to acknowledge the bank's interest.

The surrender value of a policy is its surrender value now – what the company would pay for it now if the policy were cashed in. The policy may be for £5,000 in twenty years' time, but its surrender value now may be only £100. It depends on how many premiums have been paid.

The customer's age must be admitted as correct by the company, otherwise it may make a deduction from the policy monies eventually to be paid if it finds out that the customer originally quoted his age wrongly and consequently the premium has been wrongly calculated. Age may already have been admitted, in which case a note to that effect will be found on the policy or attached to it. If it has not, the customer's birth certificate must be obtained and sent to the company with the policy so that the point can be attended to.

The banker must read the policy carefully. Not all types of policy are suitable as bank security, but the endowment policy, with or without profits is excellent, as is a whole-life policy payable on the death of the assured person.

The assurance company should be a reputable one. The policy must not be expressed in foreign currency, or payable abroad.

Land

The proof of ownership of land is called the title to land.

Because of its peculiar importance the person who owns land has to be able to prove that it came to him in a proper manner, and he has to show what has happened to the land for the last fifteen years, or even longer. Everyone has to have some interest in land, because they have got to live somewhere. If they own their own house, or if they are buying it on mortgage, or if they are renting it from someone else, or even if they have only one room in an apartment block, everyone has some claim on a piece of land.

The definition of land includes anything on it, principally, of course, houses, but trees and ponds and mines as well.

Land is state-registered and the title to registered land is evidenced by a registered land certificate. The work of registering land titles has been going on for many years, and is nearly complete. There is some land still not registered, and the title to unregistered land is evidenced by a bundle of deeds. This system is a very old one and has to be understood as a preliminary to studying the rules for registered land.

Deeds

The borrower who offers title deeds as security must deposit them with the lending bank. The banker sends the deeds to a solicitor, who will check the title of the customer. The solicitor has to read all the deeds through, seeing that the titles of the various people who have held the land link up with each other for at least the last fifteen years. This is called the 'chain of title'. The deeds may include conveyances, mortgages, or assents. A conveyance is the deed whereby the ownership of the land passes from one person to another, usually when a house is sold. A mortgage is the deed which is signed by the parties when the land is used as security. An assent is the written authority of a personal representative passing the ownership of the land to the person to whom it has been left by the deceased, or to whom it passes, or descends, on his death. The title is said to 'vest' in the new owner if it has been properly passed to him.

The solicitor has to demonstrate a good chain of title for at least fifteen years, starting with what is called a 'good root' of title. The bank taking the title from the customer, needs to be sure that the customer has a good right to it. The customer's title in turn depends on the title of the person who sold or passed the land to him, and so on. One cannot go back for ever, so the state has fixed this period of fifteen years, and a conveyance or a mortgage at least fifteen years old will be the good root – the starting point for proving the title. A conveyance or a mortgage is accepted as a good root because in either case money passed and therefore it is reasonably certain that the title was carefully checked then. The title is checked through the chain from the good root to the holding deed. The holding deed is the deed which vests the land in the present holder, who must be the bank's customer.

The solicitor has to make various searches, against the customer's name on the Land Charges Register (set up by act of parliament to record claims against land), to see if anyone has registered a claim there, and against the address of the property on the Town and Country Planning registers, to see if the property will be affected by the plans drawn up by the local authority for the future development of the area. These latter are called the 'local' searches.

All these searches must show that there is no claim registered against the property which can in any way detract from its value. Then the solicitor must see that the property is adequately insured against fire, and that notice of the bank's interest is given to the fire insurance company. In some cases banks will see to the insurance themselves.

Then the solicitor can write to the bank saying that as a result of the checks he has made he is satisfied that the bank will have a good and marketable title to the property. This is called his report on title.

The bank manager must look at the property and value it. If it is a long way away from his branch he can get another manager, whose branch is near, to do it for him. The customer must sign another of the bank's forms, this time a mortgage of the property to the bank. The mortgage can be either legal, or equitable, just as in the case of stock exchange security.

The property may be freehold, or leasehold. The landowner is said to own an estate in the land. An estate is the length of time for which an interest will exist or endure. A freehold estate is the best title to land that anyone can get, and is the nearest approach to absolute ownership.

A leasehold estate is created by a freeholder when he grants for a fixed number of years a right to another person to use and enjoy the land. The leaseholder may have a house on the land, and he may sell it in due course. The house may be sold several times, each time to a new occupier. So a chain of title develops on the leasehold side, springing from the head lease, which is the document by which the original lease was granted. When the lease reaches the end of the fixed number of years the leaseholder then in possession has to hand back the land to the descendants in title of the original freeholder, and the lease is extinguished. (Arrangements may be made in some cases to renew the lease for a further period).

When the security consists of leasehold deeds the solicitor will make the same checks as before, with one more. He must see that the ground rent is promptly paid, otherwise the freeholder can bring the lease to an end even though the full term has not been taken. This would mean the abrupt disappearance of the bank's security. Ground rent is paid four times a year. All the solicitor has to do, therefore, is to see the last receipt. Thereafter the bank must ask to see each one as it becomes available. Ground rent is rent which is payable to the freeholder by the person to whom the land has been leased.

Registered land

The system of deeds as evidence of title has disadvantages. The most serious is that the constant checking and re-checking of chains of title, as land continually changes hands, makes for a great deal of duplication of work, all of which has to be paid for.

Surely, people said, we can have a system of registration of title, like shares. The evidence of title can be a registered land certificate. Let the state investigate each title once more, for the last time. Let it then issue a certificate and guarantee it as correct. Then when land is sold all that need happen is that the state can call in the old certificate and issue a new one, just like a company does with share certificates.

This process has been going on since 1925, and it is just about finished now. What the banker usually sees now, when his customer offers land as security, is a registered land certificate. Land is graded into three types of freehold land, and four types of leasehold. The most usual titles encountered are called absolute freehold, and good leasehold.

The certificate is a copy of the entries concerning the land at the Land Registry, which is kept up to date with changes as they occur. When the certificate is issued it is up to date with the Register, but thereafter it will get out of date as fresh entries are put on the Register. Therefore there is provision for the certificate to be sent back to the Registrar at any time to be written up to date. Only titles to legal estates can be registered.

There are two ways of taking a registered land certificate as security, corresponding to the equitable mortgage and the legal mortgage. They are called 'deposit of the certificate protected by notice of deposit' and 'registered charge'.

Deposit of the certificate protected by notice of deposit

The banker takes the certificate from the customer and inspects it. Like the register of which it is a copy, it is in three parts.

The Property Register gives the index letters and numbers assigned to the land (like a car number), a short description of the property (its address), states whether it is freehold or leasehold, and gives a reference to the official Land Registry general map for purposes of identification. That part of the map which includes the particular property is copied into the back of the land certificate as a scale plan.

The Proprietorship Register gives the name, address and description of the proprietor, the date of registration, the consideration paid for the land last time it was sold, and the type of freehold or leasehold title.

The Charges Register gives details of charges affecting the land, such as mortgages.

The customer signs a form of legal charge containing provisions very similar to those found in a form of legal mortgage over deeds.

The banker must make a search to ensure that there are no prior claims against the land. He does this by sending the land certificate to the Registrar to have it written up to date. At the same time he completes and sends a special Land Registry form called Notice of Deposit. This form notifies the Registrar that the landholder has deposited the land certificate with the bank (as security for a loan) and therefore that the bank has an equitable claim against the land.

The Registrar puts this entry in the Charges section of the Register, writes the certificate up to date, to include the bank's charge, and sends the certificate back to the bank, where it is kept. The banker will see, by looking at the copy of the Charges section in the land certificate, whether his title is clear. His own notice of deposit should be entered therein, and this should be the only charge outstanding. The inside cover, where there is provision for a number of date stamps, will show the date up to which the land certificate has been made to correspond with the Register.

Thus the creation of an equitable mortgage is simple and easy, needing no solicitor's investigation. Local searches, fire insurance and valuation are attended to as with deed security. If the land is leasehold, the last ground rent receipt must be seen.

Registered charge

The customer signs a form of legal mortgage. The banker takes the customer's land certificate and makes a search on the Land Register, using a special Land Registry form for this purpose. He does not now search by having the land certificate written up to date because, as will be seen in a moment, he will send it to the Land Registrar and won't get it back.

A duplicate of the Land Registry search form is returned to the banker, and should show that there are no prior claims against the land on the Register. If this is so, the banker will take the form of mortgage, prepare an office copy of it, and send both to the Registrar together with the land certificate and the appropriate fee for registration.

The Registrar will keep the land certificate and the copy mortgage. He will make the appropriate entry in the Register, and then issue to the banker a document called a Charge Certificate, which will have the original form of mortgage stitched inside. This is the evidence of the bank's legal mortgage. The evidence of the customer's land holding – the registered land certificate – is withdrawn from circulation and kept at the Land Registry. The Charge Certificate has taken its place. When the customer has repaid, the bank will notify the Registrar that the Charge Certificate can be cancelled and the land certificate returned to the customer.

As before, the banker must attend to the local searches, the valuation, the fire insurance, and (if the land is leasehold) the ground rent receipts.

The work of the Land Registry has been decentralized and there are several District Land Registries, each handling the registration of titles within its own district. The Land Registry in London continues to be the proper office for the registration of title in its own area.

Guarantees

A guarantee is an undertaking to be responsible for the debt of another. The guarantor is to be called upon only if the principal debtor fails to repay. The guarantee is an example of collateral security. To be collaterally responsible is to be responsible as a third party, as someone other than the person actually borrowing money. If that person – the principal debtor – were himself depositing security that would be direct security.

If the security is collateral the third party cannot be made responsible if for any reason the principal debtor cannot be made to repay. If a limited company having no legal power to borrow nevertheless did so, against a guarantee given by a third party, the company could not be forced to repay because a court would hold that there was no (legal) debt, no debt that could be enforced in a court of law. So neither could the guarantor be made to pay.

To avoid this the usual bank form of guarantee has an indemnity clause and in fact should be called an Indemnity and not a Guarantee. The indemnifier is responsible whatever happens. He says to the lender, 'lend my friend £100 and I will personally see that you suffer no loss, whatever circumstances may arise'. The guarantor says only, 'lend my friend £100 and if he does not repay you, I will'.

It is for the customer to name a person who is willing to stand as a guarantor for him. The two tests for any security – valuation and saleability – still apply. The valuation to be made by the manager is an assessment of the status of the proposed guarantor, who must be considered both able and willing to pay if called upon. If the manager has any doubts he can call upon the guarantor to deposit security in support of his guarantee.

Once the guarantor has been named the bank manager must confirm by seeing him, or writing to him, that he is willing to undertake the responsibility. The guarantor's bank must be written to for a report on his standing. This is the status enquiry. The answer should state that the guarantor is considered either 'undoubted' or 'good' for the sum mentioned. Anything less positive than that will not do for an unsupported guarantee.

If the reply is satisfactory the guarantor will be invited to call at the branch, or at another branch more convenient to him, to sign the guarantee. His signature must be witnessed and he has to come to the bank so that the bank can be quite certain that the signature they are getting is genuine and not forged. The person standing to benefit is the principal debtor, so the form of guarantee must never be given to him, although he may offer to get it signed for the bank. If a form of guarantee has to leave the branch it should go for signature to one of three places only, another branch, another bank (where there is no convenient branch of the lending bank), or a solicitor known to be reliable (where there is no branch of any bank). If the solicitor is not known the bank must make a status enquiry on him before using him.

The signing of the guarantee initiates a contract of guarantee between the banker and the guarantor. Of course a contract of banking already exists between the banker and the principal debtor, his customer. The banker has duties in each case, a duty of care and secrecy towards his customer, a duty not to mislead the guarantor. If the guarantor should sign the guarantee under a serious misapprehension of any kind he may later be able to get out of it, so the banker has to take great care that the guarantor is treated absolutely fairly before he signs. This includes answering any relevant questions about the principal debtor and his account, which the guarantor may ask. The guarantor is entitled to inform himself of any fact which is important in helping him to make up his mind whether to sign the guarantee or not. However, the bank manager does not have to volunteer information. His duty is only to answer truthfully any relevant questions which the guarantor may ask. Any more, and he might breach the duty of secrecy to his customer.

The guarantee is the easiest of all 'securities' to take, only a status enquiry to make and a form to be signed. The difficulty is always to impress on the guarantor the seriousness of the guarantee – he usually thinks it is just a temporary formality. If he does get called upon he seldom pays up immediately and without fuss.

The status enquiry should be repeated every six months during the currency of the loan, for a man's position may deteriorate.

If the banker has been unable to get a satisfactory status report from the guarantor's banker, and has therefore insisted on having security lodged in support, he must see that the guarantor also signs the appropriate form of charge for whatever the security may be – a memorandum of deposit, a form of assignment or mortgage – in addition to signing the form of guarantee. The security should be perfected as though it were security for a direct borrowing by the guarantor.

Limited companies

Although it is not possible in a work of this nature to go minutely through every detail which must be seen to where the borrower is in a special class, such as executors, solicitors, unincorporated associations, and so on, something should be said about limited companies as borrowers because of their importance.

Limited companies exist as separate entities, and it is this entity which in law is borrowing from the banker, although the negotiations will be carried out by the company's agents, the directors, as it cannot speak for itself.

In all cases the first step for the banker is to check from the Memorandum of Association that the company has power to borrow, and that the declared purpose for which the loan moneys are required is within the objects of the company. Then he must check from the Articles of Association that the directors are empowered to commit the company and that no general meeting of the company to consider and authorize the borrowing is required. This is in spite of the protection given to lenders advancing money to companies which is afforded by legislation passed consequent upon the entry of this country into the European Economic Community. That legislation appears to make some of the checks mentioned above unnecessary, but it is thought that until some experience has been gained of the working of the new law it is best to play safe and stick to the old routines.

In the case of a guarantee to be given by the company, the banker must check from the Memorandum of Association that the company has power to give guarantees. A company is in general forbidden to give a guarantee to secure any loan to any person or body for the purpose of buying that company's shares or stock, nor may it, except in special circumstances, guarantee a loan to one of its own directors.

Shares of private companies are unsuitable security because they can neither be easily valued, nor easily sold.

Nearly all charges given by a limited company require registration within twenty-one days at the Companies Registry at Companies House. The exceptions are charges on stocks and shares, on negotiable instruments, on a life policy, on documents of title to goods, or on a policy issued by the Export Credits Guarantee Department of the Department of Trade.

It may be thought strange that an artificial entity such as a company can offer a life policy as security, but it is quite possible, though rare. Some companies maintain policies on the lives of the company directors, because of the special importance to the company of the work which the directors are doing. It is one of these policies which the company may offer.

The Companies House Register will contain for any company not only details of charges given by the company, but also copies of any special resolutions passed, copies of the last profit and loss accounts and balance sheet, anything which is of real importance, in fact. Any person thinking of lending to a company should, therefore, 'make a search' against it at Companies House. This is done by making a personal visit to the Registry and paying a small fee. On request one is then given access to the company's file and from that can see what charges, if any, it has already given and what its balance sheet position is. From this a prospective lender can check that any security offered has not already been charged, and, in general, what the prospects of repayment are.*

The most usual security offered by a company is its land. Every company has to have a headquarters. Land is one of those securities where a charge has to be registered at Companies House. Once on the file there, a charge is available for anyone to see. Certain charges are regularly noted in certain trade journals, and some publicity is unavoidable. Most companies strongly resent this publicity, because it allows their trade competitors to see that the company has had to borrow money. For this reason a borrowing company may well ask its banker to lend on terms that will not necessitate registration.

Such requests take the form of a proposed deposit of the registered land certificate by the company with the bank with a written undertaking to execute a formal mortgage over the land if the bank ever so requires or a proposed deposit of the land certificate with a completed form of mortgage accompanied by a request not to register it.

The effect of the relevant section of the Companies Act is that failure to register such a charge has no penalties unless the company should go into liquidation. In such an event, however, the lending banker who has acquiesced in non-registration would have to give up his security to the liquidator for the benefit of the company creditors generally. He would become an unsecured creditor.

The banker knows this, yet he wants to oblige his customer. If the company is a strong one and most unlikely ever to go into liquidation the banker will probably be happy to accept an undertaking to charge if ever required to do so, plus a deposit of the land certificate.

See p. 404. *

Debentures

A debenture is a type of security which can be given only
by a limited company. A debenture in itself is merely an
acknowledgement of an indebtedness. The usual type of
debenture found in banking business is a mortgage debenture, that is, a debenture accompanied by a charge on the
assets of the borrowing company. A fixed charge covers the
fixed assets of the company, such as its land, and a floating
charge covers the floating assets of the company, such as its
raw materials in store, or stock-in-hand. Where the mortgage
debenture is worded to provide security for any sums owing
by the company to the bank, on any account, at any time,
it is called an 'all-monies' debenture. This is the usual banking security. It is taken under seal and makes the entire
assets of the company subject to the charge. Its terms will
specify that the debenture shall be a first charge on the undertaking and property of the company. It will be drawn in
favour of the bank, will fix the rate of interest to be paid on
the loan, and will stipulate that the loan is repayable on
demand. It should include a legal mortgage over the company's real property, and the relative deeds should be deposited
at the bank. Where land is concerned the bank will take all
the steps it would take if it were taking a specific charge over
land, including the completion of the bank's form of mortgage to supplement the debenture. This form of mortgage
will have to be produced to the Chief Land Registrar when
the charge is registered with him. He will not act on the
debenture, in which the land is not described in detail.

This is the fixed charge. Thereafter the company cannot
deal in any way with any of the fixed assets without the prior
consent of the bank.

The debenture deed then proceeds to give a floating charge
on the other company assets, but the company must be left
free to deal with these, for this is necessary in its business.
One cannot take a fixed charge on the company's stock,
and forbid the company to deal with it. On the contrary,

repayment can only be hoped for if the company does deal with its stock, that is, sell it. A manufacturing company buys raw materials, converts them into work-in-progress, and then into finished stock. It then sells this stock, at a profit. With the proceeds it buys more raw materials, and starts the process all over again. The raw materials come under the 'umbrella' of the floating charge as soon as they are bought, and finished stock passes out from under it as soon as it is sold. As long as the company continues to trade normally, and as long as it continues to meet the repayments on its loan satisfactorily, and pays the interest, this process will continue. But if anything happens to cause the bank to demand repayment and to put the receiver in, the floating charge will 'solidify' or 'crystallize' and catch the floating assets which happen to be there on the day the receiver is appointed. The same thing will happen if the company ceases business, or goes into liquidation.

The bank is given power by the debenture to put in its own receiver where the company has defaulted, and he will administer the assets so as to apply them towards repayment of the bank advance. The debenture will list the events which will force the bank to take this step. These usually include failure to respond to a formal demand for repayment made by the bank, default in payment of interest by the company for a specified number of months, the cessation of business by the company, the commencement of winding-up, the attempted alteration of the company's Memorandum or Articles of Association in a manner which would be harmful to the bank's interests, or the appointment of a receiver by some other creditor or by the court.

This power to give a debenture is limited to a company. A trader with a hotel business might wish to borrow, and could suggest as part-security the stock of furniture etc. – beds, carpets, linen, everything wanted for running a hotel – which he possessed. The bank would refuse as this is not a type of security in which it is interested. But if the trader turned his business into a limited company, and gives the bank a debenture, the furniture is included along with all the other assets.

Farming advances

Country banks may find their business predominantly agricultural, for in general banks are both able and willing to meet all applications by credit-worthy farmers for short, medium and long term credit. The nature of the farming to be followed will determine the picture presented by the farmer's banking account. Arable farming will show a yearly cycle as the crops are sown and harvested: sheep-farming produces lambs annually and shearing too is done annually. At the other extreme eggs are laid daily and quickly sold, milk sold to the Milk Marketing Board will be paid for by monthly cheque, and so on.

Long-term lending must be for the purchase of a farm (becoming even more difficult as the price of good farming land continually increases) or for major long term improvements to the farm, i.e. irrigation. The security must be the deeds or the land certificate relating to the farm, and will be perfected like any other land security.

However, the valuation of such land, done either professionally or by the bank manager visiting the farm, presents a number of features which would be quite strange to a city manager accustomed to valuing houses. Although there must be a farm-house on the property, this will not normally be so important: what matters is the quality of the land and the acreage involved. The visiting manager will assess the quality of the soil. Heavy clay is difficult to break up for cultivation, on the other hand light soil dries out quickly in drought or hot weather and starves root crops of water. A good, deep, easily-worked loam is ideal.

He hopes to find that the farmland is reasonably level, with good drainage. On steep slopes water will run off before it can sink in to nourish the crops. He looks for roads which will be needed to bring manure and fertilizer in, and harvested crops out. The site should be near a source of labour if many hands are required. Farm buildings should be adequate for the type of farming intended to be pursued. A large arable farm, for example, should have grain drying and storage facilities if the farmer is to be free to sell his product at the time most advantageous to him. The farm should be a compact unit, easily worked. It should generally be in a good state of cultivation and repair, with hedges and ditches properly maintained.

Such advances are technically subject to annual review, but repayment would not normally be expected until the farm was sold.

Medium and short term or seasonal lending is usually unsecured, and normally granted by way of overdraft. The farmer is basically an honest person and the banker knows this and places reliance on it. Farming is more than an occupation – it is a way of life. The bank manager has to commit himself fully to what is a specialized situation: he must judge his borrower as a man and meet him on his farm and in the market place rather than in his own office. He will find the average farmer careless about accounts and he may have to guide him in the compilation of his annual accounts. Often a document called a stock and crop form will show the basic values of the farmer's assets, but the bank manager must know enough to check his farmer's estimates. He should do this by visual inspection when he 'walks' the farm. Even this must be arranged with care, for the farming community is a close-knit one, and an unexpected visit might well start a rumour that the farmer is in trouble.

The valuation of growing crops varies as the season progresses, so it is essential to obtain the stock and crop form at the same time each year, otherwise the figures cannot meaningfully be compared. This will be easiest if a time is chosen when the growing crops are at a minimum. The valuation of farm animals will be governed by market prices, but may be difficult where pedigree animals are concerned. The bank manager must keep in touch by reading the farming journals, keeping up with the local press, visiting the markets to note the prices obtained and by nurturing frequent contacts with local farmers. He will have the advantage of having many farms and farmers on his books, so that he can compare the performance of one with another.

It is part and parcel of the farmer's character that he tends to under-estimate his liabilities and to over-value the price his crops will fetch. He often borrows from relatives and forgets to include this debt in his figures. He tends to under-estimate his liability for income tax, and is not good at maintaining farm machinery in first-class order. He is, in fact, an optimist. Perhaps he has to be, to be a farmer at all.

When the bank manager has arrived at what he is satisfied is a fair figure for the total assets of his farming customer he can check that the overdraft taken is a reasonable one. The stock and crop figures year by year, or the audited accounts if the farmer uses a professional accountant, will indicate whether the borrowing situation is improving or deteriorating, and may suggest measures which should be taken for the future.

The vast majority of farming advances are to owner-occupiers. Farms can be let, however, and the tenant farmer is protected to the extent that he cannot be evicted unless he is judged to be farming badly, or unless he is not paying his rent. He should make improvements to the land as he farms, for instance by sowing seed and digging in manure, and if he has to leave the farm he is entitled to an allowance for such improvements, to be paid by the owner of the land. This is called 'tenant right', the compensation for the unexhausted manure and the crops left to be harvested by his successor. On the other hand, the outgoing tenant has a liability for dilapidations and this liability forms a set-off to his tenant right.

Agricultural charges

An Act of 1928 provided for the setting up of the Agricultural Mortgage Corporation (see p. 138). It also dealt with agricultural short term credits. It provided for any farmer to create an agricultural charge in favour of a bank on the farming stock and agricultural assets belonging to the farmer, as security for any money lent to him. This wording covered, and the security was appropriate to, either a tenant farmer or the owner of the holding. The agricultural charge was to be a fixed charge upon the farming stock and other agricultural assets belonging to the farmer at the date of the charge and specified in the charge, or a floating charge upon the farming stock and other agricultural assets from time to time belonging to the farmer, or both.

The sum secured was to be either a specified sum, or a fluctuating amount advanced on current account.

The floating charge would crystallize over the various assets in such circumstances as the death of the farmer, or the making of a receiving order against him, and the banker would then be entitled to put in a receiver to collect his assets.

The agricultural charge was therefore very similar to a debenture given by a limited company.

Neither the farmer nor the banker have looked upon this system with very much favour. The farmer objects to signing away his assets, as he sees it, and prefers his banker to trust him. The banker finds from experience that the cases where the security has had to be claimed show that by the time the receiver gets there, the floating assets have all gone anyway. Pressing creditors have caused the farmer to dissipate these assets in an effort to satisfy them.

Agricultural charges have to be registered within seven days with the Agricultural Credits Superintendent at the Land Registry. Very few are now registered each year.

Farming Loan Guarantees Ltd

The government recognizes the importance of the farmers' work to the nation and gives preferential treatment by way of subsidies and in other ways. Two companies sponsored by the National Farming Union and named Farming Loan Guarantees Ltd and the Agricultural Finance Federation assist farmers to obtain bank credit by offering to guarantee advances made to finance a programme of agreed improvements on the farm. A condition is that the farmer shall accept specialist advice on the best way of carrying out these improvements. The government will meet up to three-quarters of any sums which these companies have to pay to banks in cases where their guarantees are called upon.

Another state-sponsored institution is the Lands Improvements Company, which was formed more than a century ago and is still in operation. It makes loans for up to forty years to farmers for improvements to land such as drainage and irrigation, building of farmhouses, cottages and farm buildings, water supply, fencing, roads, installation of electricity and many others. The procedure is rather cumbersome. Application must be made in the first case to the corporation, after which the Ministry of Agriculture makes two surveys over the land. If the loan is granted it is secured by a rent charge over the property which covers the repayment of capital and interest over the term of years agreed.

These loans are called Improvement Loans.

Sound farm management advice is in many cases very desirable and this is available from the Agricultural Development and Advisory Service (ADAS). This body was formed in March 1971 to replace the National Agricultural Advisory Service (NAAS). The latter was a technical and advisory service of the Ministry of Agriculture which for more than a quarter of a century advised the farming community in its best interests. NAAS was very largely independent of governmental or departmental policy, and free from any commercial bias. It enjoyed a unique position of trust and confidence within the farming community. Its services were normally free. Many lending managers were accustomed to arrange for a representative of the service to give his views as one of the preliminaries to granting accommodation.

But in latter years the increased pace of technical and scientific development in farming has resulted in specialization of farming systems to a degree never before seen. As a result there have emerged large, highly capitalized farm businesses, requiring a greater depth of advice at both the technical and management level. At the same time the free services of NAAS to farmers were proving an increasing burden on the tax payer generally.

The replacement of NAAS by a state extension service such as ADAS represents a change in government policy which will result in the breaking of the close link between the individual farm and advisory service and will tend to result in the absorption of the activities of the ADAS adviser into a conventional Civil Service structure.

Advisory services are also offered by private consultants, and it seems likely that these will now increase in number.

Syndicates and co-operatives

Modern conditions are in farming as elsewhere steadily putting the small man out of business. Syndicates of farmers up to twenty are formed for joint ownership and use of farm machinery and equipment, such as a combine harvester, which is expensive, but only needed for a period once a year. A system of syndicate credit has grown up, financed by county central organizations, registered as limited companies and themselves borrowing most of the required funds from the banks.

Another co-operative activity has been the formation of groups for buying their farming requirements in bulk, and therefore at cheaper rates, and selling the produce to the market in bulk. The Agricultural Finance Federation will lend for periods of up to three years to members of a co-operative.

Lending against balance sheets

Finally we come to lending against balance sheets, but before we can appreciate what the banker is looking for in a balance sheet we must have a look at the balance sheets of customers.

Revision Test 11

Put ticks in what you think are the right boxes.

(1) The valuation of some securities can fluctuate from day to day. Does this apply to
   (a) stock exchange securities ☐
   (b) life policies ☐
   (c) land ☐

(2) Assurance policy moneys are
   (a) mortgaged by way of security ☐
   (b) assigned by way of security ☐
   (c) pledged by way of security ☐

(3) No right of sale accrues to the creditor who has
   (a) a mortgage ☐
   (b) a pledge ☐
   (c) a lien ☐

(4) The lending banker takes a pledge when the customer charges
   (a) bearer bonds ☐
   (b) a life policy ☐
   (c) shares in a limited company ☐

(5) Negotiable instruments include
   (a) bills of lading ☐
   (b) certificates of deposit ☐
   (c) registered land certificates ☐

(6) A coupon is torn off a bearer bond
   (a) to show that it is in the care of an authorized depositary ☐
   (b) each time the band is transferred ☐
   (c) each time interest is claimed ☐

(7) An Assent is
   (a) the deed which is signed by the parties to a mortgage of land ☐
   (b) the written authority of a personal representative ☐
   (c) a clause in a memorandum of deposit signed by a customer ☐

(8) Which is true?
   (a) the Property Register is a list of shareholders, kept by the registrar of a company ☐
   (b) a freehold estate is one held by an owner for a term of years ☐
   (c) where a leasehold estate is offered as security the last ground rent receipt must be checked ☐

(9) A bank taking a registered charge over land will
   (a) keep the customer's land certificate ☐
   (b) send the customer's land certificate to the Land Registry ☐
   (c) send the customer's land certificate to the Land Charges Registry ☐

(10) A floating charge is
   (a) the broker's commission on a marine insurance policy ☐
   (b) a charge over certain assets of a company ☐
   (c) a commission on a current account, which is determined according to the use made of the account by the customer ☐

Check your solutions with the answers on p. 395.
Take one mark for each correct answer.
All Revision Tests total 10 marks.

332 The Elements of Banking

Questions for discussion

1. Mention the basic requirements of any security and say how these are met in the case of (a) life assurance policies and (b) guarantees.

2. If you as a lending banker had the choice of taking company shares or land as security, which would you prefer? Give reasons for your preference.

3. Mention and describe three systems of registration which concern bankers.

12

The balance sheets of customers

The final accounts of a business, so called because they are made up only at the end of each trading year, consist of the manufacturing account, the trading account, the profit and loss account, and the profit and loss appropriation account.

Manufacturing account

The manufacturing account shows the direct cost of the production of the goods, starting with the cost of the raw materials used, and of their transport into the factory, then

Example of manufacturing account

	£		£
Materials: balance in hand 1st Jan.	1,000	Finished Stock: to Trading Account	18,500
Purchases	5,000		
Carriage inwards	100		
Fuel, light and power	300		
Wages	12,000	Materials: balance in hand 31st Dec.	500
Depreciation of plant	600		
	£19,000		£19,000

listing the three items of expense – fuel, power and labour – which are essential in the manufacture. A depreciation figure is included as a cost in this account, which recognizes the wear and tear on the factory machinery, and makes provision for its eventual replacement.

Where there is a considerable amount of work which has passed from the raw materials stage but has not, by the date of the account, reached the status of finished stock a further entry:

Work in Progress 1st Jan.	Work in Progress 31st Dec.

will be seen.

A trading concern which buys goods for resale does not, of course, manufacture them, and will not, therefore, keep a manufacturing account.

Trading account

The trading account is compiled to show the gross profit or loss of the trading in the period under review. In the case of a manufacturing company the stock will come from the factory and the amount coming into the trading account will be the same as that shown as going out in the manufacturing account.

Example of trading account

	£		£
Stock: balance in hand 1st Jan.	14,000	Sales	40,500
Stock: balance from manufacturing account	18,500		
Balance, being gross profit transferred to profit & loss account	20,500	Stock: balance in hand 31st Dec.	12,500
	£53,000		£53,000

In a trading company, as opposed to a manufacturing company, the item of stock brought forward from the manufacturing account will be replaced by 'Purchases'. 'Wages' and 'Carriage inwards' will also be shown in this account.

Profit and loss account

The gross profit from the trading account is credited to this account together with any unusual or non-recurring items of gain from sources other than normal trading – for example, a profit from the sale of land. The debit side will show the overhead and administrative charges incurred during the year, such as bank interest, interest on loan (if any), rates, rent, heating and lighting, stationery, office salaries, postage and telephone charges, directors' emoluments, bad debts

Example of profit and loss account

	£		£
Rent and rates	340	Balance of gross profit transferred from trading account	20,500
Office salaries	10,460		
Insurance	210		
Printing & stationery	460	Discounts received	1,240
General office expenses	3,120		
Discounts allowed	1,700		
Bad debts	840		
Provision for bad debts	90		
Depreciation: fixtures & fittings	70		
Balance being net profit transferred to capital account	4,450		
	£21,740		£21,740

written off, commissions, and carriage outward. The balance of this account is the net profit, on which tax is charged.

Whereas the trading account is concerned with the purchase or production of goods, the profit and loss account is concerned with the distribution of the goods.

The result of these sample accounts, which are appropriate to the business of a sole trader, shows a net profit, which is transferred to the trader's capital account. This is normally a credit, so the transfer increases the amount of the trader's

Example of a profit and loss appropriation account

	£		£
Proposed dividend	4,800	Balance of profit & loss account	
Corporation tax	5,200		
Reserve	2,000	brought forward	1,850
Balance of profit & loss account carried forward	2,000	Net profit for the year	12,150
	£14,000		£14,000

capital, i.e. the money which he has in the business which he runs.

In the case of a limited company a profit and loss appropriation account would show what actually happened to the ascertained net profit. The opening balance on the account will be a balance, adverse or favourable, brought forward from the year before. The net profit is brought into the account, and corporation tax, proposed dividends and any transfers to reserves which the directors have decided to make, are set against it. The final balance, carried forward to the following year, appears in the balance sheet as the profit and loss balance.

Balance sheets of sole traders partnerships and limited companies

When summing up a balance sheet it is important to distinguish between the figures of a sole trader, a partnership and a limited company. The balance sheet of a sole trader will disclose only those assets which are being used in the business, and will not mention the assets and liabilities which the trader may have in his private life. Thus he may own a house and a car, and perhaps have a life policy with a good surrender value. He may also have mortgage payments and hire purchase commitments to meet.

As he is fully liable for the debts of his business his creditors would in case of need have recourse against all his private assets as well as those shown in the balance sheet. Usually, therefore, the position is rather stronger than it appears to be from the balance sheet.

The basic accounts of a partnership are very similar to those of a sole trader, but with two or more partners interested in the business the final accounts must show figures denoting their respective rights as to capital and profit. The firm's balance sheet will show all the partnership liabilities and all the assets of the firm available to meet them, but as with the balance sheet of the sole trader, it will not show the private assets and liabilities of the partners.

Only the balance sheet of a company shows the complete position. Creditors have no claim beyond the assets there shown, unless the company is unlimited, or limited by guarantee.

Only the balance sheet of a company must have attached the certificate of a qualified auditor. This gives a real protection to both creditors and shareholders.

Structure of a company balance sheet

The liabilities or left-hand side of the balance sheet shows where the money has come from (or to whom it is owed) and the right-hand side, the assets, shows what has been done with the money (or who owes it). The actual words 'liabilities' and 'assets' are not always used nowadays.

The entries on both sides are arranged in order of liquidity, Some people like to deal with the most liquid items first.

others like to start with the long term items. It does not matter which method is used, as long as both sides of the balance sheet are treated in the same way.

Under the liabilities, then, we will place the share capital and then the remaining liabilities in the order of their liquidity. Long term liabilities will come first, and then current liabilities, the latter being those debts which are due to be paid within the next year.

The assets are separated into fictitious (or intangible), fixed and current assets.

LIABILITIES			ASSETS		
Capital			*Fictitious or intangible assets*		
	£	£		£	£
15,000 shares £1 each, fully paid		15,000	Goodwill		4,000
Reserve		2,000			
Profit & loss account		11,000	*Fixed assets*		
		28,000			
Long term liabilities			Factory & offices		16,000
Mortgage	2,000		Plant & machinery		6,000
Director's loan	1,000		Vehicles		3,200
		3,000			29,200
Current liabilities			*Current assets*		
Tax	650		Stock	8,400	
Creditors	8,000		Debtors	9,800	
Bank	8,150		Cash in hand	400	
		16,800			18,600
		£47,800			£47,800

Balance sheet terms defined

Liability

A liability is a debt due to be settled at some time in the future.

Asset

An asset is cash, or something which has been bought for cash, or can be turned into cash.

Fixed capital

The paid-up capital, the reserves, and any balance on profit and loss account form the fixed capital, which is the proprietors' stake. All these sums belong to the shareholders. Reserves are of various kinds. A capital reserve is the result of a profit on a capital transaction, such as the sale of a fixed asset at a figure in excess of the balance sheet figure. A revenue reserve is a sum which has been built up out of good profit and loss balances in the past.

All such capital reserves and accumulated profits can at any time be capitalized by issuing bonus shares to the members.

Also sometimes described as reserves are provisions for specific or possible liabilities, such as dividends to be paid, or taxation due. Provisions of this nature should appear as a current liability: provisions linked directly with an asset, such as a provision for depreciation of a fixed asset, should be shown as a deduction from the value of the asset.

Long term liabilities

Under this heading come liabilities which are neither repayable at short notice, nor yet of such fixed quality as the shareholders' funds, such as the company's loan capital.

Current liabilities

Current liabilities are debts arising in the normal course of business, such as debts due to trade and hire purchase creditors, or sums owing to the bank. All these debts have to be paid in the next twelve months, i.e. before the next balance sheet can be expected.

Fixed assets

All assets which have been acquired for the purpose of carrying on the business of the company, and which will not be resold, but kept in permanent use until they wear out. They will make production possible. A manufacturing company must have a factory, plant and machinery, and vehicles. The office staff must have furniture and office equipment. These are fixed assets. Without them no production would be possible.

Floating assets

Floating or current assets are those bought so that they may pass through the normal cycle of manufacture or trade and then be sold again for cash. Floating assets do not stay with the company long. They are sometimes called quick, liquid, or circulating assets.

Fictitious assets

Under this heading we speak of intangible assets such as patents, trademarks or goodwill; and fictitious assets such as preliminary expenses when a company is being formed. The money has been spent and therefore has to appear somewhere, but the fictitious asset has no value and will be written out of the balance sheet as soon as the company has made some money. Intangible assets, on the other hand, have a real value, sometimes a considerable value.

Working capital

The sum which must finance the day-to-day operations of the company is called the working capital. This can be thought of as the money which is left over after the fixed capital has been brought in and the fixed and fictitious assets bought and paid for. Another way of arriving at the same result is to subtract the current liabilities from the floating assets. The layout of the balance sheet is designed to make it easy to do this quickly.

If the company has insufficient working capital, it has

spent too much on buying the fixed assets and as a result will be permanently short of ready cash. It will be obliged to rely on trade creditors paying up promptly, or on the bank letting it go over the top of the overdraft limit. This condition is called 'over-trading'. There is no cure, except an injection of fresh cash into the company. If creditors, who have of necessity been left unpaid for too long, press their legal rights against the company there is a danger that the company will be forced into liquidation.

Straight-line balance sheet

As many, if not most, shareholders are unaccustomed to interpreting accounts, the straight line balance sheet was invented to make it easier for them to see what the figures meant.

If we take a very simple balance sheet:

	£		£
Capital	5,000	Fixed assets	5,000
Loan	2,000	Stock	2,000
Sundry creditors	4,000	Sundry debtors	2,000
		Cash	2,000
	£11,000		£11,000

we can re-write it as it appears overleaf.

In the vertical form of balance sheet the term 'capital employed' is used – this will be equal to the total of fixed and net current assets.

A more complex example of a vertical balance sheet appears on page 343.

	£
Proprietors' interest	5,000
Loan	2,000
Capital employed	£7,000

Current assets:

Stock	2,000
Sundry debtors	2,000
Cash	2,000
	£6,000

Less current liabilities

Sundry creditors	4,000
Liquid resources	2,000
Add fixed assets	5,000
	£7,000

Lending against a balance sheet

The question for the lending banker is whether the company's position, as disclosed by the balance sheet, is sufficiently strong to justify an advance unsecured in any other way, or whether, should the advance be granted, it be on the condition that security be lodged in support. One balance sheet on its own is useful, but gives only a picture at one moment in time: it is better to have balance sheets for the last three years, so that the trend of the company's business can be estimated. Three years' profit figures will show whether profits are increasing or the reverse, three years' turnover figures will show the general progress or otherwise of the company.

The banker will look first for a satisfactory liquid position. Floating assets less current liabilities will show whether the company has adequate working capital. Can they pay all their creditors without difficulty and go on with their business

in the normal manner? Other points will be whether the
balance sheet is properly certified by a qualified auditor,
what the distribution of the debtors is (well spread, rather
than a few big debts), whether proper provision has been
made for tax, and what claims there might be against the
company which would have priority over the bank. Machinery, plant and similar assets should be regularly written down
to provide for depreciation, and a reserve fund established

		£	£
Capital employed	Preference capital		1,740
	Ordinary capital		33,719
	Reserves & retained profits		46,263
			81,722
	Loan capital		63,542
			£145,264
Employment of capital	Land, buildings, plant & equipment		49,345
	Investments in subsidiaries		72,275
	Other investments		3,897
	Fixed assets		125,517
Current Assets	Stocks	16,009	
	Debtors	13,089	
	Deposits	9,835	
	Cash	876	
		39,809	
Current Liabilities	Creditors	11,788	
	Overdraft	2,054	
	Dividends	6,220	
		20,062	
Net Current Assets			19,747
			£145,264

for their replacement. Reserves, whether for a specific purpose such as future tax, or for the purpose of providing a fund for general unforeseen expenditure or loss, should be invested outside the business in sound securities bearing interest, and not left in the business as part of the working capital. If the latter is the case it is possible that the money may be difficult to get at when it is wanted.

Each balance sheet must be scrutinized in the light of the trade in which the company is engaged, but in general the amount of book debts and stock disclosed by the balance sheet would have to be considerably marked down to arrive at a reasonable estimate of what would be realized if the debts were suddenly called in or the stock sold by a forced sale. In other words, the balance sheet figures are those of a company which is a going concern. There are times, as we shall see, when it is necessary for the banker to think of the company in 'gone concern' terms, and to convert the balance sheet valuations to 'break-up' figures.

The valuations of any land and stock have usually to be taken on trust. Sometimes a professional valuation may have been available for the land, or part of it may have been sold, or bought recently, which will give a guide. The stock valuation is usually done by the directors and the figure there is likely to be an under-valuation because this reduces the profits and so the tax to be paid. The nature of the stock must be kept in mind: some articles deteriorate if kept too long, others go out of fashion. Some businesses must maintain a rapid turnover which must be based on an accurate forecast of the market, such as the manufacturers of ladies' clothing. Other businesses demand a long and careful preparation, so that turnover is slow, e.g. the manufacture of aircraft engines. The way in which the money is going to be used is important. The banker prefers to lend money for use in the business, on a short term basis. He does not want to see it used in the purchase of a fixed asset, because that will lock it up. He does not want to see it used to pay off pressing creditors, because that will take it out of the business altogether. In any case, of course, the purpose of the advance must be covered in the Objects Clause of the Memorandum of Association.

The effect of any borrowing must be either to reduce the outstanding liabilities of the business or to increase its assets, either current or fixed.

Advances to reduce an outstanding current liability

The banker asks himself, if I grant this advance, what will be its effect on the company's balance sheet? Will it have the result that the company's working capital is reduced? An advance to reduce a current outstanding liability will not affect the liquid position, because the increase in 'Bank overdraft' will be offset by a reduction in 'Creditors', both items being in the liquid section of the balance sheet. However, the banker will not be very keen to lend money to pay someone else off, perhaps only one of many pressing creditors. He could keep on doing this, each time lending more to the company to pay off creditors and so avoid its being put into liquidation by one of them. In the end the banker would wind up by having to put the company into liquidation himself as the only way of getting even part of his money back.

Advance to increase fixed assets

Advances for the purpose of investing in, say, new plant or machinery are advances for capital expenditure, not the business of the bank. The current liabilities are increased as the item 'Bank overdraft' or 'Bank loan' goes up, but there is no corresponding increase in the current assets. The increase is in the fixed assets. So the liquid position is worse and the company's working capital has been decreased.

Advance to increase current assets

In this case the liquid position is unchanged, for current assets and current liabilities will both increase by the same

amount. An advance to buy stock would be an example
under this head. A request for an advance of this nature
would be more likely to receive favourable consideration.

Now we can take two examples, remembering that the banker
never wants to be asked to advance the whole of the sum
required, but thinks that his customer ought to put something into the kitty himself as well. We must remember also
that we are coming to conclusions on one balance sheet only,
whereas the banker prefers to have some previous experience
of the company's business and for this purpose will copy
out the balance sheet figures year by year on to a com-
parative form of some kind which will permit of a detailed
analysis.

A.B.C. Company Ltd

	£	£		£	£
Capital		10,000	Land & buildings		10,670
Reserves		5,250	Fixtures & fittings		1,020
Profit & loss account		7,250	Vehicles		1,028
		22,500			12,718
Trade creditors	11,280		Stock	10,420	
Tax-current	3,460		Trade debtors	19,611	
Tax-future	3,600		Cash	1,070	
Bank	2,979				
		21,319			31,101
		£43,819			£43,819

Profit for the year (after tax) £3,319. Sales £93,000.

The company is a private one, operating as a builders'
merchants in a suburb of London. They have a busy shop,
which is always full, with stock all over the floor and very
little room to move. There is a display floor upstairs showing
various layouts for kitchens and bathrooms. Space at the
rear allows builders to come in to get their supplies, load
them up, and drive off with them. The shop is used also by
do-it-yourself individuals who are making their own improvements at home. The customers have been in account at the bank
for a number of years, and have a good reputation both with
the bank and in the town. There is an unsecured overdraft

limit of £4,000, which is fully used at times, but the account swings well and occasionally goes into credit.

The bank is asked to increase the limit to £12,500. The increase of £8,500 will finance an extension to the shop which will take in part of the space at the rear. Repayment out of profits is promised over four years.

The directors' capital in the balance sheet is £22,500. All this money must be lost before the settlement to creditors becomes endangered. There is a liquid surplus of £9,782. A comparison of stock and sales figures suggest a brisk turnover.

What will the balance sheet look like if this advance is granted? The figure for land and buildings will rise by £8,500, as will the total of current liabilities. (the bank overdraft will rise by £8,500 as well).

	£	£		£	£
Capital		10,000	Land & buildings		19,170
Reserves		5,250	Fixtures & fittings		1,020
Profit & loss account		7,250	Vehicles		1,028
		22,500			21,218
Trade creditors	11,280		Stock	10,420	
Tax-current	3,460		Trade debtors	19,611	
Tax-future	3,600		Cash	1,070	
Bank	11,479				
		29,819			31,101
		£52,319			£52,319

The liquid surplus has dropped to a mere £1,282 (£31,101–£29,819), and current tax has to be paid. Once the extension to the shop has been completed, there will be room for more stock, which will in turn increase the sales and therefore the profit. But the working capital which is required to pay for this increased stock is not there, so it is apparent that the bank advance of £12,500 is not going to be enough.

Can the directors introduce any capital from another source? The situation should be discussed with them. Obviously the question of granting any increase unsecured cannot be considered – should a debenture be suggested? Even then, would the situation be other than marginal?

These are the immediate reactions to this single balance sheet.

The repayments suggested from the increased flow of business are never going to be received if unpaid creditors put the company into liquidation. There is often a critical period in every business where the company can find itself temporarily short of working capital, but the risk to the bank asked to support it at these times must be a reasonable one. Here the shop premises appear to be unencumbered and a charge over the land as security suggests itself as a possibility, but the bank would be certain to be asked for more money as time went on and it is not easy to see how much more it would have to lend. Moreover, the bank is being asked to lend the whole of the sum required.

Now another proposition, from a similarly-sized company.

D.E.F. Company Ltd

	£	£		£	£
Capital		8,000	Plant & machinery		5,880
Reserves		1,502			
Profit & loss account		8,500			
		18,002			5,880
Current tax	3,220		Stock	18,470	
Trade creditors	34,414		Trade debtors	26,612	
			Cash & bank	4,674	
		37,634			49,756
		£55,636			£55,636

Profit for the year (after tax) £8,440. Sales £102,580.

This is a small private company engaged in light engineering, which was founded some eight years ago in rented premises. The directors are young and energetic and have built the business up by hard work and by remunerating themselves modestly so as to leave as much of the profits in the company as possible. A bank overdraft was agreed over the first five years of the company's life, since when it has been able to operate in credit. Business has continued to increase and the directors now find that the rented space is inadequate for their requirements and they judge that the time has come to build their own works. The estimated cost of this is £14,000. The directors can arrange for half of this to be found informally from family sources, and ask the bank to lend £7,000. The freehold deeds of the new workshop are offered as security. Repayment out of profits is promised over four years.

The history of the company and the quality of its management will tend to inspire confidence in the bank, together with the fact that half of the sum required is to be found elsewhere. The request is a reasonable one, one which every small company making progress will have to make at some stage or other. On the figures supplied there is a good liquid surplus of £12,122. However, the advance is again to be used to acquire a fixed asset, and therefore working capital will be cut down.

Re-writing the balance sheet to see the position after the loan has been taken, one sees that the liquid surplus will then be £5,122. Tax is to be paid, but there are enough funds in hand for this. Good security is offered. Trade creditors are rather higher than one would like to see, bearing in mind the trade debtor figure, and it may again be the case that the company should have asked for rather more, say another £2,000, or £3,000, to give them more elbow room with their working capital position. Also the bank manager will want to know whether in the new building the business is expected to require more in the way of stock, or whether the present stock will be adequate for the immediate future. Details of contracts on hand will help in assessing this. Subject to satisfactory information from the directors on these points, the bank would probably be prepared to help. Repayment will be from profits, and these, we may take it, have been increasing year by year up to this point. A forward budget, although by necessity only an estimate, will give some guidance on whether the annual repayments are feasible, and whether the number of years over which repayment is to be made is satisfactory to the bank.

Going concern and gone concern

The appraisals made so far have all been on the supposition that the balance sheet figures are those of a going concern, that the sums recorded are in fact of that worth to the continued progress of the company. If it is anticipated that the company may fail, a very different interpretation must be placed on the figures. On a gone concern footing the left-hand side of the balance sheet will remain the same, on the right-hand side there will be drastic scaling down. Figures for goodwill and cash will almost certainly disappear. Property will be conservatively written down, plant and machinery, office furniture and the like will be written in at scrap value only. Vehicles will usually come out of it reasonably well, provided they have been well maintained, for there is nearly always a ready sale. Stock will usually have to be marked down, work-in-progress will be of little value, being neither one thing nor the other. Raw materials will keep their value quite well.

Let us take a look at an example.

X.Y.Z. Company Ltd

	£	£		£	£
Capital		12,000	Freehold property	20,500	
Reserves		3,500	*Less* mortgage	16,000	
					4,500
Profit & loss account		2,000	Plant & machinery		3,500
			Fixtures & fittings		2,200
			Vehicles		3,400
		17,500			13,600
Trade creditors	13,800		Sundry debtors	9,400	
Hire purchase creditors	4,000		Stock	21,800	
Taxation	4,000		Cash in hand	900	
Bank	6,400				
		28,200			32,100
		£45,700			£45,700

X.Y.Z. Company Ltd is an old established customer of the bank which has for some years enjoyed temporary and fluctuating unsecured overdraft limits up to £6,000 to finance normal trade needs. Recently the advance has become much more solid, that is, the overdrawn balance seems to go up all the time, and the manager has had to write to the company calling their attention to the overdraft and asking for a reduction. The company manufactures transistor radios, high fidelity equipment, and electric clocks.

Its business has suffered recently from competition from abroad. The bank has been asked to increase the overdraft limit to £15,000 to finance an advertising campaign stressing the company's after-sales service (£2,000), settle pressing creditors (£3,000), and pay overdue tax (£4,000). A fixed and floating debenture on all the company's assets is offered as security.

The company's liquid surplus is poor for a manufacturing concern of this size, and unduly dependent upon stock, which stands at rather a high figure. The bank's records show that turnover at £79,000 is well down on the previous year (£108,000), while profits before tax have dropped from £11,000 to £2,000. The directors admit that the company is suffering from a temporary financial stringency, but expect trade to recover as a result of the advertising campaign. Repayments are to be out of profits over the next four years.

Further enquiry of the directors reveals that two large debtors totalling £5,000 are six months overdue, and that one half of the stock of high fidelity equipment has been in store for eighteen months. The question of a reduction in price to clear them is being discussed.

It is now clear that current assets could not raise enough to clear current liabilities, and that the bank's existing loan is in danger. Would the taking of an debenture, together with the granting of the fresh limit required, improve the bank's position? The manager decides to apply the gone-concern test to estimate the position in the event of a liquidation. He estimates the break-up value of the assets and analyses the creditors as follows:

Use to be made of the bank's advance

settlement of overdue tax	£4,000
settlement of certain pressing creditors	3,000
advertising costs	2,000

Analysis of balance sheet

	£	£		£	£
Capital		12,000	Freehold property	nil	
Reserves		3,500	Plant & machinery		350
Profit & loss account		2,000	Fixtures & fittings		220
			Vehicles		2,000
		17,500			2,570
Sundry trade			Sundry debtors	3,960	
creditors	10,800		Stock	10,900	
Hire purchase					
creditors	4,000				
Bank	15,400				
		30,200			14,860
		£47,700			£17,430

The manager considers the freehold factory to be well-sited, but specialized and difficult to adapt. He thinks there will be little if any left over after the mortgage is paid off. Plant and machinery, and fixtures and fittings, he values as scrap. Vehicles are in reasonably good conditions, but five or more years old. He values Sundry debtors by writing off the two doubtful cases and allowing 10 per cent loss on the remainder. He puts the stock in at half price, and makes no allowance for cash, which will all have disappeared by the time it is most wanted.

On this estimate the business will produce £17,430 cash assets to satisfy the creditors. This sum would all fall under the debenture, if taken, and so be available for the bank (supposing the company continued in business for twelve months after the taking of the debenture), which would in this way secure repayment in full, leaving about £2,000 over for the other creditors, who would thus get about 13p in the £.

The requirement for the company to continue in business

for twelve months after the taking of the debenture results from a section of the Companies Act which makes floating charges taken from a company within the twelve months before its liquidation void and of no effect in certain conditions. The intention is to stop certain creditors of a failing company improving their position at the expense of other creditors, as indeed the bank would be doing here.

A similar exercise to show the position if the company were to go into liquidation now shows that the £17,430 expected would first go to pay the £4,000 owed in tax. Certain creditors are by law 'preferred', that is, they are paid in full first, before anyone else gets anything. The Inland Revenue is such a preferred creditor in respect of any one year's tax owing. (We will suppose that the £4,000 is in respect of last year's tax). The remainder, £13,430, will be available for all the other unsecured creditors including the bank. They total £24,200 so the company will pay 55p in the £ and on its advance of £6,400 the bank would lose £2,880.

These figures are of course very rough. An exercise of this nature is merely to indicate the broad choices open to the bank, and to try to assess the bank's position in the worst of all possible cases.

Revision Test 12

Put ticks in what you think are the right boxes.

(1) Interest charged on an overdraft paid for the year will be shown in
    (a) the trading account   ☐
    (b) the profit and loss account   ☐
    (c) the profit and loss appropriation account   ☐

(2) Goodwill is
    (a) an intangible asset   ☐
    (b) a floating asset   ☐
    (c) a fictitious asset   ☐

(3) A bank overdraft appears in a company's balance sheet as
(a) a long term liability ☐
(b) a floating asset ☐
(c) a current liability ☐

(4) Working capital is
(a) fixed assets minus current liabilities ☐
(b) floating assets minus long term liabilities ☐
(c) floating assets minus current liabilities ☐

(5) A sum of money set on one side to meet future tax is a
(a) general reserve ☐
(b) provision ☐
(c) revenue reserve ☐

(6) A bank advance to purchase stock will
(a) reduce the outstanding liabilities of the business ☐
(b) increase the fixed assets of the business ☐
(c) increase the current assets of the business ☐

(7) A bank advance to pay tax will result in
(a) an increase in the working capital ☐
(b) a decrease in the working capital ☐
(c) no change in the working capital ☐

(8) On a gone concern basis which will show up best?
(a) plant and machinery ☐
(b) vehicles ☐
(c) work-in-progress ☐

(9) Which of the following statements is true?
(a) A qualified auditor must audit the accounts of a partnership ☐
(b) The profit and loss account is concerned with the distribution of goods ☐
(c) Net profit is gross profit less administrative and over-head charges ☐

(10) An adverse balance on profit and loss account has
the effect of
(a) increasing the fixed capital ☐
(b) reducing the long term liabilities ☐
(c) decreasing the proprietors' stake ☐

Check your solutions with the answers on p. 395.
Take one mark for each correct answer.
All Revision Tests total 10 marks.

Questions for discussion

1. As a lending banker what would you be looking for in your borrowing customer's balance sheet?

2. What circumstances can increase or decrease the working capital of a company?

3. What are the principles involved in assessing a company's balance sheet on a 'gone concern' basis?

13

Human relations in banking

Relations with customers

For the customer, the branch is the bank, and the branch manager is the personification of the bank. Under the branch manager the branch staff will go about their business in an atmosphere which will be set from the top. If the staff are happy with each other, and well led, there will be a contented, efficient air about the branch which will extend to the public side of the counter.

The customer is made to feel welcome in the branch: it is a place he enjoys visiting.

This ideal picture does in fact obtain in a number of branch banks, but not in all of them, not even in most of them. The banks have spent years in trying to break down an image very firmly held by the lower-middle and working classes, which can be summed up in the one word 'stuffy'. Such potential customers dared not even enter a bank, for fear of being made to feel embarrassed, either for lack of knowledge or paucity of resources. A further potent factor was that they couldn't find out how much it was likely to cost, but they suspected it would be too much.

Now mausoleums of dark wood and marble pillars have largely been replaced by bright and cheerful offices, with bright and cheerful cashiers, mostly girls, on the counters.

In some larger branches a receptionist is employed in the banking hall to assist or direct customers. The cashier is the first point of contact with the customer. He or she must have an easy manner, must be neatly dressed and well-groomed, and must be considerate and sensitive to the needs of the customer.

All this is in addition to the technical knowledge the cashier must have, which is important enough, but not so important as the cashier's personality and attitude.

It's how you get on with people that counts, not how much you know.

There are other points of contact between the customer and the bank besides the counter. There is, of course, the confidential interview in the manager's room; there are contacts outside the bank, often in the shape of business luncheons or visits to customers' premises or farms, there are telephone conversations, and there are letters.

Before we consider these we must think for a minute about the bank's duty of secrecy with regard to the affairs of the customer.

Banking is neither a calling, like being a priest, nor a profession, like being a doctor; but neither is it shop-keeping. It is somewhere between the two – call it semi-professional, if you like. At any rate, it carries with it an atmosphere of confidentiality. The new entrant signs a declaration of secrecy, and gradually learns what this means. It means you don't disclose to anyone the state of the customer's account. You don't discuss his affairs with anyone, not even your wife, and when you talk to your colleagues about him you do it in the office where no one can overhear you, and not over coffee in the café over the road, or in the train. You don't give his balance over the telephone unless you are absolutely certain that it is he to whom you are speaking. If a husband has a personal account you mustn't tell his wife how much is in it, and vice versa. If a customer asks for his balance over the counter you write it on a piece of paper and hand it to him folded.

You learn discretion. The customer is entitled to have his business kept secret, and he relies on this.

This duty of secrecy grew out of the business of banking, but it has been reinforced by case law. A judge once said that disclosure was permissible only in four cases, under compulsion of law, when there is a duty to the public to disclose, where the bank's interest demands disclosure, or where the customer's interest demands disclosure. Under the first of these we sometimes have to produce copies of accounts in a court of law, or report to the revenue authorities all cases where deposit interest of a certain amount is paid or credited to a customer annually, in case he is not declaring it in his income tax return.

Unfortunately these cases of compulsory disclosure seem to be on the increase. Under a law passed in 1976 a circuit judge, where he is satisfied by information on oath that there are reasonable grounds for suspecting an offence involving any form of fraud in connection with tax, may issue a warrant authorizing an officer of the Board of Inland Revenue to enter any premises (by force, if necessary) and to search for and seize documents and other articles which he believes may be needed as evidence for proceedings in respect of such an offence. It is not very likely that a tax inspector will force his way into a bank in search of information, but the mere fact that he can now legally do so is very disquieting.

A police officer is not entitled to ask for information about a customer merely because he *is* a police officer: if he wishes to inspect the bank's records he must get an order signed by a judge or a magistrate.

Interviews

If the customer wants to be sure of seeing the manager he should make an appointment. If he does not do this he cannot really complain if the manager finds it impossible to see him when he calls. Someone will see him, whether assistant- or under-manager, sub-manager or chief clerk, accountant or second clerk; whatever the description, he will be the most senior officer available. The customer may wish only to see the securities clerk or the foreign-exchange clerk if it is a question merely of picking up some documents.

Some customers refuse to see anyone but the manager. If they feel like this, that is their privilege, and the manager will suggest a suitable time, asking the customer if that is convenient for him.

By the way, there is always a manager. Don't say, 'the manager is out'. If he is, the next man down is the manager, acting, it is true, but fully able to represent the bank.

The manager should prepare himself for an interview which has been arranged in advance. He may have a record card on each customer which tells him a few facts about the customer, the date of the last interview, and brief details of what was then discussed. He will certainly have a copy of the customer's account and details of any securities and safe custodies held. He will have a quick look at the customer's correspondence file.

Without this preparation, the manager will go into the interview cold, and the customer will notice. The customer thinks he is the only one the manager has to worry about. He expects the manager to know all about him and his affairs. He will feel less important if he has to remind the manager of things which he feels the manager ought to know, and this will be bad for the bank, because the customer is not only important, he is everybody's bread and butter.

The manager may in fact remember all about the customer, but most managers have too many people on their books to be full of information about every one of them. Most managers are doing well if they can remember most of their borrowing customers.

This brings up another point. Sometimes you hear a customer say, 'I've been at that bank for sixteen years, and I've never met the manager.'

A reason may be that he has never needed to borrow. But a newly-appointed manager should make an effort to meet at least his most important credit customers (he will meet the others soon enough). He should write and say that he is the new manager and that he would be very pleased if the customer would call in to become acquainted; alternatively, he will be pleased to call on him.

At an interview the important things are that the interviewing officer should make the customer welcome, spend a few minutes in chatting generally (otherwise the customer may think that the manager's time is really too valuable and that he must state his business quickly), listen carefully with the whole of his attention, making notes as he does so, and finally ask any questions which are required to make the position clear. If the request is one which the manager can himself come to a decision on, he should then do so forthwith. If not, he should tell the customer that he will let him know the bank's decision at the earliest possible moment.

Incoming telephone calls can make interviewing very difficult. The manager can attend only to one customer at a time and he should ask his switchboard operator to divert calls during an important interview. Alternatively, he can take them, ask to be excused, and promise to ring back.

After the interview a memorandum of what passed should be completed and perhaps circulated round the senior staff to keep them informed of what is going on.

A different situation arises if an interview prolongs itself into the time set for the next interview. The manager should excuse himself, walk out to where the next customer is waiting, and apologize. He must do this personally.

A final touch is for the manager personally to escort the customer to the door.

Telephone communication

A telephone call to the bank should be answered by a pleasant voice saying, 'Southland Bank, Corn Street branch. Good morning, can I help you?'

The first impression is good. The caller's message is taken

and he is connected to the person who is going to handle it, or to the person for whom he has asked. That person has been told by the switchboard operator who the caller is, so when he lifts the receiver he is able to say, 'Good morning, Mr Brown.' In his voice he must convey a degree of interest in the customer and in his business. If he is at first unable to feel a genuine interest he should reflect that in the long run it is Mr Brown who pays his salary.

If the switchboard operator is some time finding the person asked for, she should go back to the caller to apologize for keeping him, and to explain the cause of the delay. This will reassure the caller that he has not been forgotten. The telephone is an infuriating thing at the best of times, and the caller may be in a short temper anyway. Customers are allowed to have short tempers, bank staff are not. In fact, dealing with an annoying or even rude customer is excellent character training for the person at the other end of the telephone. It is also a very difficult thing for anyone, but particularly for a young man or woman who has not had very much experience of life. Nevertheless, it is part of the job, which has to be learned like any other part.

An example. A young clerk newly transferred to a busy City office saw a customer waiting at the inquiries counter. The inquiries clerk was temporarily absent, so the young man very properly went up and said,

'Good morning, sir. Can I help you?'

'Yes,' said the customer, 'you can get me my statement.'

'Certainly. May I inquire your name?'

The customer was an important man and he was outraged that anybody at the branch should not know his name. He went red in the face.

'My name's Morgan,' he said, banging the counter, 'and don't you b——y well forget it!'

The clerk walked away without comment. He got the statement, put it in an envelope, and handed it over.

'There you are, Mr Morgan,' he said, pleasantly. 'I'm sorry you've been kept waiting.'

Mr Morgan snatched the envelope and stamped off without a word. He had achieved one thing. The clerk indeed did always thereafter remember his name, but for the wrong reason.

There are still people like this about, but as a general rule, the more important people are, the more courteous they tend to be towards their juniors. There must be a lesson in this somewhere.

Correspondence

Turning to letter writing, one can say at once that every letter from a bank to a customer is an advertisement for the bank. A good one, or a bad one. A good letter is written clearly in good English. Simple words are used in preference to important-sounding words. A conversational style is used. The customer's initials are correct and his name is correctly spelled, both on the letter and on the envelope. The latter is correctly addressed and properly stamped. The writer is polite, and friendly. The customer is addressed by name and not as 'Dear Sir'.

Dear Sir,
    I wrote to you on the 20th ult. about the matter of your overdraft. As you have not answered I am sending a copy for favour of your immediate attention.
    Yours truly,

PRIVATE
Dear Mr Jones,
    I see that I wrote to you last month and as I have had no reply I fear my letter failed to reach you. I am therefore enclosing a copy, and hope to hear from you shortly.
    Yours sincerely,

The golden rule for the writer is to try to imagine himself as the customer opening the letter and reading it. This is not an easy exercise, but it does suggest a sensible slogan – try to put yourself in the other person's place. How would you like it?

If the letter is in answer to one of the customer's it should (a) deal with all the points raised by the customer, and (b) be dispatched either on the day on which the customer's letter is received or on the following day.

There is, of course, a lot to learn about writing a good letter, and, indeed, about writing and speaking good English. Now that the schools no longer seem to treat the subject very thoroughly, the task of maintaining the standards has fallen on big business organizations. They will teach those who are willing to learn.

I hope it is apparent that banks require staff with a high sense of responsibility. The need for this starts from day one in the bank. Routine work in the early years may obscure this fact for a time, but eventually it will be recognized, one hopes, that the job carries a certain aura of integrity and is not without dignity.

Relations with staff

The strikes, lockouts, workings to rule, picketings, and confrontations which occur regularly in this country show that as a nation our employers have still got a lot to learn about the art of management. However, the banks are good employers and look after their staff both up to and after retirement better than most. As men and women in banks get older and more mature, they appreciate more fully how good the conditions are. For the young man or woman just starting in a new job, however, the immediate test of the bank is how they are received on their first day.

As with all staff matters, one has to remember that the average branch is a busy place, and most people in it are fully occupied all day long. The reception and training of new staff has to be fitted into a time table which is already heavily booked. However, a Personnel Department or Division will carry out the initial interviewing and selection, and will then appoint the new entrant to a branch, advising the manager at the same time. A pleasant custom which is sometimes encountered is for the manager to write to the new entrant inviting him or her to bring his or her parents to visit the branch in the week before the appointment is due to be taken up. They can then be shown over the branch and the new boy or girl can meet the people with whom he or she will be working. This takes away some of the strangeness of the first day.

The abruptness of the entry into branch routine is softened by a sensible system in the Midland Bank, where all new recruits join the bank at a training branch.

Banks may advertise that the minimum qualifications for entry are four 'O' levels, or some other requirements, but what they are basically looking for is a steady supply of new staff who are willing to learn, and have pleasant manners. There must be, in addition, enough suitable applicants to reach managerial level in due course. For the exceptional people this now means in their early thirties. The extraordinary diversity now offered in the banking industry means that a new recruit has a much better chance of finding the work for which he is best suited. It also means that for those who wish, and are suitable, there will be opportunities for travel abroad and exciting and interesting chances of work, as far removed from the conception of the clerk slaving away at his ledgers as could possibly be. Most women do not see banking as a career, preferring to marry and raise a family. Those who stay in the bank and progress to managerial status seem to do so on the administrative and personnel sides of banking, not in the domestic banking to be found in any ordinary branch. There are some female branch managers, but very few indeed. Their numbers may increase; after all, the very idea of a woman manager was quite unthinkable twenty years ago. But it is the men who go through to branch management.

What are the requirements?

Two have been mentioned already. Ability to get on with people, and willingness to learn. The first job is to fit into the branch and learn the branch routine, the second is to start preparing for the future by studying for the examinations of the Institute of Bankers. This is traditionally done in the evenings, either by evening classes or correspondence colleges. In recent years there have been changes in the thinking on this subject, as on most. Day release has been tried on the grounds that the young man or woman should not have to work all day and most nights also, because that leaves little time for the development of a social life. Where day release has been out of the question, half-day release has been given. These schemes have two disadvantages. The first is that in busy branches no one can be spared, therefore release has to be subject to the discretion of the manager. The second is that release is difficult to marry up with planned instruction by qualified teachers. Block release would overcome this if the banks would recruit sufficient staff to form an adequate staff reserve: greater emphasis is now being laid on this. (Block release would be where a clerk was given, say, three week's leave in a year in one go.) An alternative is for banks to leave their staff to study in any way they please, but to back them up by releasing them for attendance once yearly at the bank's own revision courses, run just before the examinations.

The application required for a young man to study consistently for a number of years is an important element in the selection of future managers. To some extent it shows the bank that the young man does not expect the bank to do everything for him, but is himself willing to contribute something to the joint venture.

The manager will have to be acceptable socially. He should have interests outside his job. The bank will therefore be pleased to see a young man who is interested in some local group which has some element of unselfish interest about it, some degree of community spirit.

A final quality which can advance or retard promotion is a certain respect for authority, or loyalty. Here we come to one of the biggest difficulties. Our young people today mature earlier and, on the whole, think more for themselves than preceding generations. Some young men have difficulty in calling anyone 'Sir', or in accepting traditions which have shaped the careers of their seniors. They do not accept that from the day of their appointment they are representatives of the bank. They do not wish to dress in conformity with the public image of the banker; in fact, the whole idea of 'conforming' is repugnant.

The bank recognizes that the young man is struggling to establish himself and to prove his manhood. It is patient. It will take a student who liked nothing better than to take part in a demonstration march, or a sit-in protest, and will hope to turn him into an employee who will do the bank credit. A man who joins the bank at seventeen and retires at sixty-five spends most of his lifetime with the bank, and will return in good measure his early training. In return he can be sure that unless he is dishonest, or persistently unpunctual, it is highly unlikely that he will ever be dismissed. He can be sure that the bank will not become insolvent, leaving him without a job. He can look forward to a pension which will be periodically raised to combat inflation. In a word, he has security.

It is the banks' misfortune that the characteristics which make the job most attractive are the very ones which least appeal to a young man. At seventeen he is perhaps not so interested in his pension rights, or in the fact that he can get a house mortgage at a privileged interest rate. The longer view comes with increased responsibility. Marriage seems to make a difference. Perhaps the purchase of a house, financed by the bank, has something to do with it. However this may be, at some point there or thereabouts the management trainee emerges.

Of course luck plays a part. The young man does not always find that all his superiors are considerate, understanding men who remember their own youth. Such older men have a duty to the younger ones. They should remember the disadvantages of youth – lack of knowledge and experience, lack of ability to handle difficult situations, not knowing what the right thing to say is. It is a poor game, to pit yourself against a junior who cannot answer back without getting into trouble, who has none of the weight on his side, who is always playing away from home. If he has done well he should be told so. If he has erred, again, he should be told so, but here there are two ways of doing it.

A young man wrote a letter to head office, to be signed by his manager. There was a spelling mistake in his written draft, unnoticed by his typist, who was even younger than he.

Here, Jones, you've got a word spelt wrong in this letter! For God's sake, man, didn't they teach you anything at school! Hurry up and get it put right! This letter's got to catch the five-thirty post.

Oh, William! This isn't a bad letter you've written, but one word is spelt incorrectly. If I let this go up to head office, where they don't know you quite as well as we do here, they might think you don't know the right spelling; whereas we know, of course, that it must be a typist's error. Can you have it put right please? I'd rather like to get this in the five-thirty post.

Deliberate obtuseness, of course, is another thing. But short of this, an error is almost certain to be made in good faith by someone trying to do his best. The speech, manners, and actions of senior officers have far more influence on their juniors than perhaps they suspect.

14

Training
and prospects
in banking

Bank courses

The central requirement of all banking is that good service should be given to the customer. This service can only be given properly if it is based on a broad commercial education. This commercial education will be carried on within the bank in the first stages of the examinations of the Institute of Bankers. The appropriate subjects are economics, accounting, legal principles and the English language, on which all else depends.

In the first place the bank will conduct an induction course on entry, to familiarize the new recruit with the structure of the organization he has joined, the career opportunities to be found within it, the salary scales to be expected, the social facilities of the bank, and the conditions and establishments of branches and departments. At the same time, or shortly after, as soon as the new entrant has settled down in the bank, there will be courses for imparting skills training, whether in the operation of machines or electronic accounting, which are inseparable from the provision of cheque and credit transfer systems.

Technical training

The next step up will see the young man or woman on the counter course, learning the duties of a cashier. There is a quite comprehensive legal background to the work of a cashier, on which has to be superimposed two other concepts: the first, the cashier as a representative of the bank, seeing many more customers than the manager does and requiring at least some of the social graces; the second, the cashier as a selling agent for the various services offered by the bank and its subsidiaries. Here the cashier must endeavour in conversation to identify a need which the customer has, whether he knows of it or not, and then to suggest the service and bring about the contact between the customer and the person who is going to supply the service, or see that it is supplied.

The courses on securities and foreign trade are the highest point of the technical training and can be said to conclude the young banker's basic training in banking techniques. When we come on to the pre-management and management courses we are dealing with education rather than training, taking education to mean the continuous development of the banker's professional background and judgement.

The technical training described is usually conducted by means of formal courses, whether residential or not, at colleges or centres staffed and run by bank staff. Any sort of training which is to be applied to the whole of the staff of the bank must surmount certain difficulties. One of these in the large clearing banks is the sheer numbers involved. Yet others are the fact that staff are in penny packets scattered in thousands of branches all over the country, and the many different levels of executive, managerial and clerical staff.

Usually the solution is the expensive one of bringing the staff in to a centre, but some attempts have been made to take the instruction to the student. Some banks maintain travelling tutors or branch training departments which can run local courses in a branch, to which clerks from nearby branches can come. Because the branch premises are wanted during the day these courses are in the evenings, unless there is a spare room, as there often is, which can be put to a daily use.

These courses must be on a small scale when the training task is viewed nationally, but they are something. Ideally any training, education, or help or assistance of any kind which is offered should be equally available for the whole of the staff. If we think of programmed learning, or unit exercise packages, or discs or cassettes, we can imagine a kind of remotely-controlled guidance which might perhaps be put under the general supervision of a local man, or, carried to its extreme, might be sent to the student in his home, or taken home by him from his branch. Experiments such as these have resulted in a well-established department of programmed learning in most of the big banks, sending out programmes to all branches from time to time. These programmes are written in the department. Some may be intended for use with teaching machines in the branch, so that if the student can be spared from his duties for an hour in the day he can study at the branch.

All these systems are initiated from the head office of the bank. Simultaneously, the new entrant is learning at his branch by being told what to do by his immediate senior – the traditional on-the-job apprenticeship. This is ideal if the business of the branch day by day will allow the senior man to exercise a sufficiently comprehensive supervision. A proper scheme of rotation of duties, limited though it must be to two or three jobs, will do much to expand the horizons of knowledge, and, incidentally, to maintain the interest of the recruit.

So the general branch staff discharge their duty to provide trained replacements for themselves. As the staff are constantly changing, so in these days are the technical aspects, always keeping up with the ever-increasing complexity of banking. One certain ability required of every bank officer today is adaptability.

Just before, or at, first management level, a whole new chapter of education begins, designed now to fit the manager into his place in the community, which looks for him to be a judge of his fellows and a leader in local matters. He is expected to give good financial advice and be the guide and counsellor of local industry, the treasurer of local groups and the supporter of local charities. In these circumstances banking becomes more than a mere job. It becomes a way of life.

Management development

For these managerial courses less formal instruction will be given. Much is done by informal discussion and seminars, a group leader seeing that a certain ground is covered. Besides the new information received, the manager will take from such a course a heightened awareness of the bank's resources and a better knowledge of the more senior officers of the bank, whom normally he might very seldom see, who have made visits to address the course and talk with them. New services provided by the bank, and the official policy on various matters, can be explained at these meetings. The central executives of the bank, too, will gain from these meetings because they will obtain valuable feed-back from their managers in the field.

These bank courses are supplemented at all levels by temporary attachments or secondings. Some young men or women may be lent for a period to a charitable organization working, say, in hospitals, or put on an Outward Bound course, things which have nothing to do with banking as such. Older men may be attached for a time to a subsidiary company, or seconded to a department of the Civil Service. There will be links with banks overseas, which may lead to reciprocal visits; there may be liaison with universities; there will be courses at administrative staff colleges.

The senior ladies of the bank may well have started as typists and will have had courses on shorthand, typing and secretarial work, later graduating to personnel duties and thereafter meeting a wide variety of people both in the course of their duties, and on courses or conferences in connection with them.

Banking as a career

The banks have first-class training programmes and they have spent much time in devising career patterns for staff able and willing to follow them. Against this there is the routine work which must be performed in the early years, and the discipline which is necessary where large numbers of employees are dealing with cash which belongs to other people. Conditions in busy branches become difficult when staff changes are frequent, the one leading to the other in a vicious circle.

How does the job seem to the outside world? Two interesting summaries were given by the Careers Information Service of the *Daily Telegraph* on 14 April 1975 and 3 May 1976, the first of these dealing with the international banker and the second with the domestic banker.

Interested in banking?

What is an international bank? The basic functions of a bank are familiar. In simple terms, it lends money at interest to individuals and companies and provides customers with a deposit taking service, paying interest on their deposits and using them to make loans to other customers, i.e. a fund-based service.

A bank also provides foreign exchange services, and certain fee-based services such as security of valuables and financial advice. An overseas branch provides similar services to customers overseas.

What is it that makes a bank international? Basically it is its ability to look after all the banking needs of its international customers on a world-wide scale. It requires a wide network of overseas branches and offices and the ability to tailor services to suit the customer's requirements.

For example, a large international company working closely with the government of a developing country may require a loan of millions of dollars to set up a new industry or develop a hydro-electric scheme. An international bank would be asked to raise such a loan, probably in Euro-dollars, together with other banks. This is a syndicated loan and is usually announced in the Press by way of a 'Tombstone' advertisement which gives the name of the borrower, the managing bank, and a list of subscribing banks.

The same operation may require the international customer company to form a local company under a 'joint venture' arrangement for which the skills of the bank's corporate finance team would be required. If the customer had a number of overseas subsidiaries or associates it could well require the services of the bank's international Money Management System Group to advise and implement the restructuring of its accounts, in order to help cash flow and reduce operating and financial overheads.

Lloyds Bank International is also an overseas commercial bank. The majority of its 10,000 employees are in Latin America, but the branch network extends also to Europe and the United States and has recently been expanded by the opening of branches or representative offices in the Far East and Middle East. The purpose of a representative office is to develop business for existing branches elsewhere, in areas where branches are not allowed or not yet established.

As in most businesses, only a minority of employees are in direct contact with the customers, the rest providing planning control and support services. Some functions such as administration, accounting, and personnel management make it possible for the basic banking operations to be carried out; other functions such as organization and methods, computer services, economic research, make it possible to perform them more effectively and efficiently.

The progress and direction of any business are influenced

by the economy of the country or countries in which it operates. When the economy is buoyant the marketing of banking services, including lending, is important. In times of economic stringency, as at present, it becomes more important than ever to make sure before money is lent that it will be secure, that is, that customers will be able to repay the loan on the due date. The functions of appraisal of credit-worthiness and loan inspection are always important. Today they are crucial.

The country's economy has an effect not only on the bank's business activities but also on its employment and recruitment policy. In the short term it is prudent to redeploy, if possible, anyone whose activities have been greatly reduced into a vacant appointment, instead of recruiting from outside. But the bank has to consider the medium and long term. Present areas of expansion are the Far East, Middle East, North America, and Europe; some of the vacancies there are filled by recruitment and others by transferring people with the right experience or aptitudes from other areas.

This in turn creates vacancies down the line which have to be filled by qualified and well-trained people willing to work anywhere in the world, and preferably with a potential for promotion as more senior vacancies become available. It is this kind of person, capable of holding a key job at an early age after only a few years in the bank, for whom recruitment and training must be planned and implemented continuously. A person with the right education and background but without banking experience can be trained in less than three years to become a junior banking officer. In exceptional cases it could be done in little more than a year.

The prospect of working in an international bank, helping to develop new financial services, working for part of one's career overseas, perhaps in areas where the Bank is a recent arrival, is a great attraction. Hundreds apply every year for the 25–30 vacancies available with Lloyds International.

What kind of candidate does a Bank such as Lloyds International look for? Most, though not all, have degrees. A recent successful candidate had a Higher National Diploma in Business Studies followed by a year as a clerk in a French bank and a year in Germany. Another had an economics degree, and an MBA and had been a trainee in an oil company. Another had a Ph.D. in engineering. The type of educational qualification is not the most important criterion, though business studies, economics, maths, and languages may be useful. What is important is adaptability, decisiveness, and an interest in economic and foreign affairs.

Some recruits join straight from school at 18 with good A levels and linguistic ability. After three years' basic training in London and after gaining a banking diploma they become eligible along with the older recruits for further training to equip them for an executive post in their twenties.

Twice a year a four-month induction course is held in London for 12–16 trainees, both new recruits and selected employees already working with us. The programme provides basic knowledge of banking, specially international and overseas, daily language tuition and an economic background to international affairs. This is followed by an on-the-job training programme, usually overseas, which lasts from six months to two years depending on previous experience, aptitude, and progress.

At the end of two years a number of the trainees will already have been for some time in their first appointment but they all return to London to complete their formal training with a three-week course in banking techniques and management and an introduction to those banking services and activities with which they are not yet familiar.

Further development is by a sequence of postings and appointments planned to give a wider experience of the bank's operations. Throughout their career executives keep in touch with modern techniques and skills by attending special courses inside and outside the bank, or being attached to departments in London or head offices overseas.

The three main areas of work are the servicing of international customers, domestic customer banking, and specialized functions such as administration, personnel, and computers. After training a likely appointment is to an overseas branch in the business function as assistant to the management or as sub-accountant in control of part of the branch's administration.

Alternatively, an ex-trainee may work in head office, perhaps in the credit appraisal department, or he may travel overseas as a member of an inspection team. Either of these appointments, principally intended to further his development, may precede a job in international banking in London or overseas or in an overseas branch. Many spend some time in their early careers in a branch in both lending and administration, and also increasingly nowadays in international banking. A few have an opportunity to work in the banking subsidiaries and associated companies. Most of them will have periods in London and overseas but in their early career it is unlikely that they will remain in the same job for more than 2–3 years.

Candidates for senior posts are likely to have had a variety of managerial experience and those who show outstanding potential are likely to reach senior executive level before they are 40. Most of those appointed to the Board in recent years have been in their forties.

International banking is a career which demands intelligence, clear thinking, human understanding, and nerve. For those who qualify there may be a rewarding future.

Working away in a bank

Lovers of Dickens, with visions of the banker perched precariously on a high stool entering an endless series of figures in some vast ledger, may be disappointed to hear that Dickens is dead. In terms of the banking world, though, his death is a comparatively recent event. Even now the clearing banks suffer from an image of stuffiness despite the various publicity campaigns to persuade the public otherwise. This popular view often extends to those who either make or contemplate making banking their career

The view is less than fair. Banking has developed considerably since the day when the Monopolies Commission described the banks as 'soporific' in the 1960s, and since that unique blend of friend and skeleton popped out of the cupboard at five-minute intervals on television screens up and down the land. Various stimuli account for the transformation, including the introduction of competition, the dramatically increased numbers of customers, the development of various services to attract both private and corporate customers, and, perhaps most important, the growing sophistication of personal, national, and international finance.

The net result is that the Clearing Banks presently operate some 12,000 branches throughout the country offering up to 200 separate services at branch level for upwards of 20 million customers. Supporting these services are the specialist divisions, such as hire purchase, merchant banking, or foreign-exchange dealing. As the services become at once more complex and comprehensive so the machinery follows suit. The banks operate some of the largest computer installations in the world which both opens a further career prospect and relieves the branches of much of the routine slog of dealing with figures.

This last point is important. Banking is not an arid profession dedicated to the processing of figures or the analysing of balance sheets. It is, perhaps primarily, a profession which deals with people and their problems. 'People' can mean the small personal account holder or, equally, the finance director of a multi-national industrial giant, but, in the end, the bank manager is assessing both the obvious practicality of a given proposition and the character and reliability of the customer; the one may invalidate the other. This being the case, staff managers are looking quite as much for an ability to get on with the public as for academic qualifications providing evidence of high numeracy. One manager actually listed the qualities he regarded as necessary in the following order:

patience, humour, numeracy, individuality or character. Others may vary the order of importance but the theme remains constant. Banking is, then, a profession for those with a flair for people as well as one for those with a flair for figures.

It is equally a democratic profession. People who work in banks do so for two reasons: they want a job or they want a career. Both categories are necessary, although it is fair to point out that for 1976 the number of 'jobs' vacant is likely to be less than in previous years, especially in large cities. The reason for this can be traced back to the present economic climate and the fact that banks offer security (as well as fringe benefits in terms of favourable borrowing rates which can be helpful in times of inflation).

Career entrants tend to enter at one of three levels: school leavers with a minimum of four O levels, preferably including English and maths; holders of at least two A levels – the subjects do not matter much but both economics and geography are looked on favourably – and graduates where, once again, the degree is of no particular relevance except in so far as an arts degree, including economics, is more likely to be appropriate than a degree in science.

All levels of entrant will follow the same training pattern and once they have reached a certain stage in their career, progress depends on their own ability and reflects neither age nor previous academic record. However, the O level entrant is paid less on joining than the A level entrant and the A level entrant less than the graduate. Once again there is good reason: A level entrant is expected to complete the training period faster than the school leaver and the graduate's training is yet more concentrated.

Most people will start their training in one of the branches. These are the backbone of retail banking, and it is here that the fundamental knowledge of banking procedures is obtained. The first job will probably be in the back rooms processing the details of the day's business, dispatching cheques to other banks, and feeding information to head office on the computers. A period in the general office follows this dealing with customer inquiries and correspondence, standing orders, and so on to the cashier's desk. It is here that the public is first met face to face, and apart from handling and being responsible for large sums of cash daily, the cashier is also the first person the customer meets and, as any public relations officer can vouch, first impressions are important, however difficult the customer. No one, incidentally, should underrate the vagaries of the general public. The case of the man who presented his cheque written on a cow is, after all, enshrined in law.

Throughout the early years, on-the-job training is supplemented by courses conducted either on a day-release basis or at a bank training centre. Further specialist training takes place upon transfer to the securities or foreign-exchange departments so that after about six years – the length of time varies according to the level of entry – the raw recruit is conversant with all aspects of branch banking.

Progress beyond the level of chief cashier depends upon the passing of the exams of the Institute of Bankers. These are in the process of being restructured and will be based on the national awards in business studies. Provision is made for exemption from parts of the syllabus depending upon qualification. For example, the O level entrant will spend some two years studying for an ONC in business studies whereas the A level holder will spend only one year on a 'conversion' course before embarking on the next stage which is an HNC in business studies. By 1978, when the new system is wholly operative, it will take a graduate some three years to gain the highest qualification, an A level entrant five years, and an O level entrant six years.

Basic training does not take place at a single branch. Banking in an agricultural community is vastly different from that conducted in an industrial community. The basic techniques may be the same, but the problems to which they are applied are not. The trained banker is a person of experience and it is clearly to the advantage of all parties that some of that experience is gained in the early stages. If you contract to join a bank and if you wish to develop a career within it, it is important to recognize that mobility is an essential feature of life.

Once the basic training has been completed, career development depends on the individual. Although, banking tends to be a one company career – transfers between banks are rare because of the confidentiality aspect – the number of occupations available is considerable. These range from branch banking services for private customers through financing industry or exports to dealing with credit cards or stocks and shares in the domestic sector. The development of world trade has led to increasing opportunities in international banking from foreign-exchange dealing to the managing of branches abroad, though numbers of openings are still not great. The growth in related banking services has obviously created a demand for persons capable of managing unit trusts, handling hire-purchase agreements, or providing full merchant banking services.

Banking services do not exist in a vacuum. Behind the keeping, providing, or transferring of money are services which you would find in any large multi-national business. Computer experts, personnel managers, property managers, publicists, and accountants are all necessary to a bank. Banking may be a one-company career, but then it also provides a broad enough spectrum of work to allow the incipient banker to switch careers without changing jobs.

Prospects for bankers are clearly good. It is unlikely that the trend towards a 'moneyless' society will be reversed, and this in itself will lead banking either into new areas or to evolving their existing services. The challenge is there and the banks are well aware that it has to be met and this can only happen if the new generation of bankers are prepared to accept it. Further rationalization of retail outlets will occur, but the United Kingdom is over banked, and this can only be of eventual benefit both to the customers and to those who work in banks.

In the unlikely event of time standing still there remains a great variety of progressive careers in a business which is not only central to the national economy but which touches everyone living in the country: provided, of course, that you like dealing with people.

Appendix

The Institute
of Bankers

The Institute of Bankers is a professional body whose members are men and women engaged in banking of every sort all over the world. It was founded in 1879, and its two main objects have always been:

(i) to provide an education in banking
(ii) to maintain the standard of the profession.

At present there are three grades of membership: ordinary members, who must be employed by a bank recognized by the Institute's Council; Associates, who have completed the banking or trustee diploma examinations; and Fellows, normally elected from senior associates who have given service to the Institute. The total of all three grades of membership is now over 110,000.

For members in their early years, the main part of their formal banking education (apart, that is, from their working experience) is provided through courses of study for the associateship examinations. For the vast majority, the Banking Diploma is the qualification which they are encouraged to obtain by their employers; for the much smaller numbers on the executor and trustee side, a separate route is available – the Trustee Diploma.

As a prelude to their studies for the associateship examinations, members – other than those who already hold a degree acceptable to the Institute, or two relevant GCE A-levels (viz. in law, economics or accountancy) – will be expected to complete Stage 1 of the Institute's educational structure. Stage 1 is intended to provide a background knowledge of the basic commercial subjects: economics, law, accountancy and English, as well as the subject of this book, 'Elements of Banking' (or Elements of Investment for 'trustee' candidates). Courses that satisfy the Institute's Stage 1 requirements include the appropriate public awards in business studies, such as the Business Education Council (BEC) National Certificate and Diploma; equivalent overseas and local commerical qualifications; and suitable recognized conversion courses (primarily for students who already hold one or more GCE A-levels).

The Banking Diploma leading to the award of A.I.B. (Associate of The Institute of Bankers) forms Stage 2 of the Institute's educational structure. Its object is to provide a knowledge of technical banking and applied business studies and it is the basic qualification for the majority of career bankers. Subjects covered in the first part of the Banking Diploma include accountancy, applied economics – with particular reference to monetary theory and practice, law relating to banking, finance of international trade, investment, and the nature of management. A link with the new public sector awards at this level is under consideration, but for the time being students are being advised to prepare for the Institute's own Stage 2 examinations. The second part of the Banking Diploma entails study for two compulsory Institute papers in the practice of banking.

Full details of Stages 1 and 2 of the Institute's educational structure are given in an Institute publication – the annual *Associateship and Optional Examinations: Regulations, Syllabus & Tuition Guide* – obtainable from the Registrar's Department, The Institute of Bankers, Emmanuel House, Canterbury, Kent CT1 2XJ.

Completing the Institute's educational structure is the new Financial Studies Diploma, providing a degree level qualification in banking and management subjects for those who are expected to achieve senior management appointments. This diploma covers subjects such as personnel management, marketing and business planning, as well as advanced banking practice. Entry is restricted (i) to Associates of The Institute of Bankers, and (ii) to holders of acceptable degrees of professional qualifications who have also taken two special introductory papers and completed a course of recommended background reading. Details of the syllabus and regulations for the Financial Studies Diploma are obtainable from the Institute Registrar's Department (see address above).

Students have a choice of methods of study for the examinations: they can attend technical college classes, take correspondence courses, or rely entirely on private study. For the majority, good oral tuition is likely to be the most effective method of study.

A system of recognition, for correspondence courses, was started in 1968 to ensure that material for the final subjects of the Banking Diploma is kept up-to-date, and that the marking of test papers corresponds with the standards expected by the Institute in the examinations. A considerable number of courses, offered by five commercial correspondence colleges, are now recognized under this scheme; because of the large volume of banking candidates, enrolment fees have been kept at a reasonable level compared with those charged for other professional courses.

Revision courses

The banks themselves offer a great deal of encouragement to their staff to complete the examinations. In most cases candidates are given study leave – a half day or a full day per week – and some of the larger banks run their own revision courses in the final subjects. Candidates overseas – who now account for a substantial proportion of the 100,000 subject-entries a year – do not usually enjoy the same facilities; since 1974, therefore, the Institute has sponsored a number of revision courses in Practice of Banking, sending tutors from the United Kingdom to a number of overseas countries.

In the UK many of the Institute's local centres (see below) run similar revision courses, and some of the examiners have recently conducted 'teach-in' sessions in Practice of Banking and other technical subjects in the larger local centres. The Institute itself provides a comprehensive service to banking teachers through regular education bulletins containing up-to-date information about the subjects they teach, and short courses for those who are teaching banking subjects.

An important feature of the Institute's examinations is that they are not 'competitive': an objective standard is set in each subject, and those who reach it pass, those who do not, fail. This means that the percentage of those passing can fluctuate from one examination to the next.

Local Centres

It is vital, of course, that any sort of vocational education should be kept up-to-date, and the Institute sets out to provide the banker with the means of doing this throughout his career. To cater mainly for the qualified members it has encouraged the formation of local centres of which there are now more than 100, with eight of them overseas. These centres each have honorary education officers, whose task is to deal with the problems of students in their areas. The main work of the centres, however, is in arranging programmes of lectures, discussions, seminars, industrial visits, and social events for its qualified members. In the past few years nearly 1,000 meetings have been arranged annually, attended each year by over 30,000 members and their colleagues in allied professions.

Other facilities

The main medium of communication with the members is the two-monthly *Journal*, which provides information on all major new developments in banking and in the Institute. The Institute also issues a wide range of other publications – especially works of reference on the practice and law of banking. Its library, with over 30,000 volumes, is well known in the financial world, and in addition to the usual services provides members with excellent postal borrowing facilities and a wide ranging information service.

The Institute is directly involved in running a number of courses for members of senior management in the banks and, in recent years, has also promoted scholarships and study-tours to enable younger qualified members to learn about banking systems in other countries.

In short, the Institute aims to provide something for everyone at every stage of his or her career in banking. In the long term the services which it offers should help its members in their careers, the banks with their profits, and, perhaps most important, improve the standard of service enjoyed by their customers.

Glossary

Acceptance A word sometimes used to denote an accepted bill of exchange, but strictly the writing across the face of a bill by which the drawee assents to the order of the drawer.

Accommodation bill A bill to which a person adds his name to oblige or accommodate another person, without receiving any consideration for so doing (in other words to lend him money).

Ad valorem According to the value, generally in connection with taxes or duties.

All monies debenture A deed of debenture express to cover all monies owing by a company at any time on any account.

Arbitrage A term formerly used to describe the activities of dealers in foreign exchange, when cross-dealing in various currencies quoted at differing rates in differing financial centres, with a view to making a profit. Now often used to describe the activities of company treasurers who are able to borrow from a bank under an existing overdraft limit and re-lend the money at a profit on the inter-bank market or on another secondary market ('Interest arbitrage').

Assignment A transfer or making over of a right to another person, as in the assignment of the proceeds of a life policy as security to a lending banker.

Authorized depositary A person authorized by an order of the Treasury to keep bearer securities in safe custody. The term arose under the Exchange Control Act, 1947, and includes banks, members of the Stock Exchange, solicitors practising in the United Kingdom, and certain other financial institutions.

Bank bill   A bill of exchange bearing the endorsement of a bank.

Bank Rate   Formerly the advertised minimum rate at which the Bank of England would discount approved bills of exchange, or lend against certain securities. Bank Rate was discontinued in October 1972 and replaced by the minimum lending rate.

Bear   A speculator on the Stock Exchange who anticipates a fall in the value of a certain security and therefore sells stocks which he does not possess in the hope of buying them back more cheaply at a later date, thus making a profit.

Bill of exchange   An unconditional order in writing, addressed by one person to another, and signed by the person giving it, requesting the person to whom it is addressed to pay, on demand or at a fixed or determinable future time, a sum certain in money to, or to the order of, a specified person, or to bearer.

Bill of lading   A receipt for goods upon shipment, signed by a person authorized to sign on behalf of the owner of the ship. The bill of lading is also a document of title to the goods. It is capable of being transferred by endorsement.

Billbroker   A merchant engaged in buying and selling bills of exchange.

Bimetallism   A currency system having a double standard, under which gold and silver coins are in circulation, containing the full weight of metal represented by their face value.

Blue Chip   A term used to describe the ordinary shares of first-class industrial companies.

Bull   A speculator on the Stock Exchange who anticipates a rise in the value of a certain security and therefore buys such stocks, not intending to pay for the purchase, but hoping to sell them later, at a profit.

Bullion   Gold or silver in bars or in specie. The term is also used to describe quantities of gold, silver, or copper coins when measured by weight.

Capital   Money used to run a business, often raised by an issue of shares: sums of invested money: the amount of money used or available to carry on a concern.

Cash   Deposits with the central bank, banknotes and coin.

Chain of title   In the proof of title to land, the sequence of deeds and documents from the good root of title to the holding deed.

Cheque   A bill of exchange payable on demand drawn on a banker.

Clean Bill A bill of exchange having no documents attached.

Clearing bank A bank which is a member of the London Bankers' Clearing House.

Consideration The price paid. The term has been defined as 'Some right, interest, profit or benefit, accruing to one party, or some forbearance, detriment, loss, or responsibility given, suffered or undertaken by the other.'

Consumer spending The current expenditure of individuals, including purchases of so-called 'consumer durable' articles, such as television, radios, washing machines and machinery for use in the home.

Currency The recognized means of making payments which circulate from hand to hand, or pass current, in a country.

D/A bill A bill with documents attached, presented for acceptance by the drawee, the documents to be surrendered against such acceptance.

Dated stock Gilt-edged stock issued by the government, having a date by which it will be repaid.

Debenture An acknowledgement of indebtedness, usually given under seal and usually incorporating a charge on the assets of an incorporated company.

Deed A written document executed under seal, evidencing a legal transaction.

Demand An authoritative claim or request. A demand draft is one payable on presentation. Current account balances are repayable on demand.

Deposit bank A bank taking money from customers on current deposit or other accounts on the terms that the money is to be repaid on demand or at the end of an agreed term: usually confined to banks which take any sum on deposit, and do not specify any minimum amount.

Deposit rate The rate of interest paid by a bank on a deposit account.

Depreciation Loss in value of assets by wear and tear, obsolescence, etc.; or normal deterioration in value which takes place during the life of an asset. Of a currency: a diminution or lessening of the power of the monetary unit over the market, the diminution being shown by a rise in prices.

Devaluation The reduction of the official par value of the legal unit of currency, in terms of the currencies of other countries.

Documentary bill A bill of exchange which is accompanied by various documents, such as a bill of lading, invoice, and insurance policy.

Domestic banking The normal course of business between banker and his customer (as opposed to 'wholesale' banking), or the banking business in this country (as opposed to international foreign banking).

Domicile A place of permanent residence: the place at which a bill of exchange is made payable.

D/P bill A bill with documents attached, presented for payment by the acceptor or drawee, the documents to be surrendered against such payment.

Drawee The person or company on whom a bill of exchange or cheque is drawn. When he has accepted a bill he is known as the acceptor.

Drawer The person who writes out and signs a cheque or bill of exchange.

Eligible liabilities The sterling deposits of the banking system as a whole, excluding deposits having an original maturity of more than two years, plus any sterling resources gained by switching foreign currencies into sterling. Interbank transactions and sterling certificates of deposit (both held and issued) are taken into the calculation of individual banks' liabilities on a net basis, irrespective of term.

Endorsement in blank An endorsement in blank consists of the name only of the payee or endorsee of a bill of exchange, written on the back of the bill. Such an endorsement specifies no endorsee, and the bill becomes payable to bearer.

Finance bill A bill drawn by a firm or company for the purpose of arranging a short-term loan. The bill is drawn by arrangement on another firm or on a bank or accepting house. No sale of goods is involved. When the bill is accepted it is discounted.

Floating pound The pound sterling left to find its own level on the foreign exchanges through the operation of the laws of supply and demand.

Foreign bill A bill of exchange drawn abroad and payable in this country; or drawn in this country and payable abroad.

Forward rate The rate at which foreign currency can be bought or sold for delivery at a future time.

Freehold An estate in land which is properly described as an estate in fee simple absolute in possession, signifying the highest type of land ownership which anyone can possess.

Gilt-edged Securities of the highest class (e.g. government stock) which are readily realizable.

Good root of title A document which deals with the whole legal and equitable interest in the land, describes the property in detail, and shows no adverse factor influencing the title. It is the starting point of the chain of title when proving title to land.

Ground rent The rent paid to a freeholder who has granted a lease on his land and/or buildings.

Hedge against inflation An investment in land or shares which is expected to appreciate in value in times of inflation, thus protecting the investor against loss due to the fall in the value of the money.

Holding deed The deed which transferred the ownership of land to the person who is now holding it.

Inflation The result of the excessive issue of paper money, so that too much money is chasing too few goods, with the result that the value of the money in terms of goods steadily falls (i.e. prices rise).

Inland bill A bill of exchange both drawn and payable in this country.

Intrinsic value Genuine or real value. When used of coin it means that the metal in the coin is worth the face value of the coin.

Investment Using money to buy something which it is hoped will bring in some return and will not lose its value.

Jobber A dealer on the Stock Exchange who carries on business with the public and with other jobbers through the medium of stockbrokers.

Leasehold The granting of the use of land by the freeholder to a lessor for a term of years.

Legal tender The authorized notes and coin which may be lawfully offered in payment of a debt in a country.

Lien A legal right to obtain goods belonging to someone else until the charges on them have been paid, or until some pecuniary claim against the owner has been satisfied.

Limited liability The limitation of the shareholders of a company of their liability for the debts of the company to the nominal amount of the shares they hold or to the amount they have guaranteed.

Long bill A long bill is a bill of exchange having a usance of three months or more.

Minimum Lending Rate The Bank of England's minimum rate of interest for lending to the money market. It was based on the average rate of discount for treasury bills at the weekly tender plus $\frac{1}{2}$ per cent and rounded to the nearest $\frac{1}{4}$ per cent above, but is no longer so calculated.

Mortgage The conveyance of a legal or equitable interest in real or personal property as security for a debt or for the discharge of an obligation.

Near money A term sometimes applied to bills, cheques, promissory notes, postal and money orders.

Offer for sale An invitation to the public to buy shares of a new issue from an Issuing House which has bought the issue from the company concerned.

Offshore funds A name given to mutual investment funds registered abroad in countries which offer tax advantages.

Open market operations The purchase or sale of securities in the Stock Exchange or Money Market by the central bank for the purpose of expanding or contracting the volume of credit.

Option forward rate The rate at which foreign currency can be bought or sold for delivery between two future dates at the option of the buyer or seller. The option is as to the precise day of completion.

Paper money Documents representing money, such as banknotes, promissory notes, bills of exchange or postal orders. (The last three of these are sometimes referred to as 'quasi-money'.)

Par The nominal value of securities, or the exact amount which has been paid for them.

Pledge A delivery of goods or the documents of title to goods, by a debtor to his creditors as security for a debt, or for any other obligation. It is understood that the subject of the pledge will be returned to the pledgor when the debt has been paid or the obligation fulfilled.

Prime bank bill A bill of exchange drawn on and accepted by a first-class bank.

Qualitative control Directives from the Bank of England to the lending banks and financial institutions as to classes of customers who may be allowed to borrow.

Quantitative control Directives from the Bank of England to the lending banks and financial institutions as to the total amount of money which they may lend.

Reserve assets These assets, to be held by banks and other financial institutions, are those which the Bank of England is ready to convert into cash, either directly or through the discount market. They comprise:

(1) balances at the Bank of England (other than Special Deposits).

(2) British and Northern Ireland government treasury bills

(3) money at call with the London money market

(4) British government stocks with one year or less to maturity

(5) local authority bills eligible for rediscount at the Bank of England

(6) commercial bills eligible for rediscount at the Bank of England (up to a maximum of 2 per cent of eligible liabilities).

Restrictive endorsement One which prohibits the further negotiation of a bill or cheque.

Retail banking The traditional course of business between a banker and his domestic customers, as opposed to 'wholesale' banking.

Rights issue The offer by a company of new shares direct to its existing members. The price is usually set below the market price of the existing shares, in order to make the offer attractive. The rights to subscribe, therefore, have themselves a market value, and can be sold.

Scrip The document or provisional certificate which is given to a person who has agreed to take up bonds in connection with a government loan and has paid the first instalment. Scrip is principally associated with the issue of bonds or debentures.

Scrip issue A capitalization of reserves by issuing fully paid-up shares free to present shareholders in proportion to their current holding.

Short bill A short bill is one which has only a few days to run to maturity, irrespective of the original tenor of the bill.

Sight bill   A bill of exchange payable as soon as sighted or seen by the drawee.

Special deposit   An instrument of monetary policy, designed to restrict credit. The Bank of England may call upon all banks and financial institutions to deposit a percentage, usually 1 per cent, of their total deposits with the Bank of England. This restricts the ability of the lending institutions to extend credit.

Speculation   The purchase or sale of shares on an estimate of whether the share value will rise or fall, with the intention of making a quick profit, or avoiding a loss.

Spot rate   The normal rate of exchange quoted in the foreign exchange markets, i.e. the rate for transactions in which the funds are to be paid over in each centre two working days later.

Stag   A Stock Exchange expression for a person who applies for shares in any new company with the sole object of selling as soon as a premium is obtainable and never intending to hold or even fully subscribe for the shares.

Stockbroker   One who purchases or sells stocks or shares for his clients on the Stock Exchange.

Tenant right   A right of the tenant of property, whether expressly stated or implied, such as a right to remove fixtures at the end of the tenancy, or to receive an allowance for seeds or fertilizer put on the land.

Tenor   The exact purport or meaning. Applied to a bill of exchange it means the purpose and intent of the bill on a construction of the words and figures used in it.

Term bill   A bill of exchange which is payable at the end of a period, as opposed to a bill payable at sight or on demand.

Token money   Coins where the value of the metal in them is less than the value attached to them by law, such as the cupronickel and bronze coins of this country.

Trade bill   A bill of exchange drawn and accepted by commercial firms.

Treasury bill   Bills issued by the treasury in return for sums of money lent to the government by bankers, brokers, etc. They form part of the floating debt of the country.

Undated stock   Gilt-edged security issued by the government on a perpetual basis and having therefore no date by which it will be redeemed.

Usance bill   A bill of exchange drawn in one country and payable in another at a term which is governed by the custom or usage of such transactions.

Wholesale banking Borrowing or lending, usually in large sums, by big banks amongst themselves through the medium of the interbank market; dealing with other financial institutions, as opposed to the retail banking, which consists of the traditional course of business between a bank and its customers.

Answers to Revision Tests

Test No. 1 1b: 2c & d: 3c: 4b: 5c: 6a: 7b: 8b & c.
Test No. 2 1a: 2b: 3c: 4c: 5b: 6a: 7c: 8a: 9c: 10b.
Test No. 3 1b: 2c: 3a: 4b: 5a: 6c: 7a: 8b: 9a: 10b.
Test No. 4 1b: 2c: 3a: 4b & c: 5c: 6c: 7a: 8b: 9c.
Test No. 5 1c: 2b: 3a: 4b: 5b: 6b: 7b: 8b: 9c: 10b.
Test No. 6 1a: 2b: 3b: 4a: 5a: 6b: 7c: 8b: 9c: 10c.
Test No. 7 1b: 2b: 3c: 4b: 5a: 6c: 7b: 8a: 9a & b.
Test No. 8 1c: 2b: 3b: 4a: 5c: 6a: 7c: 8b: 9b: 10c.
Test No. 9 1c: 2b: 3b: 4c: 5b: 6b: 7b: 8a: 9c: 10b.
Test No. 10 1a & b: 2c: 3b: 4a: 5c: 6b: 7c: 8b: 9b.
Test No. 11 1a: 2b: 3c: 4a: 5b: 6c: 7b: 8c: 9b: 10b.
Test No. 12 1b: 2a: 3c: 4c: 5b: 6c: 7c: 8b: 9c: 10c.

Supplementary
notes

Page 48

Although in theory MLR was determined by the market rather than by the Bank, it was soon found that the Bank was likely to suspend the MLR formula (as it had first done in November 1973) when the market forced the rate to an unwelcome level. On many other occasions the Bank sought to influence the price at which the discount houses tendered for Treasury Bills, thereby manipulating MLR at one remove.

Then when the Bank from time to time let the market have its head and take MLR to whatever level was thought appropriate, much confusion followed.

The decision to abandon the formula was announced in May 1978. It had become an unhappy compromise – the Bank not quite in charge, the market not really free. In future the level of MLR will be established by 'administrative decision', any change being announced at 12.30 p.m. on a Thursday. It is intended that MLR will continue to be adjusted 'flexibly', taking account of market developments. Changes in MLR require the Chancellor's approval.

Page 57

The corset was reintroduced on 18 November 1976. Over the subsequent six months the authorities set a limit of 3 per cent growth in a banking institution's interest-bearing eligible liabilities over the average level on make-up days in the three months to October 1976. Thereafter a further $\frac{1}{2}$ per cent growth was allowed in the months May–December 1977.

If a bank exceeded the limit set down, penalties in the form of non-interest-bearing special deposits were imposed on a sliding scale: if the excess growth was less than 3 per cent, 5 per cent of the excess had to be deposited with the Bank of England; if between 3 and 5 per cent, 25 per cent; and above 5 per cent excess, 50 per cent.

In May the corset was renewed unchanged for another six months, but it was removed during the second week in August.

It was again reintroduced on 8 June 1978. An institution would be liable to lodge with the Bank during November 1978 a non-interest-bearing special deposit if the average of its interest-bearing resources for the three months August–October 1978 exceeded by more than 4 per cent the average amount outstanding on the make-up days in the six months November 1977–April 1978. (The make-up days are the days when the banks work out their figures for the monthly return to the Bank of England.)

In respect of an excess of 3 per cent or less, the rate would be 5 per cent of the excess; for 3–5 per cent, 25 per cent; thereafter 50 per cent.

In August 1978 the supplementary special deposits scheme was extended for a further eight-month period. The same base was retained (average of each institution's interest-bearing eligible liabilities on the make-up days for the six months November 1977–April 1978) but the period started from the average figure of September, October and November 1978 and will end with the average figure of April, May and June 1979. The specified penalty-free rate of growth for each institution is to be 1 per cent per month of the base average.

It would puzzle anybody to remember all these figures. It is suggested that the student need only be in a position to say:

(1) Whether the corset is on or off at any particular time (e.g. the day of an examination).

(2) What it is (under the penalty system the banks must compulsorily deposit funds with the Bank of England, interest free, on a scale specified by the authorities. This effectively freezes these funds and prevents them from being used in their operations).

(3) That the corset is in effect the reimposition under another name of the quantitative directions sent out to banks before Competition and Credit Control.

(4) That it looks now as though the corset will continue to be used as one of the authorities' chief instruments for controlling the money supply.

Page 59

A draft bill to license banks was published in July 1978. Two classes

of banks are defined: recognized banks which will be able to call themselves 'banks', and other deposit-taking institutions which will need a
licence from the Bank of England before they can continue in the
business of deposit-taking, but which even then will not be able to
have the word 'bank' in their title.

The first group will generally be the major banking companies – the
clearing banks, the merchant banks, the discount houses – which are
recognized already under some existing legislation, notably the
Exchange Control Act, 1947.

The Bill also sets up a deposit protection fund guaranteeing 75 per
cent of deposits up to £10,000. Each bank will contribute towards this
a sum in the range £5,000–£300,000, according to its size.

There will be appeal machinery from the Bank's decision on
licensing to the Chancellor of the Exchequer.

Page 89

National Giro now provides foreign currency direct and also Thomas
Cook travellers' cheques. Application forms are available at main Post
Offices, where the necessary passport entries are made. The currency
and travellers' cheques are sent direct from National Giro by registered
post on receipt of the application.

The Giro Gold Card has been replaced by a cheque card and no
longer exists.

A bureau de change has been opened in Trafalgar Square Post
Office, and other services, introduced in 1978, now include deposit
accounts, bridging loans, budget accounts, personal loans and cheque
guarantee cards. These were made available to the customers of the
bank (whose name was changed during 1978 to National Girobank)
from the first day of 1979. Since 27 November 1978 all current account
customers who remain in credit have paid no charges. There is a charge
for customers who overdraw of 10p per cheque or standing order,
which is applied until their accounts move back into credit.

Page 90

An interesting experiment is that of the Midland Bank which launched
a pilot scheme in January 1978 to see if it is possible to adapt its
branch structure to the needs of the next decade. Eleven branches in
Central Tyneside and Wearside and, from March 1978, ten in the
Southampton area, are included in the experiment which involves
removal of much of the back of the office work from the branches
which are, at the same time, linked to area offices run by a team of
experienced senior managers. This releases branch management and

staff to provide a wider range of personal services tailored to customer needs, and also releases space to provide more counter service points as required, while the area offices will deal with the more specialized needs of the bank's business and professional customers. If these schemes succeed the experiment is to be extended to encompass some 120 branches in all. Other desirable consequences will follow. The bank:

(a) should avoid long-term increase in staff levels (under existing projections the banks fear that they may need as much as one-third more staff to keep pace with the growth of banking business over the next seven years);
(b) hope to make better use of existing premises and
(c) will be better placed to extend its personal banking services to the ten million or so who have no bank account.

Page 137

A year later there had been increased business in all main divisions, and although the demand for advances from larger enterprises was restrained, loans to small and medium-sized companies showed a marked up-turn. During the year term deposits of £1,000–£25,000 for 3–10 years were introduced, giving private investors the opportunity to contribute directly to industrial development.

Page 138

The new organization has been required to set high standards in maintaining, on behalf of its shareholders, close contact with the companies in which it invests. Moreover, many cases of financing difficulty are solved by packages containing both new medium-term lending and new equity funds; and the involvement of both FFI and ECI together in a joint financing package is expected to provide increased opportunities for ensuring that performance is adequately monitored.

Page 143

Perhaps it is fair to say that since the Page Report the Trustee Savings Banks have moved towards becoming a 'third force' in banking and into competition with the clearing banks, as far as personal customers are concerned.

Page 143

It is now inaccurate to talk about 'Departments' in connection with the Trustee Savings Banks. It is more accurate to refer to the variety of accounts maintained, e.g., Savings Accounts, Investment Accounts, Term Deposit Accounts and Cheque Accounts.

Page 144

The tax-free interest concession on Savings Accounts will cease to apply from November 1979. The Trustee Savings Banks have already lost the ability to register purchases of new government stocks for their customers on the National Savings Stock Register, a means by which the holder could receive the payment of interest gross. Ultimately the position of the Trustee Savings Banks in relation to tax treatment will become that of any other banking organization. Although this may cause some problems in the transitional stages, in the long run the Trustee Savings Banks would not wish to enjoy unfair advantages over their competitors.

No person may enjoy relief of tax on the first £70 in a Trustee Savings Bank and another £70 in the National Savings Bank.

Page 144

The position now is that where a minimum balance of £50 is maintained for six months there is no charge. In other cases there is a charge of 2½p for each debit item (see p. 293).

Both secured and unsecured overdrafts are now available. A list of Trustee Savings Bank services therefore now includes lending.

Page 144

The full list of the products of the Trust Company are (a) Harvest Savings Plan; (b) Family Income Plan; (c) Convertible Insurance Plan; (d) Mortgage Protection Plan and (e) Harvest Bond Plan.

Page 145

It was also the only organization to offer house mortgage facilities, but it is hoped that there will be a wider application of this much-needed service.

New lending services were generally introduced in August 1977. These were personal and bridging loans and short-term overdraft facilities. Other possibilities being considered are corporate lending and loans for house purchase. A credit card, called 'Trust card', was offered to customers from November 1978.

Page 146

The Trustee Savings Bank Association has been replaced by the

Trustee Savings Bank Central Board. The Trustee Savings Bank Inspection Committee was wound up in 1976.

Page 151

The SAYE scheme described in the text is the second issue, but this is no longer available at Post Offices, where only the Index-linked Scheme is currently available. The second issue is, however, still available from building societies, which do not, of course, offer the index-linked scheme.

Page 192

All the clearing banks are now prepared to make medium-term loans to credit-worthy customers.

Page 252

There is now no tax relief on overdrafts, but certain loans entitle the borrower to a yearly certificate signed by the banker in respect of interest charged, which may be produced to the Inspector of Taxes. Tax relief is granted on current loans for house or land purchases, or for home improvements, and there are various tax reliefs on loans incurred on or before 26 March 1974, up to a period extending to 5 April 1980. Relief for these loans can be claimed up to six years from the time the debt was incurred.

Pages 282 and 297

In 1977 there were recommendations of nationalization of the clearing banks from the Labour party's Home Policy Committee, and although these have not been officially adopted, the banks thought it desirable to conduct their own survey of how the public felt on this point. The result was a massive 'not in favour', but the opportunity was taken by those responding to press some of the things which gave them cause for complaint. Prominent among these have been poor counter service, especially at lunch time, and no Saturday morning opening. However, it is learnt that Barclays Bank are to run an experimental scheme in four of their Cardiff branches, in which opening hours will be extended until 5 p.m.

Page 287

On the continent a uniform cheque and cheque card has been developed under the Eurocheque scheme. Unlike here, the card is sold to customers by the banks for a nominal sum, say Dm 1 in West Germany. The card enables the holder to draw cash, generally up to the equivalent of £50, from bank branches, and also acts as a guarantee up to specific amounts at hotels and stores on the continent. Both the cheque and the card are slightly different from those which individual banks used to issue (and still do in places) before the advent of the Eurocheque system.

However, there is a strong move towards uniformity, which may end the individual bank's ordinary cheques and cards. United Kingdom banks have yet to decide whether they will become full members of Eurocheque and start issuing uniform cheques and cheque guarantee cards. It is because of Britain's limited membership that continentals are restricted here to using their cheque cards for cash at banks. The cards do not in Britain as a rule act as guarantee cards in shops or hotels. So any retailer who accepts a cheque backed up by one of the continental cards is taking a risk; but some shops and hotels in London will accept them.

Page 288

About a third of the credit card holders make a habit of taking credit, another third do so occasionally and one-third always pay up promptly, thus avoiding being charged interest at all. The total amount of credit in the credit card system is thought to be rather more than £250 million.

The limitation imposed on repayment of amounts outstanding, believed by the credit card companies to be a major obstacle to rapid growth, was removed in the April budget of 1978, and both Barclaycard and Access, the two major concerns in this country, thereafter asked for repayments of £5 or 5 per cent of the outstanding balance, whichever was the greater. Credit card holders are now also able to withdraw cash at any branch of any of the participating banks up to their limit, instead of the ceiling of £30 formerly in force. Two companies have about eight million cardholders between them, with much future potential. Both companies make their profit, of course, from the commission which they charge to retailers (this varies between 3 and 5 per cent) and the interest paid by those who do not clear their accounts at the end of each month; and a steady expansion is going on all the time.

Thus it was reported in the spring of 1978 that payment of rates in four country areas could be effected by either Barclaycard or Access. For a one-year trial period, the half-year or full-year rates could be paid on credit. The authorities concerned pay the companies 2 per cent or less of the payments, but for this they get immediate cash from the companies with no waiting and no collection costs. Scores of other local authorities have apparently asked for the same facility, but the companies have limited themselves to the four authorities concerned until they see how the pilot operation goes.

It does not need much imagination to see the eventual payment of all rates, gas, electricity and telephone bills by this method. In fact, another pilot scheme was reported as starting in May 1978 to allow the payment of electricity bills to one of the electricity boards by credit card.

Other news announced in the autumn of 1978 concerned Marks and Spencer, who were to launch their own borrowing plan for customers, based on credit card principles. A pilot scheme began on 1 September in six stores, four in London's suburbs and two in big southern towns. The administration is in the hands of Citibank Trust, a consumer credit company owned by one of the largest of the American banks, who decide on interest rates and run the scheme. The system is based on the revolving credit principle – customers can borrow up to thiry times what they subscribe each month. As they pay off one debt, they can contract another, so long as they do not exceed their overall limit.

Tesco is also to introduce its own credit card. Announcing this news in September 1978 Tesco's finance director said that his organization, which sells more food than any other retail group except the Co-op, was already negotiating with various finance groups. Fine Fare, too, has decided in principle to introduce its own card.

Finally, it was learned late in 1978 that the cashless society had come one step nearer, with the news that the major banks and credit card companies had set up a full-time team to look into the possibility of installing banking terminals in shops, restaurants and the like.

Page 295

When the banks wished to increase their charges they approached the Prices Commission for the necessary permission. The Commission's Report, published in April 1978, found that the efficiency of the money transmission services in this country compared favourably with those abroad, and were not in general excessively expensive. The case for raising the general level of charges was thought to depend very much on the level of interest rates, but a general approval was given subject to the charges being related more closely to the individual costs of handling the current accounts, either by paying interest on current accounts, or by relating the notional allowance for interest more closely to the changing level of interest rates.

The second of these was selected, partly because the tax authorities would have been interested in interest paid, and Lloyds, National Westminster, Barclays and the Trustee Savings Bank put their charges up during the year. Midland has an application to do so before the Price Commission.

At the time of writing (November 1978) the position is as follows:

	Minimum balance for free banking	Debit charges thereafter
Barclays	£100	13p
Lloyds	£100	12½p
Midland	£50	9p
National Westminster	£50	15p
Yorkshire	£50	9p
Williams & Glyns	£50	9p
Trustee Savings Banks	£50	5p
Co-op	Free if in credit	9p
National Girobank	Free if in credit	10p

Innovations include the decision of Lloyds to pass on some of the savings of automation by reducing the charge for cashpoint withdrawals to 7½p: Williams & Glyns do much the same by charging only 6p for standing orders. Both Lloyds and National Westminster have altered the basis on which the notional allowance set against charges is calculated – a gesture in the direction of the Prices Commission. National Westminster's allowance will be 0.5 per cent below the current deposit rate; Lloyds, 1 per cent.

Page 297 – see note to page 282

Page 321

The administration and registration of limited companies, which used to be in City Road, EC1, moved to Cardiff in 1976. In that year microfilm reading was introduced; in return for the standard search fee copies of the original documents are supplied on microfiche, which can be taken away. Full-sized copies of the filmed documents are to be available from microfilm printers which the searcher can operate himself. A reading room is provided at Companies House in City Road and facilities are available there and at Cardiff.

Index